D1743160

THE BIBLICAL LIBERATION OF WOMEN

FOR LEADERSHIP IN THE CHURCH

AS ONE ESSENTIAL FOR THE SPIRITUAL

FORMATION OF THE CHURCH

BY

KNOFEL STATON, D.D; D.MIN.

Wipf and Stock Publishers
EUGENE, OREGON

Wipf and Stock Publishers
199 West 8th Avenue, Suite 3
Eugene, Oregon 97401

The Biblical Liberation of Women for Leadership in the Church
By Staton, Knofel
Copyright© March, 2003 by Staton, Knofel
ISBN: 1-59244-196-3
Publication date: March, 2003

CONTENTS

PREFACE iv

ACKNOWLEDGEMENTS v

ABBREVIATIONS vi

Chapter 1: THE BEREAN CHALLENGE 1

Chapter 2: GOD'S LEADERSHIP INTENTION FOR WOMEN: AS

REVEALED IN CREATION AND POST-CREATION OLD

TESTAMENT TEXTS 11

Chapter 3: JESUS MODELING GOD'S INTENTION FOR WOMEN. 36

Chapter 4: THE HOLY SPIRIT'S CONTINUATION OF JESUS'

MINISTRY WITH, FOR, AND THROUGH WOMEN IN THE EARLY

CHURCH 71

Chapter 5: BAPTISM AND *CHARISMA*: TWO DYNAMICS

EMPOWERING WOMEN FOR LEADERSHIP ROLES IN THE

CHURCH 87

Chapter 6: REVISITING THE SILENT PASSAGES OF 1

CORINTHIANS 14:34-35 AND 1 TIMOTHY 2:9-11: WOMEN

MUZZLED OR UNMUZZLED? 107

Chapter 7: RETHINKING HEADSHIP IN LIGHT OF THE TRIAD IN

1 CORINTHIANS 11:3 139

Chapter 8: FROM THE TRINITY OF DEITY TO THE "BI-UNITY"

OF HUMANITY 156

Appendix: WOMEN AS ELDERS: PONDERING THE ISSUE. . . . 159

WORKS CITED. 163

PREFACE

Denying women the role of pastor, preacher, elder, deacon, or teacher of men is universally practiced in my church affiliation, the Christian Church (independent). Some leaders in this tradition argue that a woman may sing a solo in a congregation with men present provided she is not singing Scripture, such as a praise chorus from a Psalm or the "Lord's Prayer."

While not denying the value of traditions that helped shape some of my spiritual understandings, I have determined to approach Scripture on any topic hermeneutically, exegetically, and holistically rather than be cemented to past positions. This approach to Scripture includes considering the immediate literary context, the theme context of the book or letter in which a passage is placed, the cultural context, and the holistic biblical teaching that covers the topic being studied.

The New International Version will be used throughout the paper, unless noted otherwise.

I will use the small "c" with church when referring to a congregation and the capital "C" when referring to the universal Church or to a specific name/denomination.

The word "independent" is not technically nor legally a part of the nomenclature of the Christian Church; however, it is often used to differentiate it from the Christian Church (Disciples of Christ). The two fellowships were originally one. Today they are more like distant sister fellowships instead of being identical twins. Throughout this dissertation, the legal designation of Christian Church without an adjective will be used.

ACKNOWLEDGEMENTS

Although this is my 35th book, the writer of Proverbs stated it well, "As iron sharpens iron so one man sharpens another" (NASB). Seldom have I written anything as a lone ranger; and that was certainly true throughout this book. Many different persons sharpened my thinking by sharing their encouragements and challenging thoughts. So while only one name appears on the title page, several have been co-thinkers with me. I am particularly indebted to three people who excited me about doing biblical studies and modeled a hermeneutics that changed my life. These three are Dr. Marion Henderson, Dr. Harold Songer, and Dr. Frank Stagg. Over the past several years several other sharpeners motivated me not only to continue to do biblical research, but also to re-think my hierarchical view of the place of women in leadership, which I held for over three decades of my adult life.

Dr. Earl Grant, Director of the Doctor of Ministry program, Associate Dean of Curriculum and Programs, and Professor of Church Development and Intercultural Studies at the Haggard Graduate School of Theology of Azusa Pacific University encouraged me to tackle this issue academically. My doctoral mentor, Dr. Sarah Sumner, who has an holistic understanding of the women issue, has been consistently and significantly helpful. We spent many hours sharing our concepts with each other. Not only is she biblically and theologically grounded, but also is relationally irenic and analytically fair with those who differ from her. I am grateful to the following who read selected chapters and gave encouragingly helpful response: Dr. Earl Grant; Dr. Donald Thorsen, Professor of Theology at Haggard Graduate School of Theology; Dr. Richard J. Foster, Professor of Spiritual Development and Director of Renovare; Dr. Roger White, Professor of Education at Azusa Pacific University; Dr. H. Newton Maloney, Senior Professor of Psychology at Fuller Theological Seminary; and Dr. Eddie Elliston, Provost at Hope International University.

I am also deeply indebted to my wife, Julia, for her encouragement, support, and many years of dialoguing with me about the value of women and their role in the Church and culture. She is truly a sharpening partner. My many discussions with Dr. Gary Tiffin, Provost at Northwest Christian College, Eugene, Oregon, have been iron-sharpening times.

My deep thanks to all of you, and to you the readers.

Knofel Staton
Hope International University, Fullerton, California 92831
2003

knofelee@earthlink.net

ABBREVIATIONS

Ac	Acts
ATR	*Anglican Theological Review*
AUSS	*Andrews University Seminary Studies*
BIB SAC	*Bibliotheca Sacra*
BJBL	*The Bulletin of the John Rylands University Library*
BJS	*Brown Judaic Studies*
BQ	*Baptist Quarterly*
CBQ	*Catholic Biblical Quarterly*
CEV	The Contemporary English Version
Chic. Stud.	*Chicago Studies*
Co	Corinthians
Col	Colossians
CJ	*Conservative Judaism*
CTJ	*Calvin Theological Journal*
CS	*Christian Standard*
CT	*Christianity Today*
CTR	*Criswell Theological Review*
DDSR	*Duke Divinity School Review*
DIR	*Direction*
Dt	Deuteronomy
Ecc	Ecclesiastes
ECR	*The Ecumenical Review*
Eph	Ephesians
Ex	Exodus
Ga	Galatians
Ge	Genesis
Heb	Hebrews
HOR BIB TH	*Horizons on Biblical Theology*
IJT	*Indian Journal of Theology*
INT	*Interpretation*
Is	Isaiah
Jas	James
Jer	Jeremiah
JES	*Journal of Ecumenical Studies*
JTSA	*Journal of Theology for Southern Africa*
Jn	John
Ki	Kings
KJV	King James Version
Lk	Luke
LXX	*Septuagint*
Lv	Leviticus
M.	*Mishnah*
Abot.	Aboth

M. Ber.	Berakoth
M. Git.	Gittin
M. Ket.	Kituboth
M. Kid.	Kiddushin
M. Naz	Nazir
M. Ned.	Nedarim
M. Sheb.	Shebiith
M. Yeb.	Yebamoth
MCM	*Modern Churchman*
Mk	Mark
Mt	Matthew
NASB	New American Standard Bible
Ne	Nehemiah
NTS	*New Testament Studies*
Nu	Numbers
Pe	Peter
Phm	Philemon
Php	Philippians
Pr	Proverbs
Ps	Psalms
Rev Exp	*Review and Expositor*
Ro	Romans
Sa	Samuel
SBLSB	*SBL Sources for Biblical Study*
SJT	*Scottish Journal of Theology*
SRSR	*Studies in Religion/Sciences Religieuses*
ST	*Theological Studies*
TCNT	The Twentieth Century New Testament
TDNT	*Theological Dictionary of the New Testament*
TEV	Today's English Version
Th	Thessalonians
Ti	Timothy
TJ	*Trinity Journal*
TTJ	*Trinity Theological Journal* [Singapore]
USQR	*Union Seminary Quarterly Review*
WTJ	*Westminster Theological Journal*
Zech	Zechariah

CHAPTER 1

THE BEREAN CHALLENGE

From the day I was born through high school graduation, I attended a very conservative Bible believing church. Throughout high school Miss Mabel Caddy was my Sunday School teacher and Shirley DeArmond (now Powell), a recent Christian College graduate, was my youth director. Consequently, these two women were my primary Bible teachers until I left for military service and then soon for Korea during that "forgotten war." But I suppose my church still viewed me as a boy rather than a man.

Throughout those youthful developing years I never saw a woman serve as a greeter, help distribute the Lord's Supper, baptize anyone, serve as an usher, help take up an offering, and certainly not speak to the congregation. Therefore, I left my hometown thinking it would be wrong (biblically liberal) for any woman to serve in any of those capacities.

After serving eight years in the Air Force and being an FAA senior air traffic controller at O'Hare airport, I enrolled in and graduated from a conservative Bible College, and was ordained for ministry. Men only conducted my ordination interrogation. Professors throughout my seminary education did not address the issue of women leaders in the church, partly because that was not a hot button topic in the early sixties. Later as a Bible College Professor and then head of a Seminary's New Testament Department, I taught others the way I was taught (by both formal education and informal experiences) that male headship meant male authority and that women, while not inferior, were always to remain subordinate to men.

At the age of forty-seven, I moved to California to commence the presidency of a Christian College. But a couple of Sundays later several things happened that initially bothered me. In fact, some of those things did more than just bother me—they shook me. As I walked through the door, I was joyfully greeted by a woman who handed me the bulletin, a woman led the worship service and taught us some new songs from the Psalms, another woman baptized her son, and yet another woman baptized an adult man (also a father baptized his daughter, and the male preacher baptized another person but those baptisms did not concern me at all). I was sitting next to the aisle when it happened. I looked up and there she was—a *woman* server holding the communion trays and offering the Lord's Supper to me. I sat stunned for a second or two—a woman distributing the Eucharist! Should I take it from her?

On the way home, I remember inwardly asking myself the following questions: (1) Is it right for a woman to be an usherette in a theater, but wrong to do the same in a Christian worship service? (2) Is it right for a woman to serve a man dinner on an airplane or in a restaurant and receive a tip, but wrong for her to serve the Lord's Supper in a worship service? (3) Is it right for a woman sitting next to me to offer the communion trays to me, but wrong if she stands in the aisle offering it? (4) Was it right for Miss Caddy or Miss DeArmond to teach the Bible to me when I was 18 just out of high school, but wrong for either one of them to teach me after I returned from Korea (hopefully being considered a man by then)? (5) Was it right for Miss Corrine Jessup to teach me both English and Speech in high school and encourage me to enter the teaching/preaching ministry, but wrong for her to share with me any of her insights about the Bible even though she was a marvelous biblical student?

So at the age of forty-seven, after being committed to one tradition about the roles of men and women in the church, I was faced with the Berean challenge. We know about that challenge, don't we? In fact, we can review the difference between the Thessalonian response when their tradition was challenged and the Berean response (Acts 17:1-13). The Thessalonians listened to Paul's reasoning from Scripture, but were not challenged to study the issue because Paul's scriptural conclusions did not square with the way they developed their theology (formal education and informal experiences). Consequently, the Thessalonians remained frozen to their tradition and lead a mob-kind of opposition against a fellow member in their religion. But the Bereans, who no doubt developed their theology the same way as the Thessalonians did (formal education and informal experiences), were open to studying the Scriptures to prevent them from placing tradition above Scripture, and thus using tradition to interpret Scripture rather than vice versa.

Being exposed to a different tradition by either experience (such as a woman serving the Lord's Supper) or by formal education can become the catalyst for us to either grow through study or growl through traditions, to be changed through study or to be chained to a position without study, and to become more certain of our traditional position through further study or to be critical of it because of additional study.

I decided to leap into the Berean challenge by examining Scripture to discover whether or not the traditional roles of women that I was taught and observed squared with God's intention. I admit that it is more comfortable to salute a monument to tradition than a movement toward a different position, to be frozen to it than to be freed from it, to be chained than to be changed—especially when the movement, the freedom, and the change are not consistent with the way I had taught, written, and for which I was nationally known in my denomination. It is probably difficult for most of us to hit the eject button and bail out of traditions we have been trained to pilot. It is possible that many of us fall in love with our traditions and equate that love with our love for our Lord.

The Issue

The content of this book is the result of my journey with the Berean challenge. It is about women and ministry, issues that are exegetically complex and emotionally volatile. As with many fellowships, my church denomination is experiencing a quandary concerning the role of women in the Church. During the late 19th and early 20th century, women shared identical leadership roles with men.[1] But after splintering from the Disciples of Christ in 1927 (a split that was not related to the role of women), the Christian Church (independent) gradually eliminated women from teaching/preaching leadership functions if men were present.

However, today there is a growing unrest among members concerning the lack of women in leadership roles as evidenced by written responses to articles in the Christian Church's periodicals that prohibit women leaders from teaching/preaching roles. The unrest comes from two analytical bases: (1) Inconsistencies: prohibiting women leaders in congregations while allowing women to be authors and editors of biblical lessons which would be taught by men to men in Sunday School classes; women leading workshops in Christian Church conventions attended by men; women students being admitted into various accredited Bible colleges and seminaries;[2] refusing the ordination of women to congregational ministries while endorsing women as military, hospital, and industrial chaplains. (2) The growing perspective that the Bible does not prohibit women from teaching/preaching or holding other leadership roles.

Thesis

The thesis developed in this book is **although women are restricted from leadership roles in many churches, it is God's intention for them to be included along with men**. The liberation of women is demonstrated by God's intention in creation; the modeling of God's intention through Jesus' life; the continuation of God's intention through the Spirit's leading the apostolic Church; the role of baptism and charisma for leadership; the meaning of "headship"; and an evaluation of those "silent passages." The development and application of this thesis is necessary for the advancement of spiritual formation toward Christ likeness in the individual and the Church.

---

[1] Forty-one women preachers are listed in the 1907 *Yearbook of the Disciples of Christ*. At that time the Disciples of Christ included the fellowship presently identified as the Independent Christian Church.

[2] "Christian Colleges, 1998-99," *CS* 134 (February, 14, 1999): 148-149. In this report women make up 49.5% of students in the Bible colleges and 29.1% of students in the seminaries.

Other Authors

Due to the influence of the feminist movement, literature about the role of women in the Church has mushroomed, particularly since the beginning of the 1970's. The most helpful literature comes from three sources – journals/periodicals, topical books, and comprehensive commentaries. I have read the appropriate sections in the books and the textual sections in the listed commentaries. I have also researched all the periodicals/journals abstracted over the past 38 years in the New Testament Abstracts and have read the articles listed in the bibliography.

Primarily the literature focuses on the role of women from the creation narratives in Genesis, 1 Corinthians 11:2-16, 14:34-36, 1 Timothy 2:9-15, and Galatians 3:28. The literature acknowledges that male and female were created in the image of God and share spiritual equality. However, the literature indicates significant differences concerning the following:

1) The correct meaning of the words head, covering, uncovering, and authority in 1 Corinthians 11:2-16.

2) The social roles of males and females. If the role of females is subordination to males, scholars disagree about the meaning, scope, and object of the subordination. Is the subordination voluntary or demanded? Is it to certain male leaders, to every male, or to only their own husbands? Scholars also disagree over the origin of female subordination – from the order of creation or from the fall? Is the male's (or husband's) rule in Genesis 3:16 descriptive or prescriptive? If prescriptive, should the subordination continue or should it be reversed with the initiation of the new creation in Christ?

3) A woman's right to speak. Some writers argue that a woman can speak freely in all circumstances; however, others claim she is not to speak if men are present. Some assert that women may speak if men are present provided the content is not biblical or doctrinal truths; however, others argue against that assertion, allowing women to speak biblical or spiritual truths provided the content is not false doctrine.

4) The propriety of women teaching in the Church assembly or elsewhere. Some writers argue against a woman speaking in an official assembly of God's people – either a house-meeting, Bible-study or worship service; however, others argue she may speak anywhere at any time to anyone.

5) The proper rendering of the word "silent" or "esuchia" in 1 Timothy 2. Some argue that it refers to absolute silence,

while others suggest it refers to a quiet-peaceful demeanor. Some suggest the woman's silence means on thing in 1 Timothy 2 and something else in 1 Corinthians 14.

6) The identity of women in both 1 Timothy 2 and 1 Corinthians 14. Does the identity refer to the female gender or to wives in both passages; or to the female gender in one passage and to wives in the other passage?

7) The proper application of 1 Corinthians 14:34-35 and 1 Timothy 2:9-15. Do the verses apply universally or to only specific circumstances in a 1st century church?

Although the quality of the literature varies, the most striking common weakness is the failure to review the respective texts contextually, especially the literary context, i.e., how the sections fit into the immediate context and theme (or big picture) of the respective biblical book. Most writing about the 1 Timothy passage view the big picture being the presence of false teachers; however, that picture does not fit all sections within that document. I argue that false teaching is neither the big picture of 1 Timothy nor the issue in 2:9-15. Many writers argue that the cultural context of the passage includes Gnosticism; however, a developed Gnostic system did not exist in the environment of early Christianity. However, some philosophical ideas present in the latter part of the 1st century helped crystallize the formation of Gnosticism in the 2nd century.[3]

Most journal/periodical articles and books dealing with this issue are framed within either the egalitarian or the hierarchical (complementarian) approach with none that I have read opting for an alternative angle. I did not begin my research with the intention of looking for an alternative view, but that emerged from the research. I did not come up with a label that describes a different handle, although not necessarily an alternative position, until after I had finished the research. The label/term is "bi-unitarian" with the rationale for that term running throughout the book and is summarized in chapter 8—From the Trinity of Deity to the "Bi-unity" of Humanity.

In this book, I occasionally relate the liberation of women to the spiritual formation of the Church.

Theological Presuppositions

The presuppositions that frame my research follow:
1) The Bible is the inspired revelation from God and is authoritative for all Church doctrine.

---

[3] See the substantive research by Arthur Darby Nock, *Early Gentile Christianity and Its Hellenistic Background* (New York: Harper & Row Publishers, 1964), xiii-xvii.

2) Scripture is the primary source for concluding the appropriate role of women in the Church.
3) The non-biblical resources are secondary and are subject to Scripture, not vice-versa.
4) Paul's writing about the role of women is consistent with God's intention, Jesus' model of that intention, and the Spirit's continuation of that intention in leading the early Church's liberation of women recorded in the book of Acts.
5) The Church is the continuing body of Christ.
6) The more the Church conforms to the intentions of God, the teachings and examples of Jesus, and the models of the foundational Church in Acts, the more she advances toward maturity (spiritual formation toward Christ likeness).

Methodology

I will be analyzing and interacting with my primary source—the biblical texts, and secondary sources—literature from various scholars.

I will not respond to source, form, textual, and redaction criticism when dealing with the primary source. I will, however, seek to understand what the biblical author meant by what he wrote and what that means for readers today. In doing so, I will consider the intentionality of the author by considering how the text relates to the holistic composition (the umbrella theme/purpose) of the book in which it is located, and also how it relates to the immediate literary context into which the author positioned it. I will also consider the cultural context to which the author addressed and to which the topic of the text was relevant as well as the *Sitz im Leben* of the first intended audience. Grammatically, I will deal with the meaning of the original language— word meanings and syntax. Although the lexicological approach is helpful, it is not determinative. Therefore, I will consider how words were used in their contexts, and how the author used the same words in other writings. I will also apply the holistic biblical position concerning the role of women in religious communities. That is, I will seek to integrate what appear to be restrictive or exceptional passages about the functions of women to the over-all biblical teaching concerning women with (or without) those functions.[4]

My secondary sources include scholars who hold identical, similar, different, and opposing positions from my conclusions. I value the research and writing of these scholars as fellow Christians and committed disciples of Christ. Their writings help me appreciate the

---

[4] See my developed exegetical and hermeneutical approach in Knofel Staton, *How to Understand the Bible* (Cincinnati, OH: Standard Publishing, 1978) and *Hearing God: 8 Steps to Understanding the Bible* (Cincinnati, OH: Standard Publishing, 1993).

complexity of this issue, and serve as catalysts for me to analytically review my own research and conclusions. I will interact with the secondary sources through the lens of how I understand the meaning of the primary source, the biblical text. While I will disagree with some, I affirm our unity in Christ amid our diversity, and thus as fellow members of Christ's Body.

The scope of my research includes reviewing forty years (1830 through 1970) of articles in the voluminous issues of the *Millennial Harbinger*, thirty-eight years of articles abstracted in *New Testament Abstracts*, all the articles published by the Council on Biblical Manhood and Womanhood in the *CBW News*, all the articles published by Christians for Biblical Equality from 1987 to the present in the *Priscilla Papers*, and a representative selection of books written by leading scholars holding either the hierarchical or egalitarian position.

I did not discover many articles published by the Council on Biblical Manhood and Womanhood or by Christians for Biblical Equality that broke new ground from what was already published in journals and related books. However, both of the above sources introduced me to a library of books to which I turned.

I grew in my respect for evangelical scholars who hold differences of interpretations and conclusions from each other and me. However, we all hold more in common than in conflict such as our high view of God, Christ, the Holy Spirit, the acceptance of the trinity, the inspiration and integrity of the Bible, dependence upon the Bible as the primary source for making conclusions.

Liberation and Spiritual Formation

Spiritual formation refers to both individual Christians and the corporate Church making progress toward conforming to Christ likeness (Romans 8:29). Today's Spirit liberates us for that process, "Now the Lord is the Spirit, and where the Spirit of the Lord is, there is liberty . . . we all with unveiled face beholding as in a mirror the glory of the Lord, are being transformed into the same image. . ." (2 Corinthians 3:17-18). The Church is the body of Christ, "the fullness of him who fills everything in every way (Ephesians 1:23). Individual members in the body are to help, not hinder other members mature in Christ's fullness in order to continue His priorities and practices – character and conduct on earth.

Developing various disciplines that aid that process such as prayer, meditation, silence, worship, visualization, fasting, study, giving, and so on is beyond the perimeters of this writing; however, ministry,[5] a focus of this writing, is one of the spiritual formational practices that is related to liberating all Christians to function as fellow ministers – the ministry/priesthood of all believers (1 Peter 2:5,9).[5]

The apostle Paul affirmed that leaders are to equip all members for service, which is essential for the body of Christ "to become mature attaining to the whole measure of the fullness of Christ." It is only as each member does its part that the body can build itself up in love (Ephesians 4:11-16). In Christ, people are "created to be like God in true righteousness and holiness" (Ephesians 4:24). Righteousness refers to proper relationships and holiness to commitment to God's kind of relationships. God's Spirit and charisma equip Christians to imitate the likeness of God (Ephesians 5:1-2). But doing so requires the process of maturing – spiritual formation.

Paul also wrote that each Christian has charisma for the common good to be used to help the church grow out of immaturity. No specific gift is gender specific. Each person is to be liberated to use the gift(s) to strengthen, encourage, and comfort one another which builds up the church (1 Corinthians 3:1-3; chapters 12-14, especially 12:4-8 and 14:3,12).

Paul unpacked the statement that no one should think more highly of self than he/she ought. Then the diversity of gifts can be tapped from the diversity of all kinds of members to do the many "one anothers" (Romans 12:3 through chapter 16).

Seeing people the way God does (2 Corinthians 5:15-16) and emancipating them from any internally and/or externally caused fear from or reluctance to using their gifts is essential for the Church to grow up (mature) into God's goal for us – to be like Christ. When the local church body is not engaged in the kinds of releasing ministries that God intended, Jesus demonstrated, and the early Church continued, she inhibits the spiritual formation of its members and thus of the holistic body. ALL MEMBERS regardless of their gender, ethnic, educational, economical, or any other social identity are to be liberated to share in ministry, for no ministry is biblically restricted from any category of people BECAUSE of any biological or sociological linkage.

It is possible for individual congregations to measure their maturity level by how they perform certain disciplines and rituals while neglecting God's desire to liberate all categories of people for both leadership and ministry into which baptism ordains, charisma equips, and God calls us. To not free people to serve hinders the Church's ministerial and evangelistical witness to the world.

---

[5] Richard Foster, *Celebration of Discipline: A Path to Spiritual Growth* (San Francisco: HarperSanFrancisco, 1998.), 126-140. Foster lists and discusses service/ministry as one of the four outward disciplines.

A Global Concern

The "State of World Population Report 2000" released by the United Nations on September 19, 2000 attacked the global bias and abuse against women. Women around the world are routinely denied access to education and health care. The report revealed that at least one in three women has been beaten, coerced into sex, forced to have 80 million unwanted pregnancies each year and 50 million abortions—20 million of which are unsafe, and abused in other ways. At least 60 million young girls, mostly in Asia, are listed as "missing," as a result of infanticide, neglect or other factors. This report further revealed that "as many as 5,000 women and girls are murdered each year in so-called 'honor' killings by members of their own families."

In some cultures, women are often seen as commercial assets. For instance in the province of Sanliurfa in Turkey, a groom has to pay so-called head money to his potential bride's family before he marries her. But if she is dishonored, the family forfeits that income. Mahmut Ozyavuzlar, an ethnic tribe leader in the town of Harran 30 miles south of Sanliurfa, stated, "It is true that we view our girls as commercial assets, to be traded or sold." Some girls can be worth as much as $50,000 depending upon their looks. In the Mus province, 28 girls within six months killed themselves after being forced into such marriages. Ozyavuzlar noted, "Better perhaps they kill themselves than run away and dishonor their families. Otherwise, it would fall upon the family to erase the stain."[6] The same article disclosed a "virtue that only a man can possess" which is to kill a woman or a girl. In Sanliurfa, a city of 500,000 people, an eleven-year brother slit his teenage sister's throat on the town square in broad daylight because someone dedicated a love ballad to her over the radio. The girl was a virgin who did not even have a boyfriend. A 17-year-old husband slit his 12-year-old wife's throat because she had gone to the movies without his permission.

According to an Israeli newspaper, a Tel Aviv rabbi ruled that in the midst of a withering heat wave a man could divorce his wife for rolling up her sleeves past her elbows in public. It is not uncommon in India for a husband to disfigure his wife's face with acid, and then divorce her for ugliness in order to marry again for another healthy dowry. The Iranian law demands the death penalty for adultery and for women failing to cover themselves from head to foot. A 53-year old woman named Faribah, was imprisoned and received 80 lashes for allowing her headscarf to slip back a little from her forehead as she was stacking groceries in her car. Horrible examples of how women are viewed and mistreated are legion around the world.

The "State of the World Population Report 2000" from the U.N. Population Fund noted that discrimination and violence against women

---

[6] *Los Angeles Times*, September 10, 2000.

"remain firmly rooted in cultures around the world." The report added, "Passed down from one generation to the next, ideas about 'real men' and 'a woman's place' are difficult to change."

Is it possible that missionaries in those countries are saying very little about such treatment of women partly, if not largely, because missionaries may harbor a lessoned view of a woman's valuable contributions in a man's world? Is it possible that what is viewed as the Church's value or non-value and use or non-use of women may unintentionally (or perhaps intentionally in some cases) help maintain an ungodly abuse of women locally and globally?

Perhaps a hundred years from now historians will record the ironies of ironies—that companies did more for liberating women to a place of value and freedom to use their abilities and charismata than did the Church. And commercial companies elevated women for money (profit) while the church did not do so for their Master.

Seeing a problem is not unrelated to solving it. For a problem cannot be solved correctly unless it is understood and addressed correctly. I hope to offer fresh insights for the Christian Church which may have a potential for impacting our cultures both locally and globally with the relational characteristics of our Heavenly Father demonstrated perfectly by His incarnated Son, and continued by the incarnated Holy Spirit in Christians.

However, I realize that engaging males and females in equal ministries is not the ultimate solution. Both males and females can bring to co-ministries a competitive stance against the other gender, self-serving attitudes for turf protection, and accusations that the other gender is being unfaithful to the text and thus to God. I am hoping that re-visiting the texts can elevate our spirits to God's so we can more easily rise above our opinions and demonstrate loving relational attitudes that feed unity amid diversity that accepts the other gender's essentiality and contributions for the spiritual formation of the Church toward the maturity of Christ likeness.

CHAPTER 2

GOD'S LEADERSHIP INTENTION FOR WOMEN: AS REVEALED IN CREATION AND POST-CREATION OLD TESTAMENT TEXTS

Introduction

While many in the restrictive hierarchical tradition use I Timothy 2:11-15 and many in the equalitarian tradition use Galatians 3:28 as the springboard and normative text for the use of women leaders, God's intention for creating women and His subsequent use of women in the Old Testament are foundational for the Church today.

In this chapter I will develop the thesis that it was God's original intention for women to be included as leaders along with men. Thus shared leadership of women with men is essential for the spiritual formation of both individual members and the corporate Church. To deny women leadership roles not only marks spiritual immaturity, but also maintains a level of immaturity in Christians and the Church.

Community as God's Intentional Design

Community and the Nature of God

There are many different Hebrew words for God in the Scripture[1], which reveal ways God disclosed Himself to people[2].

The first word for God in Genesis is the plural word, *Elohim.* Zlotowitz suggests this refers to the plurality of majesty of the one God.[3] Cohen related the plural name to "the many forces which spread throughout Genesis" from the one God.[4]

The plural word for the one God suggests that God would not create a world of disunity, but one of connectedness. One of Judaism's most respected scholars, Samson Hirsch, noted that the plurality of things in

---

[1]H.B. Kuhn listed 20 different Hebrew words "God, Names of." *The Zondervan Pictorial Encyclopedia of the Bible*, 1975, vol. 2, 760-766.

[2] *Ibid.*, 766.

[3] Meir Zlotowitz, *Bereishis: Genesis: A New Translation with a Commentary Anthologized from Talmudic, Midrashic and Rabbinic Sources.* vol. 1A (Brooklyn: Mesorah Publications Ltd., 1986), 33.

[4] A. Cohen, ed., *The Sonicino Chumash: The Five Books of Moses with Haphtaroth* (London: Soncino Press, 1947), 1.

the world were created and joined in a unity from the one God's plurality of characteristics.[5]

Many Christians relate *Elohim* to the community nature of the plurality of *personae* in God.[6] Gilbert Bilezikian links the "original community of oneness" to the mutuality and equality of the trinity.[7] Jewett notes that God is not *deus solitarius* (solitary God), but *deus triunus* (the triune God), i.e., God-in-relationship.[8] Several of the same terms that describe the Father are also used to describe the Holy Spirit and the Son. Thus God's nature is demonstrated by unity amid diversity within Himself. The Father, Son, and Holy Spirit were co-creators of the cosmos.[9] Partnership in community relatedness is an essential characteristic of God.[10]

Community and the Nature of Humans

> God made the wild animals according to their
> kinds, the livestock according to their kinds, and all
> the creatures that move along the ground according to
> their kinds. And God saw that it was good. Then God
> said, "Let us make man in our image, in our likeness,
> and let them rule over the fish of the sea and the birds
> of the air, over the livestock, over all the earth," and
> over all the creatures that move along the ground." So
> God created man in his own image, in the image of
> God he created him; male and female he created them.
> God blessed them and said to them, "Be fruitful and
> increase in number; fill the earth and subdue it. Rule
> over the fish of the sea and the birds of the air and
> over every living creature that moves on the ground."
> (Genesis 1:25-28)

---

[5] Samson Raphael Hirsch, *The Pentateuch: Genesis* vol. 1, 2d ed. trans. Isaac Levy (Brooklyn: Judaica Press Ltd., 1989), 3.

[6] Kuhn, 765-6.

[7] Gilbert Bilezikian, *Community 101* (Grand Rapids: Zondervan Publishing House, 1997), 16-18.

[8] Paul K. Jewett. *Man as Relationship from a Theological Point of View* (Grand Rapids: Eerdmans Publishing, 1975), 35; however, these are terms Karl Barth used to not only describe the nature of God, but also of humans created after the pattern of the triune relational nature. *Church Dogmatics.* vol. III. Part 4 eds. G.W. Bromiley and T.F. Torrance (Edinburgh: T & T Clark), 117.

[9] See the activities of the Father in Ge 1; the Holy Spirit in Ge 1:2, Ps 104:30; and Jesus in Jn 1:3 and Col 1:16.

[10] Stanley J. Grenz and Denise Muir Kjesbo, *Women in the Church: A Biblical Theology of Women in Ministry* (Downers Grove, IL: InterVarsity Press, 1995), 155.

Every time God created a life-form (animal, fish, fowl, plants), He described its essential ontological characteristic with the declaration "according to their (or its) kind."[11] Repeating this 3 times in verse 25 was the composer's crescendo in His creation opus as revealed by the first word in verse 26, "then" which introduced the "apex of God's creation."[12]

By saying, "Let us" God revealed His *pluralis majestatis*, i.e., God speaking of Himself in the fullness of His essence.[13] He was consulting with Himself, i.e., the trinity.[14] Gerhard Hasel believes the distinction of personality in "Let us" expresses "an intra-divine deliberation among 'persons' within the divine being."[15]

Greenhalgh's research of "Let us" indicates that God's use of this term is a partnershipping term not only among the parties of the "Let us", but also among the people God created in a divine-human partnership.[16] Therefore, the male and female created in God's image were surely intended to share a loving co-existence of mutuality with cooperative equality.

Genesis 1:26 reveals the first time God did not use the formula "according to its (or their) kind" when He created a life-form. Instead God said, "Let us make man in our image, in our likeness..." That was God's way of saying, "according to **my** kind. "Man" comes from the Hebrew, *adam*, which can be used for a person's name, the male gender, or for humankind without being gender specific. In Genesis 1:26, *adam* refers to people with both genders as demonstrated in 1:27, "male and female he created them", and in Genesis 5:2, "He created them male and female and blessed them. And when they were created he called them 'man'." N'tZiv noted that the etymology of the Hebrew word *adam* means "to resemble".[17] Since God's nature is connectional (a community

---

[11] This was expressed 9 times in 5 different verses: Ge 1:11, 12, 21, 24, 25.

[12] Gordon J. Wenham, Genesis 1-15. *Word Biblical Commentary* vol. I (Waco, TX: Word Books Publisher, 1987), 38.

[13] C.F. Keil and F. Delistzsch, *Commentary on the Old Testament I: The Pentateuch. reprint* (Grand Rapids: William B. Eerdmans Publishing Company, 1981), 62.

[14] John Calvin, *Commentaries on the Book of Genesis.* vol. 1, trans. John Kind. reprint (Grand Rapids: Baker Book House, 1993), 92. See also Terence E. Fretheim, "The Book of Genesis: Introduction, Commentary, and Reflections." *The New Interpreter's Bible* (Nashville: Abingdon Press, 1994), 345.

[15] Gerhard Hasel, "The Meaning of 'Let Us' in Gen 1:26," AUSS 13 (1975): 65.

[16] Stephen Greenhalgh, "Creative Partnership in Genesis," SCRB 22 (1992): 9-14. Greenhalgh relates the inclusion of partnership here by the "Let Us" formula elsewhere such as in Ge 11:3-4 and 11:7.

[17] Zlotowitz, 69.

of unity), people were created to represent God's kind of community living with God's community kind of relational characteristics.[18]

"In our image, in our likeness" confirms this, for image and likeness are parallels.[19] Image and likeness do not introduce exact replicas of God, but effective reflections of God.[20] Since both male and female constitute the *"adam"* in verse 26, both are "equally godly, of equal worth, neither more in the likeness of God than the other."[21]

Image *(tselem)* indicates some formal representation or copy while likeness *(demut)* indicates resemblance. To be in God's image/likeness is to be God's responsible representative on earth[22] with the capacity of enjoying a cooperative relationship with God and one another.

Wenham concludes that God created people to be His vice-regent on earth – His representatives as the copy of God Himself.[23] But just what aspect of God are people in His image to represent, to reflect, to mirror? It is God's relational character – His love. Every commandment in the Old Testament is fulfilled by love.[24] Emil Brunner describes *imago dei* this way,

> True humanity is not genius but love, that love
> which man does not possess from or by himself but
> which he receives from God, who is love. True
> humanity does not spring from the full development of
> human potentiality, but it rises through the reception,
> the perception, and the acceptance of the love of God,

---

[18] Samson Hirsch noted, "God created people to be His representatives, His agents on earth." *The Pentateuch*, 130.

[19] Calvin affirms the parallelism, 93-94. Derek Kidner notes that there is no "and" between the two descriptions which connotates that image and likeness reinforce one another. *Genesis: an Introduction and Commentary. The Tyndale Old Testament Commentaries* (Downers Grove, IL: InterVarsity Press, 1967), 50.

[20] Jewett, 21.

[21] Hirsch, 119.

[22] Fretheim connects functionality to being in the image of God – "to mirror God to the world." 345.

[23] Wenham, 32.

[24] There are 613 such commandments, but each deals with a proper relationship with God, or self, or others, or things. See Mt. 7:12, 22:35-40; Ro 13:8-16; Ga 5:13-14. The Old Testament describes itself as the covenant of love and of peace. See Dt 7:9; 1Ki 8:23; Ne 1:5, 9:32; Nu 25:12; Is 54:10; Eze 34:25, 37:26.

and it develops and is preserved by abiding in
communion with the God who reveals Himself as
love.[25]

Jewett refers to being in God's image as an *analogia re ationis* –
analogy of relatedness.[26] Wenham suggests that God expects men and
women to imitate Him in daily living.[27] Brunner agrees, for :o be in the
imago dei is to reflect God's character – His kind of rule – t1e rule of
love and not as an arbitrary master over each other, for *imago dei* is
relational.[28] Barth related the male/female relationship to the trinity when
he wrote, "By the divine likeness in Genesis 1:27 there is ur.derstood the
fact that God created them male and female, corresponding :o the fact
that God Himself exists in relationship not in isolation."[29] G-entz notes
"God is the social trinity" . . . "unity-in-diversity . . . from which
"human mankind as male and female emerges."[30] Thus "humans-in-
relation or humans-in-community ultimately reflect the *imago dei*."[31]

Community as Male and Female in Partnership:
Genesis 1:28

God created both the man and the woman with privilege[32] and
purpose[33] without a hint of ontological or functional superiority or
inferiority of either.[34] The five responsibilities[35] were given in the plural,
"you", i.e., to both man and the woman. One gender is not elevated
above another. Snyder rightly observes that this text does nat place the

---

[25] Emil Brunner, *The Christian Doctrine of Creation and Redemption*.
Dogmatics vol. 11, trans. Olive Wyon (Philadelphia: The Westminster Press,
1952), 58-59.

[26] Jewett, 36.

[27] Wenham, 39.

[28] Brunner, 68-69.

[29] Barth, 117.

[30] Grentz, 154.

[31] *Ibid.*, 171.

[32] The privilege – in His image (v 26a) and with His blessing (v 28a).

[33] The purpose – to extend God's loving care of His creation (v 28b; 2:15).

[34] R.M. Davidson, "The Theology of Sexuality in the Beginning: Genesis 1-
2" AUSS 26 (1988): 7.

[35] Mainly two with parallelisms "you be fruitful, you increase in number,
you fill the earth, you subdue it, you rule over...." To rule is from the Hebrew
mashal, which means to serve, not to abuse. See Brigitte Kahl, "Human Culture
and the Integrity of Creation: Biblical Reflection on Genesis 1-11," ECR 39
(1987): 130; and Fretheim, 346.

woman in subordination to the man. Instead, God communicated a joint-rule as stewards of God.[36] Brown notes that no division of labor is suggested such as women alone are to provide babies while the men alone are to rule over the things of the earth.

Eve was not restricted to home responsibilities while Adam was released to extended roles.[37] All tasks were to be done in partnership. Genesis 1 "democratizes this royal image so that all humanity belongs to this sphere, and inter-human hierarchical understandings of the image are set aside."[38] Snyder concurs, "the only way man and woman can possibly relate fully and harmoniously together as God intends is through mutual submission."[39] To assign headship to one or the other is to introduce something the text ignores.[40]

It appears that restricting many (if not most) job distributions to only one gender is more determined by culture and tradition than by creation and charisma. Distributions restricted to only one gender only can eventually communicate inequality of the sexes. Pamela Scalise notes that God intended the solidarity of humanity to be demonstrated partly by male and female enjoying joint responsibilities.[41] Jewett notes that humanity, which is not shared, is *in*humanity.[42] That does not mean we do not function as individuals, but that we reflect God's image individually in relationality.[43] But "the idea of woman as man's *fellow*-worker militates against the idea of the woman's role as a permanent nurse and housemaid."[44] Brown makes an incisive contribution:

> Is it possible that the "image" of God is fleshed
> out in humanity via maleness and femaleness? In other
> words, is it possible that the state of unity and
> fellowship and equality enjoyed by the persons of the

---

[36] Howard A. Snyder, *Liberating the Church: The Ecology of Church & Kingdom.* reprint (Eugene, OR: Wipe and Stock Publishers, 1996), 227.

[37] Judy L. Brown, *Women Ministers According to Scripture* (Kearney, NE: Morris Publishing, 1996), 24.

[38] Fretheim, 345.

[39] Snyder, 228.

[40] James Hurley, *Man and Woman in Biblical Perspective* (Grand Rapids: Zondervan, 1981), 172. However, Hurley later contradicts this position.

[41] Pamela J. Scalise, "Women in Ministry: Reclaiming Our Old Testament Heritage," Rev Exp 83 (1986): 7.

[42] Jewett, 36.

[43] Mary J. Evans, *Women in the Bible* (Downers Grove, IL: InterVarsity Press, 1986), 13.

[44] W.R. Domeris, "Biblical Perspective on the Role of Women," JTSOA 55 (1986): 58.

trinity was meant to define male-female relationships? Is that what it means to be in the image of God?

. . . If it is true that the fellowship between Adam and Eve, consequently between men and women in general, is a primary or even a partial means through which God's image is to be visible in humanity, then several compelling ramifications must be noted. Human sexuality would be at the very center of the Christian doctrine of "man." The differences between men and women are to reflect the distinctions between the persons of the trinity. The equality and dignity of each member of the triune God and the complementariness and unity with the Godhead are essential traits of God that are to be reflected in the male-female relationships of humanity. There should be no attempt to disregard one's sexuality or to devalue or degrade the other, not on the part of men or women. Such posturing would distort or prevent rather than reflect the image of God. . .

. . . The seriousness of homosexuality and lesbianism becomes quite clear. Each is a blatant denial of the very means through which an individual is to rightly reflect God's image. The male chauvinism that has been a blight upon society since antiquity *and* the radical, secular feminism with equal venom are *both* dramatically opposed to the will of God. Each disrespects the opposite gender as to negate any possibility of men and women reflecting the harmony that exists within the Godhead.[45]

She further adds "perhaps the *re*-creation that occurs at salvation gives the church what was originally made available at creation, namely, the capacity for men and women to reflect the harmonious relationship that exists with God."[46]

The "Godufactured" Male: Genesis 2:7

Male and female were both created in the image and likeness of God, but not "godufactured"[47] simultaneously. While Genesis 1 views the creation of humans as the apex of God's creation, chapter 2 views the apex of earthly community with male and female created for each

---

[45] Brown, 20-21.

[46] Ibid., 21.

[47] This is a term I coined and use in teaching to describe God's meticulous care in forming the original man and woman. The term parallels the precision of manufactured products.

other. "For this reason a man will leave his father and mother and be united to his wife, and they will become one flesh." (2:24) Genesis 2 does not challenge nor contradict Genesis 1, but gives a re-run of the creation of humans with added specific details. Recording the fact that the male was created first reveals the *sequencing* of the appearances of the two, not the *superiority* of one over the other. The Bible does not consistently give sequencing special status. The first heaven and earth are not superior to the second heaven and earth; nor is the first creation superior over the second; the first birth over the second; the first Jerusalem over the second; the first Adam over the second; nor the first human (male) over the second (female).

Genesis 2:7 reveals the "how" of the "what." The "what" being the *ontological* characteristic of people – in the image and likeness of God with their *functional* capacity. We were "godufactured" according to God's kind (ontological) so we could relate according to God's way (functional). The ontological and functional merged when God breathed into Adam "the breath of life." The Hebrew word for breath is *neshamah*, one of two Hebrew words for "spirit."[48] "Breath of life" is the same terminology Paul used centuries later when referring to the Holy Spirit.[49] Keil and Delitzsch refer to "breath of life" as the seal and pledge of our relation to God – of our godlike dignity.[50] Paul, described the Holy Spirit as the Christian's seal, pledge, and guarantee.[51]

Just what is the Holy Spirit? It is the extended earthly presence of God.[52] Paul referred to the Spirit as the presence of God[53] as did John[54]

---

[48] *Neshamah* and *Ruah* are translated as spirit, wind, and breath in the Hebrew Bible. Wind and breath relate to God's Spirit in that breath is evidence of life, and wind emphasizes power. *Neshamah* and *Ruah* are used interchangeably to refer to God's Spirit in several places. See Is 42:5, Ps 104:29-30, Job 33:4, Zec 12:1.

[49] Ro 8:2.

[50] Keil and Delitzsch, 63.

[51] 2 Co 1:22, 5:5; Eph 1:13, 4:30.

[52] See the Hebrew parallelism of presence of God and Spirit of God in Ps 51:11 and 139:7. God was present in the preaching and writing of the prophets via His Spirit (2 Pe 1:20-21). God was enfleshed in Jesus via the conception of the Spirit (Mt 1:20 = "God with us," 1:23).

[53] Eph 2:20 "And in him you too are being built together to become a dwelling in which God lives by his Spirit."

[54] 1 Jn 3:24 ..."And this is how we know that he lives in us: we know it by the Spirit he gave us."

and Peter.[55] But what aspect of God's presence do we receive with the indwelling Holy Spirit? We receive God's relational equipment for community living: love, joy, peace, patience, kindness, goodness, faithfulness, gentleness and self-control.[56] We were "godufactured" according to His kind so we could relate according to His way via His Spirit. All responsibilities and relationships of that first male were (are) to flow from and be expressive of love, God's basic relational characteristic.[57]

The "Godufactured" Female: Genesis 2:18; 2:22

Humans are social beings[58] who need each other.[59] So the "not good" became "very good" after God created the woman[60] as man's help. Translating the Hebrew *ezer* as "help" or "helper" can be culturally misleading, for it can connote someone who is subordinate to another.[61] Some have made such an interpretation. Keil and Delitzsch concluded that "created for the male, the woman was made subordinate to him from the very first."[62] Ortlund maintains that because she is his helper, "a man, just by virtue of his manhood, is called to lead for God. A woman, just by virtue of womanhood, is called to help for God."[63]

Others, however, see no implication that "help" refers to the status of the one who helps.[64] *Ezer* is used 20 other times in the Old Testament, 16 of which refer to *God* as our help.[65] Thus it is used more often to

---

[55] Ac 5:3-4. See Peter's interchange "lied to the Holy Spirit" (v. 3) and "lied to God" (v. 4).

[56] Ga 5:22-23.

[57] 1 Jn 4:16.

[58] Calvin, 128.

[59] Letha Dawson Scanzoni and Nancy A. Hardesty, *All We're Meant to Be: Biblical Feminism for Today*. 3d rev. ed. (Grand Rapids: William B. Eerdmans, 1992), 23.

[60] Ge 1:31.

[61] Davidson, 115.

[62] Keil and Delitzsch, 103.

[63] Raymond C. Ortlund, Jr., "Male-Female Equality and Male Headship: Genesis 1-3," in *Recovering Biblical Manhood & Womanhood: A Response to Evangelical Feminism*. eds. John Piper and Wayne Grudem (Wheaton: Crossway Books, 1991), 102.

[64] See Fretheim, 352: Davidson, 15.

[65] See Ex 18:4; Dt 33:7, 26; Ps 33:20; 70:5; 115: 9, 10, 11.

refer to a "superordinate" help than to a subordinate one.[66] *Ezer* is a relational word that describes a characteristic of God that mirrors God's *imago*. To be in God's image is to help another with love.[67] It is to become great by serving.[68]

For the woman to be a help "suitable for him" was evidently revelational to Adam. "Suitable for" is a translation of the Hebrew, *kenegdo*, which literally means "according to what is in front" of him,[69] which has two nuances. The first nuance pictures her as one who corresponds to him as his equal counterpart.[70] In her, Adam could recognize the humanity that was his.[71] Thus the facing of each other communicates an horizontal relationship of equality, not a vertical one of superiority to inferiority as in an hierarchical chain of command.

The second nuance of *kenegdo* spotlights the sexual difference, for what is "in front of" the man to which she corresponds includes his sexual difference from her. In their sexuality, they are unlike each other, and in that unlikeness they need each other not only to "be fruitful and increase in number," but also to partnership with their non-reproductive differences in caring for God's creation. Because male and female are different, they need one another,[72] and the creation and culture need both. Male and female are to correspond to each other both sexually and socially. To blur the gender differences, to pretend they do not exist, and/or to subsume or subordinate one as a subset under the rulership of the other is to potentially weaken the *imago dei* in both. Erikson noted that "a truly emancipated woman . . . would refuse to accept comparisons with more active male proclivities . . . even when . . . it has, or precisely when, it has become quite clear that she can match

---

[66] However, Ortlund states that God subordinates himself to us with his help, 104.

[67] Kidner, 65.

[68] See the biblical theology of greatness in Mt 20:25-28; Lk 22:24-27; Php 2:5-11.

[69] William E. Hull, "Women in Her Place: Biblical Perspectives," Rev Exp 72 (1975): 13.

[70] Davidson, 15-16.

[71] Keil and Delitzsch, 86; Hull wrote that this word emphasizes that she was "a kind of mirror of his humanity",13. See also Franklin S. Page, "Toward a Biblical Ethic of Women in Ministry," Ph.d. diss., Southwestern Baptist Theological Seminary, September, 1980, 83; and Wenham, 68.

[72] Brunner, 64.

man's performance and competence in vast spheres of achievement. *True equality can only mean the right to be uniquely creative.*"[73] (italics mine)

Woman being formed from the male does not imply subordination to the male any more than does man being formed from the dust suggests his subordination to it.[74] Perhaps God formed her from Adam's rib as sort of a show-and-tell of His intention for their side-by-side partnership,[75] which Adam seemed to have affirmed in his exclamation, "this at last is bone of my bone and flesh of my flesh."[76] While not stated, Eve surely received God's "breath of life" as did Adam, for both were created in the image and likeness of God, which affirms God's Spirit in both.

Brunner noted that "existence-in-community" is part of true humanity because "God is love, and in God's very nature there is community - man must be able to love: thus man has to be created as a *pair* of human beings. He cannot fully realize his nature without the other one: his destiny is fellowship in love."[77] Karl Barth captured our interdependence by stating that "man's being is in its root fellow-humanity" and "humanity which is not fellow-humanity is inhumanity." Man was created to participate in a "radical relativisation."[78] As God does not exist independently from the relationship of the Father, Son, and Holy Spirit, we cannot be fully human by living apart from other humans. Humans are simply neither autonomous nor self-sufficient. The word "good" (the Hebrew word *tob*) in Genesis 1 described different aspects of God's creation functioning "according to their kind." That is, each life-form was acting and reacting as it was designed to do; however, the male-in-aloneness from another person was not.[79]

The "Community of Unity"

After six days of God's creative activity, His intention for a "community of unity" on earth became the cultural context of life in the garden. A community of unity existed among all life forms. The Darwinian concept of the survival of the fittest was nonexistent. Adam

---

[73] Erik Erikson, *Identity Youth and Crises* (New York: W.W. Norton & Company, 1968), 290-291.

[74] Davidson, 16.

[75] *Ibid.*, 17.

[76] Ge 2:23.

[77] Brunner, 64.

[78] Barth, 117, 120-121.

[79] Thus God's announcement, "It is not good for the man to be alone." (Ge 2:18)

and Eve enjoyed community with not only the animals, but also with God, each other, and the surrounding environment. Adam enjoyed an harmonious community with Eve. When he first saw her, he excitedly exclaimed, "this is now bone of my bones, and flesh of my flesh; she shall be called 'woman', for she was taken out of man."[80] He did not see her as a competitor, but as a companion; not as property to control, but as a partner to caress.

Adam and Eve also enjoyed a "community of unity" with their own individual selves. "They were both naked, and they felt no shame."[81] Each had a healthy self-esteem – no sense of inferiority or superiority. The two also shared a "community of unity" with things. There was no greed for, or prioritizing of the beautiful gems, gold, onyx stone (and no doubt many more), and of the aromatic resin. Riches in abundance and without impurities surrounded them.[82] Absent was "what is mine is mine and I will keep it from you" or "what is yours is mine and I will take it from you." Absent also were battles or struggles between the natural elements.

What a community! God's will was being done on earth as in heaven—a life of unity amid diversity without animosity. Only when both male and female work together and live in a mutuality of community did God say creation was "very good" (Genesis 1:31). Hirsch noted that "the human role will never be sound as long as the first fundamental virtue of life is not considered with seriousness of both sexes; as long as . . . men should allow themselves things that are not to be permitted to girls and women."[83] And for Hirsch, the fundamental virtue of life is that the breath of God's life makes people partakers of God's nature and character[84] as they share equality in God's likeness.[85] Drawing from the *vilnagaon*, Scherman stated that something may be good in isolation, but not when it is combined with another thing,[86] as is man and woman.

---

[80] *Ibid.*, 2:23.

[81] *Ibid.*, 2:25.

[82] Zlotowitz, 97.

[83] Hirsch, 72.

[84] *Ibid.*, 55.

[85] *Ibid.*, 33.

[86] Scherman and Zoltowitz, 9.

The Community Shattered

God did not create the woman so man would have an object to subdue/dominate. He created people to lovingly and caringly subdue/dominate things, and to love God and one another. But Satan turns that around by tempting, deceiving, and guiding people to subdue/dominate over each other (and try to do so over God) and to love things. That reversal of love and domination was the rootage of dysfunctional relationships in the garden that has continued throughout the planet to this day.

From Unity to Disunity

The text does not suggest that Satan[87] approached Eve because she was either stronger or weaker than Adam. To suggest that Adam was with Eve *during her dialogue with the serpent* is possible, but is not textually clear. To suggest that Eve received God's command about eating from the tree of the knowledge of good and evil secondhand from her spiritual leader, Adam, is reading too much into the text. The total conversations of God with Adam and Eve are surely not recorded in Genesis. To suggest that Eve distorted God's word by adding "and you must not touch it" is as subjective as it is to suggest that one of the Gospel writers distorted God's word by adding words to Jesus that another did not include. Since God spoke directly to Eve *after* she sinned, there is no reason to suspect that He did not also do so *before* she sinned. Is it not more like God to communicate His commands clearly to *both* Adam and Eve since He confronted *both* about their disobedience? Both disobeyed God; God confronted both; both experienced spiritual death; both were expelled from the garden;[88] both continued to live with dysfunctional relationships; and both were credited with disobedience in apostolic writings.[89]

The primary nuance of "death" is separation. And the death they initially experienced was the separation of God's Spirit living within. Sin separates from God's inner life (Isaiah 59:2) which *is* death (Ephesians 2:1-2: Romans 6:23). The reality of sin and its holistic results are recorded. The community of unity, which was dependent

---

[87] See Rev 12:9 for the identity of the serpent in Ge 3:2 being the devil - Satan.

[88] Ge 3:8-13; 16-19.

[89] Eve in 1Ti 2:14 and Adam in Ro 5:14-19.

upon humans daily expressing the character of God (*imago dei*), became a chaos of disunity in the following ways:

1. Instead of companionship (unity) with God, the couple hid from Him, with fear – the beginning of phobias.
2. Instead of enjoying a healthy self-esteem, the couple was ashamed of their nakedness and covered themselves – the beginning of inferiority complex, low self-esteem, and lack of transparency demonstrated today by mask-wearing which feeds independence rather than interdependence.[90]
3. Instead of unity with each other, they played the blame game. Adam blamed both God and the woman while Eve blamed the serpent – the beginning of projections, refusing responsibility and accountability. To blame is to b-lame.
4. Instead of unity within nature, the harmonious cosmos was thrown into disharmony – the beginning of the survival of the fittest and the struggles for subsistence.[91]

From Cooperation To Competition: Genesis 3:16

Is the statement, "he shall rule over you" prescriptive or descriptive? Was that announcing a post-fall development or the pre-fall continuation? Regardless of which side one takes, it is likely that the battle between the sexes[92] began after the fall with some of the issues described in Genesis 3:16, ". . . I will greatly increase your pains in child bearing; with pain you will give birth to children. Your desire will be for your husband, and he will rule over you." Below is a broad sweep of positions taken:

1. The woman's subordination is an ordinance of creation.[93]
2. The text is a reaffirmation of the woman's subordination and is a blessing for her when she faces difficulties.[94]

---

[90] Hull noted that instead of life in mutuality – the God-given reciprocity, they attempted to achieve their destiny separately evidenced by both covering up self, 72.

[91] See the relationship of imbalance of nature to man's sin in Ro 8:19-21 and the restoration of nature's unity through God's plan to unite *all things* in Eph 1:10 and Col 1:20. The initial promise of restoration was made at the time the imbalance began, Ge 3:15.

[92] Susan T. Foh, "What is the Woman's Desire." *WJT 37* (1974-75): 382.

[93] James Hurley, 218-219; and several others.

[94] Stephen B. Clark, *Man and Woman in Christ: An Examination of the Roles of Men and Women in Light of Scripture and the Social Sciences*. (Ann Arbor, MI: Servant Books, 1980), 35; and many others.

3. The woman's subordination is a result of the fall as one of the evil consequences of sin.[95]
4. Submission of the wife is not a creation ordinance, but is prescriptive due to the fall.[96]
5. The woman's subordination is a blessing for her, but is neither a creation ordinance nor a post-fall prescription.[97]

I will consider some of these positions from the following different angles:

1. God's plan for humanity has not changed, but disobedience caused a fundamental change in the nature of humans and their relationship to God; but the joint responsibilities of dominion and procreation were not revoked.[98]
2. Being separated from God's indwelling Holy Spirit as His interior equipment for relatedness results in ungodly relationships.
3. Genesis 3:16 does not describe the way things were supposed to be, and thus is not to continue for all times.[99]
4. The fact that women with increased pain and men working with physical struggle and sweat are today being reduced and even eliminated by painkillers and equipment such as air-conditioned cabs suggests that Christians need to rethink the longevity of the man's rule over women if that means domination.

Genesis 3:16 seems to introduce competitive *attitudes*. The two relational attitudes that can be viewed as competitive are, "your desire will be for your husband", and "he shall rule over you." The Hebrew word for desire, tesh*uqua*, is used in only two other places in the Old Testament. The first describes something functioning as a master over another,[100] and the second describes the sexual desire of a husband for his wife.[101] Because of its use in the next chapter, some believe "desire"

---

[95] Jewett, 114; and many others.

[96] Francis Schaffer, *Genesis in Space and Time: Flow of Biblical History.* (Downers Grove, IL: Inter Varsity Press, 1972), 93-94; and several others.

[97] John Otwell, *And Sarah Laughed: The Status of Women in the Old Testament.* (Westminster Press, 1977), 18.

[98] Scalise, 8.

[99] Hull, 14.

[100] Ge 4:7 sin's desire is to master a person.

[101] Ss 7:10.

in 3:16 describes the wife's goal to control her husband.[102] Others believe "desire" is a promise that the pain in childbearing will not so severe that women will stop having sexual intimacy with their husbands.[103] Others understand that "desire" refers to the woman's instinctive inclination or passionate desire toward her own husband.[104] Others believe "desire" describes women distancing themselves from God by transferring their service alliance from Him to a slave allegiance for their husbands.[105]

It is not possible to objectively decide the primary context and object of Eve's "desire." Applying the same connotation as used 15 verses later (mastery over) is attractive, but it is also attractive to use the Song of Solomon's connotation (sexual desire)[106] because it describes a wife-husband intimate relationship, which is the Genesis 3:16 context. Perhaps it is not too far off to suggest a combination of the two, i.e., the possibility that the wife might use her sexual desire to get her way (master) over her husband.

Whatever we do with her "desire" needs to be done with the man's "rule." That is, if her desire is a negative response, then the man's rule is also negative. If one is positive, both are positive. If one continues a pre-fall relationship, both do. If one is the consequence of the fall, both are. Exegetical support is lacking for dividing the two into opposite categories as some do.

---

[102] Fah maintains that her desire to control her husband means the man can no longer rule easily, but must fight for his headship. Thus the woman "has corrupted both the willing submission of the wife and the loving headship of the husband," 382; see also Ortlund, 107-109; Calvin takes the position that she exceeded her proper bounds, 172; George Knight also believes the woman corrupted the relationship, George Knight III, "Male and Female Related He Them," *CT* IXX (April 9, 1976): 710.

[103] Rabbinic commentators view the desire as sexual. See Hirsch who translates teshuqa as longing, "and unto they husband shall thy longing be," 84. See other rabbinic views along the same line in Zlotowitz, 130-131. See also Gentile commentators – Wenham, 81; Davidson, 45; Hermann Gunkel, *Genesis*. trans. Mark E. Biddle (Macon, GA: Mercer University Press, 1977), 21.

[104] F.F. Bruce, 1 and 2 Corinthians, New Century Bible (London: Oliphants, 1971), 136.

[105] John Skinner, A Critical and Exegetical Commentary on Genesis. The New International Critical Commentary (Edinburg: T & T Clark, 1910), 30. See also Scanzoni and Hardesty, 43.

[106] "I belong to my lover and his desire is for me . . . come my lover . . . let us spend the night. . . ." Song of Solomon 7:10-11.

The issue gets stickier with the second issue, "he shall rule over you." Several believe this is a *continuation* of the wife's subordination to her husband;[107] however, no one with this position views the rule as dictatorial.[108] Schmitt linguistically supports the view that the woman's "desire" and the man's "rule" are positive services,[109] thus both are serving each other – she by her desire and he by his rule. Others view man's rule as a *consequence* of the fall not as a continuation of the pre-fall relationship.[110] Bruce believed the rule refers to the husband taking advantage of the wife's passionate desire toward him "so as to dominate her."[111] I do not see human hierarchy in the first two chapters of Genesis. Those chapters do not suggest a top-down chain of command, but mutuality – a side-by-side relationship[112] with joint decisions and activities based upon unity and respect for the diversity of giftedness and abilities of each. Page is correct, "when reciprocity was broken hostility resulted."[113] Kahl adds,

---

[107] Calvin sees the continuation implied by the fact that she was created to be man's help, 103, 172; Foh views the continuation as part of the created order since Adam was created first, 378 n.14; Wenham believes the man had pre-fall authority by virtue of the fact that she was made from man and was twice named by man, 81; Ortlund states that "nothing can change the fact that God created male headship as one aspect of our pre-fall perfection," 109; plus many others – in fact all complementarians. It is not appropriate to cite God's words to Adam, "Because you listened to your wife . . ." as evidence of his rulership coming from the creation. The issue is not listening to a wife, but yielding to temptation from what she said. Elsewhere God told Abraham to do what his wife tells him. See Ge 21:12.

[108] Keil and Delitzsch captures the view of many – that the man is not to be a despot crushing the woman into a slave, but a rule of that esteems and loves her, 103.

[109] John J. Schmitt, "Like Eve, Like Adam: MSL in Gen 3, 16," *BIB* 72 (1991): 1-22. For Schmitt, service is the key. He states that nowhere does the Old Testament direct wives to obey their husbands, 1-2.n.3.

[110] Hull states that this situation is a "tragedy permitted by God as the price of mankind's freedom to fall was transformed by Him at infinite cost," 14; see also Kahl, 133; Brown, 53; Jewett, 22; Grenz, 120, 165-169; Fretheim, 363; Phyllis Trible, *God and The Rhetoric of Sexuality* (Philadelphia: Fortress Press, 1978), 128; Martin Luther, *Lectures on Genesis: Chapters 1-5* (St. Louis: Concordia Publishing, 1958), 200-203. Plus several others – in fact all egalitarians.

[111] Bruce, 136.

[112] Kahl, 137.

[113] Page, 87. Skinner notes that man's rule was not the intention seen in Ge 2:18, 23; 83. Jewett calls his rulership a perversion of the humanity of the male, 22.

Any human culture absolutizing itself at the
expense of other human beings . . . undermines the
integrity of creation and thereby becomes self-
destructive . . . Humanity needs a fundamentally new
self-perception based on a co-existence, cooperation
and communication rather than confrontation and
competition . . . there is no other way to help the
"oikoumene," the inhabited earth, habitable, no other
way for humanity to survive. Human culture must be
humanized to be a global peace culture, thus
establishing the preconditions for more justice and a
reintegration of creation. The next revolution facing
humanity is a revolution to world peace.[114]

Since the renewal of the Holy Spirit initiates the new creation,
Christians should renounce systemic relationships that reflect the
consequences of the fall. Mollenkott highlights this concept,

It is ridiculous enough for the secular world to
uphold male dominance while seeking relief from all
the other sad results of the fall. But for *Christians* to
support male domination is the height of folly! . . .
Even if Genesis 3 *had* been meant as a prescription of
what fallen civilization of necessity had to be like, it is
clear that uniting with Christ is supposed to move us
out of the old order into a completely new order.[115]

The consequences of sin are reversed and should be renounced by
the character of the "new creation" person. If Genesis 3:16 does not
cement suffering in child delivery as unchangeable (and it is not for all
women of all cultures, throughout all earthly time); and if sweating for
working the ground is reversible (for not all men in all cultures
throughout all earthly time); and if women are free to work the soil with
or without sweating, then Genesis 3:16 does not require men (husbands)
to rule women (wives) for all cultures throughout all earthly time.

Stanley Grenz shares a beneficial insight:

. . . God creates the first human pair in order that
humans may enjoy community with each other. More
specifically, the creation of the woman is designed to
deliver the man from his isolation. . .

We should not be surprised that the image of God
ultimately focuses on community. For the doctrine of
the Trinity makes clear that throughout all eternity God

---

[114] Kahl, 137.

[115] Virginia Ramey Mollenkott, *Women Men & the Bible* (Nashville:
Abingdon, 1977), 134.

is community. . . Consequently, neither the male as such nor the isolated human is the image of God. Instead humans in-relation or humans-in-community ultimately reflect the *imago dei*. Such human fellowship encompasses diversity and illustrates mutuality. . . .

The *imago dei* includes man in fellowship with woman. . . . Men and women think differently; they approach the world differently. These fundamentally different outlooks toward others, life and the world mean that each sex needs the other in order to fulfill the various dimensions of human life.

This understanding of the divine image constitutes a strong foundation for affirming the participation of men and women in all areas of church life. . . . No congregation can genuinely expect to complete the mandate given by the Lord if its structures allow only the male voice to be head in planning and decision-making.[116]

From Community to Chaos (From Valuing to Violence)

Without the indwelling Spirit, the first couple evidently drew upon external models for interpersonal relationships. The survival of the fittest that eventually emerged in the animal kingdom could have become one model to copy. Eventually "every inclination of the thoughts" of people was "evil all the time." God was grieved He made humans and his heart was filled with pain,[117] because His intended community turned community into chaos and replaced valuing God and one another with violence.

The resulting description is graphically pervasive, "now the earth was corrupt in God's sight and was full of violence. God saw how corrupt the earth had become, for all the people on earth had corrupted their ways."[118] Both the consequential desires of women and the rulership of men were corrupt. So God started anew with Noah and his family, but eventually people shifted from serving the earth and one another to trying to storm heaven in order to make a name for them.[119]

---

[116] Grenz, 171-172. See also 151-156 for Grenz's argument against the subordination of Jesus within the Trinity as the model and mandate for women's subordination to men.

[117] Ge 6:5-6.

[118] *Ibid.*, 6:11-12.

[119] *Ibid.*, 11:1-4.

The Call of God for Community

The Two-Sided Call: Genesis 12:1-3

God's call began with one man, Abram, "leave your country, your people . . . and go to the land I will show you." God's call to Abram included two aspects – like a two-sided coin. Both sides/aspects are needed for the authentic call to be heard and heeded. The two aspects are privilege and purpose. Privilege is what God wants to do *for* us. Purpose is what He wants to accomplish *through* us.

The privilege aspect:
> I will make you into a great nation,
> I will bless you;
> I will make your name great . . .
> I will bless those who bless you; whoever curses you I will curse

The purpose aspect:
> and you will be a blessing . . .
> and all peoples on earth will be blessed through you.

Did you catch the purpose? "All peoples on earth will be blessed through you." All peoples refer to all categories and subsets of humanity – ethnic, age, occupation, gender, weight, height, cultural status, IQ, physical, and mental health, etc. God's dream is to bless all people *through* people – His people.[120]

The Reductionistic Response

Through subsequent centuries, God's people eventually emphasized the privilege aspect and deemphasized the purpose side. By the time Jesus came, God's people stigmatized humanity with labels that led to exclusion and conflict rather than to inclusion and community (certain occupations,[121] people with health problems, the poor,[122] the non-Jews, women, the immoral, etc.). Most people had no clue what the real God was like, especially that He is an inclusive God with the consistent characteristic of love.

---

[120] A "top gun" Hebrew, Paul, quoted the purpose side of the call and referred to it as the gospel announced in advance to Abraham (Ga 3:8). Peter announced that Christians inherited what was said to Abraham. "Through your offspring all peoples on earth will be blessed" (Ac 3:25).

[121] Such as shepherds, tanners, and tax collectors.

[122] The theology that people were sick and poor due to displeasing God was developed through the AD centuries.

God's Correctives to Reductionism

While God permitted His people to reduce inclusiveness to exclusiveness, He shared many teachings and examples to reveal how God's people can be a blessing to all categories of peoples. He established many laws for helping the poor, condemned the rich who neglected the poor, established laws to protect women from being accused falsely and from being sexually abused and used, permitted divorce because of the harshness of men, commanded care for the widows and orphans, and honored Gentiles who helped His people. All four women in Jesus' genealogy were non-Jews.[123] He sent Jonah to a violent, anti-godly Gentile nation. He reminded His people "It is too small a thing for you to be my servant to restore the tribes of Jacob and bring back those of Israel I have kept. I will also make you a light for the Gentiles that you may bring my salvation to the ends of the earth."[124] Throughout those pre-Jesus centuries, God used women in significant ways to counter the growing and spreading prejudices against them.

Pre-Christian Inclusiveness Of Women: God's Challenge To Reductionism

Without the renewal of the Holy Spirit dwelling in people, it is not possible for any culture of any era to holistically and consistently liberate women to their pre-fall status and partnership role with men. The renewal of the Holy Spirit for all is dependent upon the life, sacrifice, and ascension of Jesus with the resulting regeneration of people. But until that time would come, God instituted many ways in the pre-Christian era that liberated women.

God blessed Sarah as a mother of all nations, and the writer of Hebrews credited her faith to conceive.[125] God told Abraham, "Listen to whatever Sarah tells you."[126] God sent an angel to minister to Hagar.[127] On another occasion, God Himself visited and spoke to her.[128] Twice God sent an angel to visit Samson's mother. On one occasion, an angel was sent to her in response to Samson's father asking for instructions.[129]

---

[123] Tamar, Rahab, Ruth, Uriah's wife (Bathsheba), Mt. 1:3-6.

[124] Is 49:6.

[125] The NIV changed Sarah's faith to Abrams' in Heb 11:11, but without manuscript evidence for making that change.

[126] Ge 21:12.

[127] *Ibid.*, 16:7-12; 19.

[128] *Ibid.*, 21:17-19.

[129] Ju 13:6-7; 13:8.

Some women protected and saved the Hebrew nation from being annihilated. Midwives risked their lives to stop Pharaoh's plan to gradually eliminate the Hebrews,[130] Queen Esther intervened to save the immediate execution of all God's people and ordered Jews to fast.[131] Abigail was considered wiser than her husband and was praised for serving David and giving him wise advice.[132] The Shunamite woman was more spiritual than her husband when she ministered to Elisha.[133] Rahab protected the Hebrew spies in Jericho,[134] and was included in the genealogy of Jesus and in the " Hall of Fame" of the faithful.[135] Deborah was God's chosen person to deliverer the Hebrew nation from foreign oppressors. She was the combined military, spiritual, and civic leader of the nation, and was the only judge who was also called a prophet. Although she was married, she was the leader of men with final authority over the nation.[136] An unnamed woman convinced David's general not to destroy a whole city because of the rebellious actions of one person.[137] A young Israelite girl, captured by the Syrians, saved her master's life.[138] Johosheba saved Joash from being murdered.[139]

A few women were prophets, whom God inspired to speak His word to both men and women. There is no hint they were under the supervision of males. Among the female prophets were Miriam, whom God sent to lead Israel along with Moses and Aaron;[140] Deborah; Huldah, with whom King Josiah consulted (instead consulting with Jeremiah or Zephaniah) which resulted in a national spiritual repentance and a return to God's word and way;[141] Isaiah's wife,[142] whom, Gill suggests may

---

[130] Ex 1:17-21.

[131] Est 4:15-16; 5:1; 8:17.

[132] 1 Sa 25:32-33.

[133] 2 Ki 4:8-37.

[134] Jos 2:1-22.

[135] Mt 1:5, Heb 11:31.

[136] Jn, chapters 4-5.

[137] 2Sa 20:16-22.

[138] 2 Ki 5:1-19.

[139] 2 Ki 11:2-3.

[140] Mi 6:4; Ex 15:20.

[141] 2 Ki 22-23.

[142] Is 8:3.

have co-authored Isaiah with her husband.[143] Two of the five premonarchical prophets were women.[144]

Condemnations against female prophets suggest the existence of many other female prophets.[145] However, the condemnations did not restrict *females* from prophesying, since the condemnations were set within the context of *identical* condemnations against *male* prophets.[146] If the condemnations against female false prophets meant there could be no *female* prophets, then neither can there be *male* prophets. The Ezekiel passage affirms God's acceptance of both male and female prophets in Judaism on the one hand and His rejection of false prophets regardless of their gender on the other hand.[147] We have no evidence that God restricted women from leadership[148] or muzzled them from speaking to and teaching men. That Israel rejected women leaders because of gender alone lacks biblical support.[149] The only named woman prophet whose advice was rejected was Noadiah because she was prophesying falsely, as were some male prophets.[150]

In addition to the above, women were allowed to be Nazarites,[151] served with priestly functions at festivals,[152] experienced theophanes,[153]

---

[143] Deborah Menken Gill, "The Female Prophets: Gender and Leadership in the Biblical Tradition." Ph.d. diss. Fuller Theological Seminary, June 12, 1991, 45-46.

[144] Miriam and Deborah along with Abraham, Moses, and Aaron.

[145] Ez 13:12-23.

[146] Ez 13:1-16; 14:9-11.

[147] See Nancy R. Bowen, "The Daughters of Your People: Female Prophets in Ezekiel 13:17-23." *JBL* 118 (1999): 417-433. Bowen argues that the condemnations were to disconnect the post-exilic religious life of the Hebrew people from pre-exilic pagan practices (witches, sorcerers, divination's, etc.), which had been led by both male and female prophets.

[148] The only leadership restricted to women were the priesthood and Levites. Although there is no clear reason stated in the text, perhaps the restriction included (1) the woman's ceremonial cleanness during her menstrual times; (2) to distance God's religion from the pagan cults (3) the physical strength needed to sacrifice large animals. However, this should not be applied to women leaders in the Christian era any more than we would restrict a handicapped person, a Gentile, or a poor person from leadership, for none of those were priests also.

[149] Grenz, 67.

[150] Ne 6:14.

[151] Nu 6:2.

[152] Dt 12:12, 18.

[153] Ge 3:13; 16:8, 18:9; Ju 13:3.

served the tabernacle,[154] could associate with men,[155] and had free access to the house of the Lord.[156]

Two Old Testament books are named after women.[157] Proverbs concludes with a description of an excellent woman who held the confidence of her husband and the praise of her children. She was not only involved in domestic activities, but also in diverse activities such as dealing in real estate, having a home-based business, marketing her product, engaging in retail, planting a vineyard, and participating in benevolence to the poor.

In summary, several women filled leadership roles with men and spoke inspired words in the form of prophecies, advice, songs, prayers, advice, commands, orders, and so on.

God looked beyond His B.C. use and appreciation of women to the Christian era by prophesying that the reductive treatment and prejudices against various categories of people, including women, were to be reversed by the coming of the Spirit and the genesis of the Christian Church.[158]

Summary

1. God is the "community" God, characterized by mutual relationships within the trinity.
2. God created the first male and female equally in His image and likeness.
3. The first male and female were given the same initial service responsibilities on earth without gender differentiation.
4. Both male and female are to reflect God's nature in daily living.
5. The image of God is fleshed out in the co-partnering of the male and female.
6. God put His Spirit in the first created persons.
7. The Holy Spirit is the presence of God – His relational characteristics.
8. Eve extended God's characteristic help, ezer, for Adam.
9. There is no superiority or inferiority in being an ezer.
10. When the pair sinned, they became separated from the indwelling Spirit and thus depended upon other resources for community living.

---

[154] Ex 38:8.

[155] Ge 24:10-27; Ru 21:1.

[156] 1 Sa 1:7.

[157] Ruth and Esther.

[158] Joel 2:28-32 which Peter quoted as evidence that the last days, the Christian era, has begun, and thus prejudices that could keep people from serving or from being saved were to end. See Acts 2:17-21.

11. The community of unity became a chaos of disunity.
12. God eventually called all people to Himself with privilege and purpose. The purpose is relational – to bless all categories of people.
13. Through the centuries, the Hebrew people reduced all categories by excluding most people.
14. The exclusiveness affected the way women were viewed and used in culture.
15. God taught many correctives against reductionism that included caring for the poor, Gentiles, and women.
16. God used women in a different leadership roles.
17. No gender specific was connected to leadership except priests and Levites.

Conclusion

The church that excludes women from leadership roles hinders people from authentically knowing and representing the inclusive God.

The *imago dei* liberates all God's people for ministry in accordance with their gifts. Only then will we holistically put flesh to Jesus' prayers, "Thy kingdom come, thy will be done on earth as it is in heaven," and, "Not my will, but yours be done."

CHAPTER 3

JESUS MODELING GOD'S INTENTION FOR WOMEN

By the time Jesus came most of the world did not understand what the Creator God was like. His people had not been a beacon of light to the Gentiles. Consequently, God incarnated Himself in human flesh through Jesus.[1] Jesus declared, "whatever the Father does the Son also does;[2] "I do nothing on my own, but speak just what the Father has taught me;[3] and "anyone who has seen me has seen the Father."[4] This chapter will develop the thesis that the church should liberate women to share leadership with men because of Jesus' ministry to, with, and through women.

This chapter will give evidence that Jesus continued God's intention for women by liberating them to various roles and ministries. The chapter will spotlight the cultural restrictions of women, significant women in the pre-ministry life of Jesus, and Jesus' liberating words and works for and with women. The chapter will conclude that Jesus' liberation of women is to continue in the on-going body of Christ, the Church.

Jesus as Liberator

Pre-Ministry Hints of Liberation

We do not need to wait until Jesus began His ministry to anticipate His liberating mission. His genealogy in Matthew included Gentile women and many immoral people. His earthly parents were quite poor.[5] When Jesus was forty-five days old, Simeon announced that Jesus would be a revelation for both Gentiles and Israel.[6] A prophetess, Anna, spoke about Jesus.[7] Gentile Magi worshipped Him before He was two years old.[8] He experienced an exodus from Egypt, which was linked to

---

[1] Mt 1:23, "and they will call him Immanuel" - which means, "God with us."

[2] Jn 5:19.

[3] Jn 8:28; 12:49-50.

[4] Jn 14:9.

[5] As seen by giving only two birds when presenting Jesus to the priest – an exception from a lamb for those in poverty. Lk 2:24 and Lk 5:11, 12:8.

[6] Lk 2:28-32.

[7] Lk 2:36-38.

[8] Mt 2:1-12.

Israel's.[9] He grew up in Galilee, a region known as the "Circle of the Gentiles", and in the small village of Nazareth, which was degraded by Jewish people in Judea.[10]

Jesus' Liberational Baptism

God's announcement at Jesus' baptism foreshadowed a liberating ministry, "This is my Son" came from Psalm 2:7 which was a Jewish royal Psalm used when coronating a new King. By using this, God announced His coronation of Jesus as King of kings. But then God linked that passage to a suffering servant passage, Isaiah 42:1, "In whom I am well pleased." By linking the royal text with the servant text, God declared that Jesus would be God's King to serve all kinds of suffering people that would bring liberation to them but suffering to Jesus. Today Christian baptism is also liberating by (1) freeing us from sin, (2) uniting us to God and to one another,[11] and (3) ordaining the baptized to continue Jesus' kind of ministry. Baptism liberates us so others can and hopefully will experience liberation through us.[12]

Jesus' baptism was the genesis point of His ministry. He began ministry the same as He ended it by relating to and identifying with the plight of sinners.[13] Jesus came with good news for the world's **troubled** people.[14] Although He was a Jew by race and a peasant by class, none of that limited Him from serving **all** kinds,[15] nor from establishing a new kind of community in line with God's original intention in creation by modeling that the sociological issues dividing people were not factors with or from God.

Jesus' "Libertarian" Inauguration Sermon

Jesus gave His inauguration speech, which spotlighted the conditions of people and the characteristics of His platform.[16] He read

---

[9] Mt 2:14-15.

[10] Jn 1:46.

[11] Ro 6:2-4, Ga 3:27-29.

[12] Michael L. Cook, "The Image of Jesus as Liberating for Women," _Chic Stud_ 27 (2'88): 136-150.

[13] He related to and identified with sinners in baptism (to which sinners were submitting by confessing their sins) and on the cross (between two thieves).

[14] Leon Morris, Luke: _An Introduction and Commentary_, revised (Grand Rapids: Eerdmans Publishing, 1990), 117.

[15] Cook, 141.

[16] Lk 4:16-27.

from another servant passage[17] announcing that He would be serving and liberating those who had been marginalized and excluded – the poor, prisoners, blind, and oppressed.

This speech revealed God's plan, Jesus' purpose, plans and pattern for His ministry.[18] Frank Stagg believes this is the keynote passage framing the theology of Luke- Acts, because it introduced not only what Jesus did, but also what Luke developed in his two-volume work.[19] Fitzmyer believes this speech foreshadows Luke's emphasis on social issues.[20] Luke positioned it at the beginning of Jesus' public ministry to "encapsulate the entire ministry of Jesus and the reaction to it."[21]

Through this "blueprint" sermon, Jesus declared that cultural and religious taboos would have no part in His manner and ministry.[22] Bock suggests the people categories listed and illustrated in this speech reach the full range of human needs.[23] However, Allen Black argued that women were not one of the oppressed groups, because they were not specifically mentioned among the oppressed or excluded in Luke-Acts.[24] But Black ignored the religious and cultural place of women in Judaism, and the fact that Jesus illustrated the opposed with a woman's situation.[25] Bock notes that a woman in this inauguration speech was the last person Jesus hearers would expect to respect.[26] However, this speech was not about liberating **women only**, but also **all humans** without distinction.[27] Jesus' speech reversed the reductionistic life proclaimed and practiced

---

[17] Is, chapters 61 and 58.

[18] Darrell L. Bock, Luke vol., 1:1-9:50. Baker Exegetical Commentary on the New Testament (Grand Rapids: Baker Books, 1994), 394.

[19] Frank Stagg, *Studies in Luke's Gospel* (Nashville: Convention Press, 1967), 40-41.

[20] Joseph A. Fitzmyer, *The Gospel According to Luke* (I-IX), The Anchor Bible (Garden City, NY: Doubleday & Company, 1985), 532.

[21] Ibid., 529.

[22] Anne McGrew Bennett tied the cultural restrictions to "the old taboos." *From Woman-Pain to Woman-Vision: Writings in Feminist Theology* (Minneapolis: Fortress Press, 1989), 28.

[23] Bock, 401.

[24] Allen Black, "Women in the Gospel of Luke," in *Essays on Women in Earliest Christianity*, ed. Carroll D. Osburn (Joplin, MO: College Press, 1993), 455.

[25] Lk 4:25-26.

[26] Bock, 408.

[27] Evelyn and Frank Stagg, *Woman in the World of Jesus* (Philadelphia: Westminster Press, 1978), 106.

by both religious and cultural traditions in his day and with a view to our day.

Jesus came "to restore the human race to its original purpose, men and women alike."[28] And He demonstrated it by consistently living a "praxis of inclusive holiness of all kinds of people"[29] in order to initiate a new kind of community – a new society.[30] He came to include the excluded, to lift up the put-down ones, to magnify the value of the marginalized ones, to honor those who were shamed, and to shame those who dishonored others.

Jewish Women in Jesus' Day

Jesus' ministry with, for, and through women sharply contrasted normative Jewish mores of His time.[31] While tracking the directional flow of the Greek, Jewish, and Roman influences on culture is difficult to trace and to pin point, there is little doubt that Alexander the Great's influence on Greek culture was paramount in shaping a large chuck of the thoughts, practices, and principles affecting the perceived and practiced value and roles of women in Jesus' era. The persistent and penetrating infiltration of Hellenism broadly and deeply spread through geographical, philosophical, sociological, and theological boundaries. It

---

[28] Stephen B. Clark, *Man and Woman in Christ: An Examination of the Roles of Men and Women in Light of Scripture and the Social Sciences* (Ann Arbor, MI: Servant Books, 1980), 38.

[29] Cook, 144.

[30] *Ibid.*, 145.

[31] James Hurley, *Man and Woman in Biblical Perspective* (Grand Rapids: Zondervan Publishing, 1981), 90.

is likely that many of the different positions about women recorded in the *Mishnah* were formed and fueled by Greek influence.[32]

Much of our information about the place and role of women in Jewish culture comes from *The Mishnah*, which was codified 150 years after Jesus' death, but spanned four previous centuries, by having been kept accurate and current through oral tradition. For some, *The Mishnah* enjoyed the same authority as the written word, and for others it was second only to the Hebrew Scriptures. *The Mishnah* linked Palestinian and non-Palestinian Judaism with integration in spite of broad geographical distances separating members. While some question using

---

[32] **General influence of Hellenism:** H.E. Dana, *The New Testament World* (Nashville: Broadman Press, 1937); Everett Ferguson, *Backgrounds of Early Christianity* (Grand Rapids: Eerdmans Publishing, 1987); Werner Foerster, From *The Exile to Christ: Historical Introduction to Palestinian Judaism*, trans. Gordon E. Harris (Philadelphia: Fortress Press, 1966); Charles Guignebert, *The Jewish World in the Time of Jesus* (New York: University Books, 1959); Martin Hengel, *Judaism and Hellenism*, vols. 1 and 2. Trans. John Bowden (Philadelphia: Fortress Press, 1974); Eduard Lose, *The New Testament Environments*, trans. John E. Steely (Nashville: Abingdon, 1976); Jerome H. Nehrey, ed., *The Social World of Luke-Acts: Models of Interpretation* (Peabody, MA: Hendrickson Publishers, 1991); Arthur Darby Nock, *Early Gentile Christianity and Its Hellenistic Background* (New York: Harper & Row, 1964); W.O.E. Oesterley, *The Jews and Judaism During the Greek Period: The Background of Christianity* (Washington, NY: Kennikat Press, 1941); John J. Pilch and Bruce J. Malina, eds., *Biblical Social Values and their Meanins* (Peabody, MA: Hendrickson Publishers, 1993); Richard Rohrbaugh, ed., *The Social Sciences and the New Testament* (Peabody, MA: Hendrickson Publishers, 1996); Emil Schurer, *A History of the Jewish People in the Time of Christ*, trans. Sophia Taylor and Peter Christie (Peabody, MA: Hendrickson Publishers, 1980); Victory Tcherikover, *Hellenistic Civilization and the Jews* (New York: Atheeneum, 1959); C.D. Yong, trans., *The Works of Philo: Complete and Unabridged* (Peabody, MA: Hendrickson Publishers, 1993); **Influence of Hellenism specifically related to the value and role of women:** Averil Camerson and Amelie Kuhrt, eds., *Images of Women in Antiquity* (Detroit, 1985); P.V.M. Flesher Oxen, *Women or Citizens? Slaves in the System of the Mishnah* (Atlanta: Brown Judaic Studies CXLIII, 1988); T. Friedman," The Shifting Role of Women from Bible to *Talmud: Judaism* 36 (1987): 479-87; Tal Ilan, Jewish Women in Greco-Roman Palestine (Peabody MA: Hendrickson Publishers, 1996); Sarah B. Pomeroy, *Goddesses, Whores, Wives, and Slaves: Women in Classical Antiquity* (New York: Schocken, 1975); *idem., "Texvikai; Kaimosikoi:* The Education of Women in the fourth Century and the Hellenistic Period," American *Journal of Ancient History* 2 (1977): 51-68; Rosemary R. Ruether, ed., *Religion and Sexism: Images of Women in the Jewish and Christian Tradition* (New York: Simon and Shuster, 1974); C. Ryder-Smith, *The Biblical Doctrine of Womanhood in its Historical Evolution* (London, 1923); Elizabeth Cady-Stanton, *The Women's Bible* (New York, 1985); Leonard Swidler, *Biblical Affirmations of Women* (Philadelphia: Westminster Press, 1979); Judith R. Wegner, "Philo's Portrayal of Women – Hebraic or Hellenic?" in *Women Like This: New Perspectives on Jewish Women in the Greco-Roman Period*, ed., Amy-Jill Levine (Atlanta, 1991): 41-66.

The Mishnah for understanding the Jewish role of women in Jesus' day, it is probably one of our best sources and should not be discredited.

Comprehensively reviewing *The Mishnah's* teaching about women is beyond the scope of this paper, because it consists of sixty-three sections or tractates grouped under six major divisions, one third of which is devoted to women issues in the "Nashim."[33] Below is a sketch of the Jewish situation of women gleaned from *The Mishnah*:

Some Rabbis taught that men would experience evil if they talked much with women.[34] Women could not be a witness in most court cases,[35] but at times in a few cases.[36] Yet some would not accept them in any case. Women were normally bypassed for receiving inheritances.[37] A wife could be obtained by intercourse, money, or writ.[38] An under-aged daughter could not refuse marriage arranged by her father.[39] A husband could divorce his wife if he found another woman more beautiful,[40] or she raised her voice while scolding him.[41] Women did not normally eat with men.[42] Prayer was uttered at meals providing three people were present, but a woman was not counted as one of the three.[43] Some Rabbis thought that sharing the Law with a daughter was to teach her lechery,[44] but some Rabbis taught their daughters anyway. Women were not required to make the pilgrimages to Jerusalem for the festivals,[45] and were exempt from studying the Torah.[46] Some Rabbis were against even

---

[33] *The Mishnah*. Trans. Herbert Danby (London: Oxford University Press, 1933). Each reference will be prefixed with "M." for Mishnah, followed by the section in which the reference is located.

[34] M.Abot. 1.5.

[35] M.Sheb. 4.11, Yeb. 16.7.

[36] M.Sot. 9.8; 6.4.

[37] M.Ket. 4.1-2

[38] M.Kid. 1.1.

[39] M.Ket. 4.4.

[40] M.Git. 9.10.

[41] M.Ket. 7.6.

[42] M.Kid. 70a.

[43] M.Ber. 7.2.

[44] M.Sota. 3.4.

[45] M.Naz. 1.1, M.Ber. 3.3.

[46] M.Sot. 3.4.

mothers teaching their children.[47] In a few situations, women could divorce their husbands.[48] The primary honor for a Jewish woman seemed to be in her home.[49]

The Jewish prayer, "Blessed be He who did not make me a Gentile, blessed be He who did not make me a woman. Blessed be He who did not make me an uneducated man (or a slave)" appears in three different pieces of Jewish literature.[50]

The role of non-Jewish women in the Greco-Roman world was quite mixed. In some locations women were used primarily as men's pleasurable sex objects and for producing sons. Divorcing them was encouraged; In Athens women were considered inferior to men and were secluded from the public; however, in Rome upper class women engaged in commerce and public life.[51]

Because the cultural norms of the day were predominately not favorable toward women, Margaret Howe noted that Jesus' relationships with women were surprising.[52] Jesus' value of women seemed to be without precedent in contemporary Judaism. Krister Stendahl noted, "all the way from circumcision to burial rites it is only the male who is an Israelite in the true sense of the word."[53] While denying that Jesus was revolutionary in regard to social roles and customs for men and women relations,[54] Clark affirmed that Jesus relating to women with love, respect, teaching, healing, and without contemptuous speech had no parallels during the two centuries before Jesus was born and during the century while he lived on earth.[55] Jesus broke through some barriers by going beyond accepted norms, and doing so contributed to spiritual and

---

[47] M.Kid. 4.13

[48] M.Ned. 11.12.

[49] *Ibid.*, 9.1.

[50] Leonard Swidler, *Biblical Affirmation of Women* (Philadelphia: Westminster Press, 1979), 154-155. For the sources see Aida Besancon Spencer, *Beyond The Curse* (Peabody, MA: Henrickson, 1985), 56.

[51] Grant R. Osborne, "Women in Jesus Ministry," *WTJ* 51 (Fall, 1989): 263-265. See also Luis Schotroff, *Let the Oppressed Go Free: Feminist Perspectives on the New Testament*, trans Anne Marie S. Kidder (Louisville: Westminster) John Knox Press, 1993), 80-91.

[52] E. Margaret Howe, *Women & Church Leadership* (Grand Rapids: Zondervan Publishing House, 1982), 19.

[53] Krister Stendahl, *The Bible and the Role of Women: A Case Study in Hermeneutics.* trans. Emilie T. Sander (Philadelphia: Fortress Press, 1966), 27.

[54] Clark, 242-243.

[55] *Ibid.*, 249-250.

social changes for women."[56] He came to liberate people from: (1) the reductionistic practical theology of God's people, (2) having little or no value and thus being of little or no use, (3) cultural and religious traditions that excluded them from many involvements.

The purpose of Jesus' liberation ministry was to restore God's original intention for community by incarnating in His own life God's two-sided call to Abraham: (1) privilege—conceived of the Holy Spirit, and (2) purpose – blessing and restoring all kinds to share equal value and use. Jesus consistently balanced God's privileges to Him with God's purpose through Him. His on-going body, the Church is called to do the same.

Women in Jesus' Pre-Ministry Life

Matthew and Luke seemed to hint that Jesus would significantly include women by mentioning some prior to His public ministry.

Women in Jesus' Genealogy: Matthew 1:1-6

That Jesus will liberate women from an inferior status is foreshadowed by the genealogical listing of four women who were Gentiles (two strikes against them) with three of them well known for some obvious immoral activities (three strikes against them).[57]

Janice Anderson believes these four women prepared the way for the Spirit's conception of Mary.[58] Osborne believes they were included to demonstrate that God had already broken down gender barriers and intended Jesus to continue to do so through His manners and ministry.[59] Matthew bracketed his Gospel with his inclusiveness of women in the beginning of his writing (the genealogical listing) and toward the conclusion (the tomb experience). For David Hagner, including these Gentile women also foreshadows Jesus ultimately including all Gentiles to God's grace, love, and forgiveness.[60]

---

[56] *Ibid.*, 251.

[57] Mt 1:3-6. Tamar gave birth to twins by incest with their grandfather (v3); Rahab was a prostitute in Jericho who hid spies and lied (v5); Bathsheba became pregnant by an extra marital affair with David (v6).

[58] Janice Capel Anderson, "Matthew: Gender and Reading," *Semeia 2* (1983): 9-10.

[59] Osborne, 271.

[60] David A. Hagner, *Matthew 14-28*, Word Biblical Commentary, vol. 33b (Dallas: Word Books, 1995), 10.

Elizabeth: A Disgrace Withdrawn, Then Filled with the Holy Spirit:
Luke 1:5-25; 39-45

In the Jewish culture, a woman's primary function was child
bearing. Those without children were stereotyped as disgraced, forgotten
by God,[61] and being punished.[62] However, Luke introduced Elizabeth as
spiritually equal with her husband priest, Zechariah, for both were
"righteous in the sight of God."[63]

Elizabeth was the only woman in the New Testament called
righteous, a label given to only five men. While Zechariah needed a sign
to believe God's promise about the birth of a son, there is no indication
Elizabeth doubted. Luke may have intentionally contrasted Elizabeth's
faith with Zechariah's.[64] Elizabeth interpreted the birth as a
compassionate act of God who took away her disgrace.[65] Elizabeth acted
courageously by naming her son and in doing so disregarded the peer
pressure on the one hand and obeyed the command from heaven on the
other hand.[66] Reid views the peoples' reaction to Elizabeth's
proclamation as evidence she was "a special agent of God, who leads
others to the source of grace."[67] Elizabeth was certainly filled with the
Holy Spirit.[68]

Anna: From the Silence of Woman to a Revelation Given: Luke
2:36-38

Since we have no evidence of any activity of Hebrew prophets
during the intertestamental period, it is surprising to read about an active
Jewish prophetess affirming Jesus as the Messiah. While some pair her
with Simeon, the text distinguished her from him in characterizing her
as a prophetess, but not Simeon. As one who foretells a future reality,
she was in line with several others God used such as Miriam, Deborah,

---

[61] See Ge 30:23; Is 4:1, 25:8, 1 Sa 1:9-11.

[62] Morris, 79.

[63] Lk2:6 (NASB).

[64] Letha Dawson Scanzoni and Nancy A. Hardesty, *All We're Meant To Be:
Biblical Feminism for Today*, 3d ed. (Grand Rapids: Eerdmans Publishing, 1992),
72.

[65] Lk 1:25.

[66] *Ibid.*, 1:60-61.

[67] Barbara E. Reid, *Choosing the Better Part? Women in the Gospel of Luke*
(Collegeville, MN: The Liturgical Press, 1996), 80.

[68] Lk 1:41.

Huldah, Isaiah's wife, Queen Esther and Abigail. It is not surprising to read that she was a "vessel for revelation from God."[69] She spoke about God to all, which no doubt would have included men.[70] Bock also noted that she was totally focused on serving God.[71] In doing so, she foreshadowed Jesus allowing women to talk to men about Him and Peter's pentecostal announcement that women would be prophetesses in the Church.[72]

Jesus' Mother: Highly Favored: Luke 1:26-28

Little is known about Mary's background, but her response to the angel was one of the finest models of discipleship. She listened, believed, and responded with humble commitment, "Be it done to me according to your word."[73] She then immediately served the needs of another.[74] She was willing to be stereotyped and misunderstood by her parents, fiancé, and others; to lose her fiancé; and to risk being stoned.

Morris contrasted her with Zechariah who needed a sign to believe the impossible, but Mary did not.[75] Fitzmyer depicted her as one who heard the word and acted upon it and thus foreshadows women being included in Jesus' later announced extended family.[76]

Mary was certainly not a reclusive, shy, or passive female; for she traveled ninety miles in her last month of pregnancy, delivered Jesus in a strange place, put Jesus on the carpet because He remained behind in Jerusalem when he twelve years old, approached Jesus to do a surprising miracle in Cana, attempted to take Jesus home after He had begun His ministry, was at the cross, remained in hostile territory for fifty days after the crucifixion, and was present on the day of Pentecost.[77] Mary was also a meditative person,[78] an important discipline for spiritual formation. No wonder she was highly favored by God which linked her

---

[69] Bock, 251.

[70] Lk 1:36-38.

[71] Bock. 252.

[72] Ac 2:17-18, 1 Co 11:5.

[73] Lk 1:38 (NASB).

[74] *Ibid.*, 1:39-45.

[75] Morris, 82.

[76] Fitzmyer, 341.

[77] Scanzoni and Hardesty, 73.

[78] Lk 1:29, 2:19.

with some of God's great men in the Hebrew Bible,[79] which was significant in a patriarchal culture.

The first three women in Jesus' early life were free to communicate revelations from God. Each prefigured Jesus' mission of emancipating other women to speak.[80] It is significant that women were first to believe Jesus was the Messiah; first to anoint

Him for burial; to arrive at the tomb; first to tell others He had risen; among the first to wait for His promised Holy Spirit to initiate the Church; and among the first to be persecuted as Christians.

Women in Jesus' Ministry

Jesus included women in many culturally surprising ways that model how His ongoing body, the Church, should continue what He began.

Women as Traveling Disciples: Luke 8:1-3

A disciple in the first century was not only a student of another, but also one committed to adopt and assimilate the philosophy, practices, and priorities of the mentor.

Including women disciples was radically different from contemporary Judaism.[81] While Rabbis refused to teach women and generally assigned them to an inferior position,[82] Jesus had no problem including them with the men as disciples in His "traveling seminary."

There is no way to know exactly how many women were in this traveling

group, for there were " many others" besides those named. Some may have left their families to become disciples of Jesus, since at least one was a wife. If they left their families, they would have resembled the twelve who evidently did the same.[83] That does not necessarily mean they totally abandoned their families, for later the apostles traveled with their wives,[84] and perhaps some of their wives were among the many other women in this traveling school of Jesus. However, one of Jesus' invitations for discipleship is a willingness to leave behind whatever

---

[79] Those "favored ones in Old Testament included Noah (Ge 6:18), Moses (Ex 33:12-17), Gideon (Ju 6:17), Samuel (Is 2:26).

[80] Reid, 94

[81] Fitzmyer, 696.

[82] Morris, 164.

[83] See Mk 1:20, 10:28.

[84] 1 Co 9:5.

might hinder following.[85] Stendahl suggested these women might have been following the Jewish tradition of sacrificing everything.[86]

These women were not just traveling locally but also widely, for later they were in Jerusalem with Jesus and the twelve.[87] They were not just add-ons to do only services for Jesus and the twelve, but also were fellow students with the twelve. They must have been with Jesus when He talked about His death and resurrection, because the angel at the tomb said, "He is not here; He has risen! Remember how he told you, while he was still with you in Galilee."[88] That statement suggests Jesus taught significant theology to these women as well as to the twelve apostles.[89] It is not unlikely they were part of "the women" who waited in Jerusalem for the Holy Spirit to empower them after Jesus' ascension[90] and were members of the subsequent prayer groups.[91] They may have been among those who were persecuted, scattered, and preached about Jesus as they traveled.[92] It would not seem unlikely that those who had been especially taught by Jesus were some of the women gifted to prophesy as announced on the day of Pentecost,[93] especially since the angel and Jesus had earlier commissioned them to tell the apostles about Jesus' resurrection.[94] It is even possible they were among the seventy sent by Jesus to minister to people throughout the area.[95]

That Jesus taught these women certainly linked them not only with the twelve, but also with Paul who received his message from Jesus.[96] Jesus made no statement that suggested that one gender was more or less capable than the other in receiving, processing, and correctly handling intellectual theological content.

These women were not only students, but also servants for they continually helped Jesus and the twelve with their financial means. The

---

[85] Mk 10:29, Lk 14:26-27, Lk 12:51-53.

[86] Stendahl, 27-28.

[87] Mk 15:41, Mt 27:55-56.

[88] Lk 24:6-7. That these included the women of Lk 8:1-3 is clear, for they were named in Lk 24:10, and referred to in Ac 13:31.

[89] Kari Torjesen Malcolm, *Women at the Crossroads: A Path Beyond Feminism and Traditionalism* (Downers Grove, IL: InterVarsityPress, 1982), 65.

[90] Ac 1:14, 2:1.

[91] *Ibid.*, 4:23-26, 12:12.

[92] *Ibid.*, 8:3-4, 22:4-5.

[93] *Ibid.*, 2:17-18.

[94] Mt 27:7; Mk 16:7; Lk 24:10.

[95] *Ibid.*, 10:1-20.

[96] Ga 1:12.

Greek verb for serving stressed repetitive actions. The word "helping" and "contributing" in the NIV is the Greek word διακovoς from which the word "deacon" comes. While we cannot conclude that they were official "deacons," the later use of this same word for deacons may suggest that the eventual development of deacons did not originally exclude anyone on sociological grounds.[97] The action of these women supports the doctrine that disciples were not just to be students, but also to serve from what they learn.

While it was not unusual in first century for women to financially support Rabbis, it was unusual for them to travel with the Rabbis they supported.[98] Jeremias noted that women leaving their homes to follow Jesus was "an unprecedented happening in the history of that time, so Jesus overthrew custom when He allowed them to leave home to follow Him."[99]

It is too much to suggest as Brown did that Jesus was economically dependant upon those women,[100] or that these women "were the backbone of His ministry," and "if it weren't for their support Christ's ministry would have been greatly hindered."[101] Women certainly responded to Jesus and contributed to His ministry,[102] but we do not know the extent of their services.

Mary and Martha: Resident Disciples: Luke 10:38-42

Evans believes this passage records the best-known example of Jesus teaching women.[103] Because our culture regularly accepts women eating with men, engaging in conversation, and being taught by men, we may miss the revolutionary significance of this event in Jesus' day. While some Rabbis prohibited teaching the Torah to daughters,[104] others

---

[97] Phoebe called a diakonos in Ro 16:1, perhaps the women in 1 Ti 3:11 were female deacons (deaconesses).

[98] Bock, 713-714.

[99] Joachim Jeremias, *Jerusalem in the Time of Jesus: An Investigation into Economic and Social Conditions during the New Testament Period* (London: SCM, 1969), 376.

[100] Ann Brown, *Apology to Women: Christian Images of the Female Sex* (Leicester: InterVarsityPress, 1991), 139.

[101] Boyd Luter and Kathy McReynolds, *Women as Christ's Disciples* (Grand Rapids: Baker Books, 1997), 70.

[102] Bock, 710.

[103] Mary Evans, *Women in the Bible* (Downers Grove, IL: InterVarsityPress, 1983), 50.

[104] M.Sot. 3.4.

considered it a religious duty to do so.[105] Consequently, the rabbinic picture is somewhat mixed.

However, it is likely this episode is revolutionary from several perspectives such as: (1) it would have reversed the position of many, if not most, Rabbis. Bock noted that Jesus teaching Mary in this manner was a startling event in a culture where women did not receive formal education from a Rabbi.[106] (2) Women were not to serve meals to men unless other servants were present.[107] (3) Jesus suggested a woman's role does not have to be restricted to her domestic functions.[108] (4) It would be unusual for a Rabbi to teach a woman privately in a house.[109] (5) Jewish women were not even allowed to touch Scripture.[110]

While Jesus commended Mary's decision to learn from Him and seemed to criticize Martha's decision to work for Him, He was not downplaying preparing/serving a meal. After all, Martha was doing what Jesus would do in the upper room. Jesus' answer to Martha was a tender reply.[111] The problem was not in the activity but in the attitude that brought anxiety to Martha. Martha was serving. The word, *diakonian*, spotlighted discipleship. Jesus described her disposition in two significant ways: *meriminas*, which means to be pulled in different directions – to worry, and *thorubaze*, which means to be disturbed. Stagg thinks her problem was not that she was "in charge of the meal, but the meal was in charge of her."[112]

Jesus' reply, "Mary has chosen what is better, and it will not be taken away from her," did not eliminate domestic responsibilities. While Mary chose to prioritize the taught word in that situation and Martha chose the tough work, Jesus did not make the two exclusive of one another.

Luke placed this encounter immediately after the parable of the Good Samaritan, who was commended for his activity. Contextually linking the two events suggests that service is not a substitute for learning, nor is learning a substitute for service. In fact, this is one part of a three-part section in Luke which communicates a beautiful balance

---

[105] M.Ned. 4.3.

[106] Darrell L. Bock, *Luke, vol. 2, 9:51-24:53* Baker Exegetical Commentary on the New Testament (Grand Rapids: Baker Books, 1996), 1037.

[107] Ben Witherington III, *Women in the Ministry of Jesus* (New York: Cambridge University Press, 1984), 67, 101.

[108] Spencer, 60.

[109] Witherington III, 107.

[110] Stagg, *World*, 118.

[111] Morris, 209.

[112] Stagg, *World*, 141.

for disciples: (1) serving – the Good Samaritan; (2) learning – Mary and Martha; (3) praying – the disciples' request, and Jesus' answer.

It is inappropriate to use this encounter to play off being contemplative against being active.[113] Jesus held a high regard for both the contemplative and the activist, as Jesus Himself modeled both. However, in this situation Jesus took the position of a Rabbi and Mary of a student sitting at the Rabbi's feet,[114] and a disciple at the mentor's feet.[115] Her decision to be an attentive student was not to be taken away from her at that time or from other persons at any time due to any sociological identities or labels. Permitting her to become a learner may have been the first time such an option was shared with a woman in Jesus' day.[116]

In a sense, both sisters represent the Church,[117] for the Church needs the balance of meditations and movements, of passivity and activity, of learning and laboring, of silence and service. We all need both work with food and the food of the word.

Jesus' reply to Martha did not seem to upset her nor cause a rift between her and Mary. Later the roles were reversed, for Martha learned from Jesus in a Socratic style of teaching/learning, while Mary stayed at home.[118] In this later situation, Martha was aware of and discussed significant theology with Jesus.[119] She called Jesus "the teacher" not "the critic", and made one of the clearest confessions in the Gospels.[120] Perhaps Martha gleaned that theology in the Luke 10 encounter, as she may have stopped being distracted and sat at Jesus' feet along with Mary.[121]

Jesus invited women as well as men to be "theologians", who would not just learn but also teach.[122] This brief passage opened that door for women, which the Church should not close. To do so is to

---

[113] Kirschbaum, 81-82.

[114] Stagg, *World*, 118.

[115] Bock, vol. 2, 1037.

[116] Witherington III, 51.

[117] Kirschbaum, 80.

[118] Jn 11:17-32.

[119] Jn 11:24-27.

[120] Brown, 144. See the confession in Jn 11:28.

[121] Spencer, 58.

[122] This passage alone does not prove women should teach. See James A. Borland, "Women in the Life and Teachings of Jesus," in *Recovering Biblical Manhood: A Response to Evangelical Feminism*, eds. John Piper and Wayne Gruden (Wheaton: Crossway Books), 113-123.

hinder the spiritual formation of women members, which in turn hinders the spiritual formation of the corporate Church. There is no gender restriction to the strategy of Ephesians 4:11-16 and 1 Corinthians 12.

Liberating Women to do Teaching and Evangelizing Activities

The Samaritan Woman: As an Evangelizing Disciple:
John 4:1-42

This encounter included the most intense conversation recorded between Jesus and a woman, and was longer than Jesus had with any man including Nicodemus in the preceding chapter. Ruth Tucker may be correct when she regarded this encounter as "the best illustration that Jesus viewed women as capable as men in assimilating theological truths."[123]

Jesus continued to break several Jewish traditions, some of which follow: (1) If a man talks religion with a woman, he would inherit Gehenna;[124] (2) Forbade a man to be alone with a woman who was not his wife;[125] (3) It was a disgrace for a scholar to speak with a woman on the street; [126] (4) Strict social mores against Samaritans; (5) Prohibited drinking from a Samaritan vessel.

By placing this encounter immediately after Jesus' encounter with Nicodemus, Luke revealed several contrasts:

Nicodemus	The Samaritan Woman
A Male	A woman
A Jew	A Samaritan
Came at night	Came at midday
A ruler	A "nobody" in society
Respected	Shunned
Confused	Not confused
No recorded response	Significant response
Discerned Jesus as a teacher	Discerned Jesus as a prophet and the Messiah
Brought no one to Jesu	Brought many to Jesus
Evidently just left	Left on a mission
No social stigma against him	Five husbands and and living with a man without marriage

---

[123] Ruth A. Tucker, *Women in the Maze: Questions & Answers on Biblical Equality* (Downers Grove, IL: InterVarsityPress, 1992), 81.

[124] M.Abot. 1:5.

[125] M.Kidd. 5:12.

[126] Jeremias, 360.

Ritually clean from Jewish view	Ritually unclean from Jewish view
Named.........................	Unnamed

Jesus' interaction with her was the pure with the impure, the righteous with the unrighteous, the clean with the unclean, the sinless with the sinner, the moral with the immoral, the mono-racial with the multi-racial, and the sexually pure with the sexually tainted. But none of that made a difference with Jesus. He reversed the reductionistic practices of the Jews and illustrated another fulfillment of His inauguration speech.

Jesus was not offended by her discussing theology with Him.[127] This woman had keen spiritual discernment[128] as seen in the fact that she knew Jewish theology, "I know that the Messiah . . . is coming. When He comes, He will explain everything to us."[129] She progressed from calling Jesus "sir" to "prophet" to "Messiah"[130]—a movement that Nicodemus did not make. Her insight was clearer than many Jewish leaders.

The woman left her container, went back into the village to report to the people her conversation with Jesus, and invited them to consider Him as the Messiah. While Jesus told some men to not yet tell others about Him,[131] He did not suggest that to this woman. Evidently Jesus had a different opinion from others about women teaching

Men (the Greek word for people in 4:28 is *anthropos,* which can be translated "men" or "people" without being gender specific.) Jesus also had a different spin about women teaching men than some today have gleaned from 1 Timothy 2:9-15 and 1 Cor. 14:34-35. This woman's activity was evangelistic,[132] and many believed in Jesus because of her testimony.[133] In a sense, she began the first village-wide revival recorded in the New Testament documents, foreshadowed later evangelism in Samaria,[134] and the role of females prophesying.[135] Her response paralleled that of Andrew when he met Jesus.[136]

---

[127] Tucker, 81.

[128] Evans, 52.

[129] Jn 4:25.

[130] Jn 4:11, 19, 29.

[131] Mt 16:20.

[132] Stagg, *World,* 117.

[133] Jn 4:39.

[134] Ac 8:4-25.

[135] *Ibid.,* 2:17-18; 21:9; 1 Co 11:5.

[136] Jn 1:45.

This woman did what Jesus' male apostles did not do. They went into the same village, but brought only food out to Jesus. Jesus contrasted her response to theirs when He said, "Do you not say, 'Four months more and then the harvest'? I tell you, open your eyes and look at the fields! They are ripe for harvest. Even now the reaper draws his wages, even now he harvests the crop for eternal life, so that the sower and the reaper may be glad together. Thus the saying 'One sows and another reaps' is true. I sent you to reap what you have not worked for. Others have done the hard work, and you have reaped the benefits of their labor." This woman was the sower who did the "hard work." It is possible that this woman's witness helped to prepare for the Samaritan revival led by Philip in Acts 8.

By this encounter, Jesus opened the door for women evangelists, which the Church should not close. To close it is to interfere with the spiritual transformation of both the individual and the corporate Church.

Women Instructing Men: Matthew 28:5-10;
Mark 16:1-11; Luke 24:1-12 John 20:1-18

Both the angels and Jesus commissioned women to tell the apostles that Jesus had risen. While on that mission, these women were "apostles" in the general meaning of that word.[137] While some today would not have allowed women to teach men because of Eve's deception,[138] Jesus did not model that logic. At the cross and the tomb women remained stronger than men since the apostles abandoned Jesus, while women remained close.[139] Bruner asked, "Was the Lord's commissioning of women a mistake?" He correctly argued that the "call of women to be the first resurrection messengers should be considered in studies of women's ordination."[140] These women not only told the apostles, but also all the "others," a masculine word that included other men. While some men evaluated the women's news as nonsense,[141] Reid suggested that receiving the women's message as nonsense "can serve to

---

[137] The verbal meaning of an episkopos is someone (or thing) sent on a mission by a higher authority, and while on the mission is to do and say what the one in authority dictated. Epaphrodites and Barnabas were each called an episkopos in this general useage. See Php 2:25 and Ac 14:14.

[138] Thomas Schreiner, John Piper, Wayne Grudem, Raymond Ortlund, Jr., Page Patterson, and others.

[139] Frederick Dale Bruner, *Matthew: vol. 2:The Churchbook 13-28* (Dallas: Word Publishing, 1990), 1080.

[140] *Ibid.*, 1079.

[141] Lk 24:11.

ritualize the grief that Christian women have experienced for twenty centuries when their faithful and true witness is dismissed as 'nonsense'. It can move believers to choose the better part by taking action to ensure the faithful preaching of women be heard and accepted in our day."[142] Even though the apostles did not believe the women, the validity of their report was not weakened. In fact, Jesus criticized the apostles for not trusting their report. While there are many differences among the four Gospel writers concerning the details surrounding the resurrection, that women were the first to report the resurrection appears in all four Gospels. In light of Jesus commissioning them to tell others, it is paradoxical that women's right to teach or preach has been so vigorously challenged by many today. Should not Jesus' response to those women then be a strong affirmation for women today, and for men giving them the kind of opportunity Jesus did?

In commissioning women to be the first full Gospel messengers to men (life, death, burial, and resurrection), Jesus opened the door for Christian women to continue to teach men as well as women, and foreshadowed the Holy Spirit gifting women to speak throughout the Christian era as announced in Acts 2:17-18, " . . . your sons and daughters will prophesy . . . both men and women . . . will prophesy." If teaching is a primary function of a pastor today, then it is not inappropriate to suggest that Jesus liberated women to be pastors. The English word "pastor" appears only in Ephesians 4:11; however, the same Greek noun, *poimen*, is translated "shepherd" 17 times to introduce several different functions including teaching (feeding others—God's sheep—the food of the Word), thus stressing servant-leadership.

In liberating women to teach (pastor), Jesus opened a door the Church should not close. Only as each gifted part of the body of Christ (the Church) does its part, can the whole church advance in spiritual transformation toward Christ likeness (Ephesians 4:11-16).

Liberating Women to Dignity

While every interaction between Jesus and women restored some aspect of dignity, following are some additional categories of dignity Jesus recouped:

Women Not Being Viewed as Sex Objects: Matthew 5:27-32

Jesus altered a popular concept that a woman's primary worth was sensual. On several occasions he contrasted the common perception that women should be treated as sex objects. Some of those included

---

[142] Reid, 204.

forgiving the woman caught in adultery; allowing the sinful woman to anoint Him; allowing other women to serve Him; and commissioning women to tell the apostles about the resurrection.

Nowhere is this more apparent than in His statement, "But I tell you that anyone who looks at a woman lustfully . . . " The Greek construction *pros epithumesai* literally means to look **for the purpose** of lusting. This is not describing a man who when seeing a beautiful woman thinks, "Wow," and gets a bit excited. It is describing the person who plans to continue looking for the purpose of visually and internally treating her as a sex object for his enjoyment. He literally adulterates her in his thoughts. Such a plan is to be stopped at its source – the eye or the hand. A person is to nip it in the bud. Job said, "I have made a covenant with my eyes not to look lustfully at a girl."[143] This teaching lifted women out of the stigma of being second-rate[144] playthings for the pleasure of men. Stagg powerfully commented that this kind of look treats a woman as an adulteress, but Jesus liberated women from this subjective stigmatism made by male mental constructs.[145]

Jesus expanded his valuable view of women in His teaching about divorce. A man is not to divorce his wife for **any and every** reason, including seeing another woman more beautiful than his wife. The man who divorces her, except for *porneias* (from which our word, "porno" comes) will be responsible for the woman's adulterous stigma. Jesus, the real macho-man, lifted women from this gutter kind of thinking. Liberating women from being viewed as sex objects frees them to make contributions with their *charismata* that males with identical *charismata* can make. *(Charismata*—gifts is the plural for *charisma*—gift)

No Gender Double Standards: John 8:1-11

Although Jesus' encounter with this woman is not in the earliest manuscripts, it is consistent with His attitudes, actions, and announcements. It was accepted by the early Church as authentic, since it was transmitted orally until included in the written record. The story was well known in the second century and is hardly a story that the Church would have invented.

This episode reveals more about the misconduct of the accusers than about the accused. The woman was **caught** in the act of adultery. The leaders may have staked out the "Holiday Inn" of that time to catch her. They brought her to Jesus at the most public and crowded place in Jerusalem in order to trap Him publicly. If Jesus voted against executing

---

[143] Job 31:1.

[144] Evans, 45.

[145] Stagg, *World*, 132.

her, they could accuse Him of rebelling against the Law of Moses. If He said to stone her, He would violate the Roman law, which prohibited executing someone for adultery.

It is an ugly scene. The woman was a fellow member in Judaism who at that moment may have become one of the loneliest and most forsaken persons in Jerusalem. She was with her religious leaders who were publicly shaming her. In this regard, she paralleled what Jesus Himself would face on the cross.

While Jesus stooped down to write on the ground, the accusers kept repeating their question. Then Jesus put them on the spot, "If anyone of you is without sin, let him be the first to throw a stone at her."

What Jesus wrote evidently challenged and canceled the double standard of those accusers, for the law of Moses called for both the man and the woman to die.[146] In that day adultery lowered the dignity of women, but heightened the delight of men. What a double standard!

Those Jewish leaders used her as a worthless object for the purpose of trapping Jesus, but Jesus ricocheted their ploy and forced them to look at their own worth – without sin? No! They trapped her in order to trap Him, but fell into their own ambush.

Jesus and the woman had something in common, for they were both opposed by the same kind of religious leaders. Jesus' question and their exit suggested that not one accuser was less guilty than she. Jesus was the only one who had the right to throw the first stone, but did not.

Is it possible that Christian women today in the same church with their brothers in Christ can feel unwanted, tainted, and used by being assigned roles that men would not stoop to do? The issue for some women today may not include being caught in adultery, but being caught doing such a "bad thing" as functioning as a leader in the church by using their *charismata* as men do. Do we "stone" women's dignity today by making them feel like lesser people with lesser abilities than men? And if we do, what does that do for or against spiritual transformation of all included?

Being Models of Jesus/God: Luke 15:1-32; Mark 12:41-44; Luke 21:1-4

When Jesus was criticized for eating with sinners, He told three illustrations each of which revealed both His and His Father's view of people (Luke 15:1-32). He used a man and a woman to reveal the kind of God/Father a sinner has – a Father of love, forgiveness, acceptance, and joy for both genders.

Jesus could have modeled Himself and the Father by using the

---

[146] Dt 22:22.

analogy of two socially accepted men, but He chose a male shepherd and a female housekeeper,[147] both of whom were low on the social scale. Both the male and female saw value in what was lost; both looked until they found what was lost; both invited others to celebrate what was found; and both equally represented how God acts and reacts.[148]

Many are comfortable identifying the searching, loving, and forgiving God with the male shepherd. But some are uncomfortable identifying God's kind of actions with the female housekeeper. But both the shepherd's and the housekeeper's activities preview what all Christians are to do – actively seek the lost and celebrate redemption.[149] All Christians are to do for sinners what the shepherd did for the sheep and what the woman did for the coin. Neither sheep nor coin had a gender connotation. That is, the shepherd did not go for just a male sheep nor did the woman go for just a coin with a female image on it. To suggest that either men or women search and speak/teach to only their own gender is difficult to support from the examples of Jesus, the use of both genders by God, and the holistic biblical teaching. Both men and women were included as recipients of the Great Commission,[150] and as new creations in Christ are representatives of God in His reconciling mission.[151]

Jesus had no problem using women as models of God's character.[152] Another example is a widow who was the poorest of the poor.[153] About her, Jesus said, "I tell you the truth, this poor widow has put more into the treasury than all the others. The other people gave out of their wealth; but out of her poverty she put in everything she had to live on."

Osborne contrasted this widow with the scribes who in the literary context devoured widows.[154] Stagg added, "The leaders were willing to sacrifice someone else – widows. But she was willing to sacrifice herself."[155] Bock noted that her heart was better than the others, for while

---

[147] Reid, 185-186. It is going too far to suggest as Reid did that using the woman portrays God as a woman, for God is neither male nor female.

[148] See the celebration connection in verses 7, 10, and 22-24.

[149] Reid, 189.

[150] Mt 28:18-20.

[151] 2 Co 5:16-20.

[152] Gilbert Bilezikian, *Beyond Sex Roles: What the Bible Says About A Woman's Place in Church and Family* 2d ed. (Grand Rapids: Baker Book House, 1990), 87.

[153] Morris, 321.

[154] Osborne, 268. See the passage prior to the widow's offering in Mk 12:38-40.

[155] Stagg, *World*, 107.

they devoured widows for self-advantage, she gave back to God from selflessness,[156] and was disadvantaged because her gift was "food out of her mouth."[157] The amount she gave was the minimum allowed by their law,[158] but was the maximum offered by her love. If the description is taken literally, she put in everything, and thus sacrificed more than all the others combined.

Jesus lifted the dignity of this humble woman, for she modeled what Jesus would do on the cross —sacrifice Himself with trust in God, "Into Thy hands, I commit My spirit."

This widow preceded Christians in the early Church who had the *charisma* of generosity,[159] such as those in Macedonia.[160] The Church today is not opposed to women using their *charisma* of generosity, but some are opposed to women using their *charismata* of teaching and preaching. To oppose the latter is to oppose what Jesus allowed when He gave the green light for various women on various occasions to speak to men.

Being a Model of Faithful Praying: Luke 18:1-8

This parable linked this woman to the episode of the Pharisee and the sinner praying, which immediately followed.[161] The unjust judge parallels the pharisee who looked down upon the tax collector. The tax collector parallels the woman, for both of them shared a lower rung on the Jewish social ladder. In a sense, this woman is analogous to many women in the Church today who are denied positions of influence, and are not treated with the same dignity as their male brothers.

All this widow had going for her was that right was on her side.[162] Jesus used this woman as a model of faith and asked, "However, when the Son of Man comes, will He find faith on the earth?" In context, the woman persistently asking which all Christians are to also do modeled the faith that will or will not be found.[163] This woman became a prototype for the kind of faith God wants in every person – male and female.

---

[156] Bock, vol. 2, 1647-1648.

[157] Stagg, *World*, 107.

[158] Morris, 322.

[159] Ro 12:8.

[160] 2 Co 8:1-5.

[161] Lk 18:9-14.

[162] Morris, 287.

[163] Bock, vol. 2, 1444.

Another aspect about this parable is easily overlooked. The faith Jesus might not find when He returns is modeled by the unjust judge who did not permit the woman to enjoy her rights. The judge denied her rights by dominating over her as her superior. While this woman foreshadowed persistent praying in the early Church as seen in Acts, the unjust judge foreshadowed reluctance to give women a rightful place of influence in the Church.

From Genetic-Related Labels: Matthew 15:21-28

Luke intentionally placed this encounter immediately after reporting unbelief of pharisees and scribes.[164] Bruner called this encounter a kind of "Gentile Gethsemane" for Jesus.[165] While at first it seemed as though Jesus was reluctant to minister to any Gentile, that was not the case because He earlier ministered to a Gentile centurion.[166] So was He hesitant because she was a woman and the centurion was a man? Not at all, for Jesus had earlier ministered to women[167] and shared a parable in which a woman's action was a key example.[168] The reluctance was possibly due to the fact that Jesus was in predominately Gentile territory, and Gentiles there might press Him to abandon His mission for the Jews.[169] The word "only" (verse 24) is not in the Greek text. Literally Jesus said, "I was not sent except. . ." (Greek,—*ei me*) His point was that His mission was to be to the Jewish nation **first**, but not **only**, as seen in inauguration speech, ministry to other Gentiles, and in His Great Commission. Apostolic writing stressed the inclusion nature of Christianity.[170]

Jesus was more reluctant to submit to pressure from His apostles than from the Gentile woman, for He refused their advice and accepted her address. This woman's persistent asking expressed her faith in Jesus. Jesus' first response (silence) may have come across as an "unanswered" prayer, but she asked again. His second response, "I was not sent except first to the lost sheep of the house of Israel" (my translation from the Greek), may have been disappointing to her, but she asked again. His third response, "It is not good to take the bread of the children and toss it to the small house dogs" (my translation), may sound to us like a final

---

[164] Lane, 259. See Mt 15:1-20. See also James Hurley, 85.

[165] Bruner, 555.

[166] Mt 8:5-13.

[167] *Ibid.*, 8:14-17; 9:18-26.

[168] *Ibid.*, 13:33.

[169] Bruner, 552.

[170] Particularly in Ro, Ga, and Eph.

unkind denial, but not to her ears. The word Jesus used for "dogs" was not the scavenger type that belonged to no one, but instead the small house lap dogs. Bruner suggests this symbolically put this Gentile under the same roof (in the same house) as the Jews,[171] instead of being neglected and abandoned to the streets.[172]

Because Jews referred to Gentiles as "dogs" (the scavenger kind of unwanted ones), this woman may have been accustomed to receiving that label; however, Jews never used the diminutive, "little dogs – lap dogs" when referring to Gentiles. This may have been the first time this woman ever heard a Jew refer to a Gentile with the kind of dog they valued, loved, hugged, and cared for. By the use of that word for dogs, Jesus lifted this Gentile woman to a valued and loved position within the family. Later, Paul affirmed that Gentile Christians would indeed be in the same family as Jews,[173] and would break bread around the same table with them.[174]

In those days, people used bread to wipe their hands (as we use napkins today) and would then toss the bread on the floor. At times, children wrapped some food inside the bread to treat their pets. This woman, aware that what housedogs received from the table was beneficial, connected that to what Jesus was able to provide. In fact, "crumbs" from Jesus would have more power to heal her daughter than the best "meat" from other sources. Jesus replied by complimenting the woman, "You have great faith." Her faith contrasted both the reaction of the pharisees (earlier in this chapter) to Jesus and also the reaction of the apostles in this specific circumstance. Her faith demonstrated several things: (1) She came to Jesus; (2) She initiated the interaction; (3) She kept asking for help; (4) She interceded for the problem of someone else; (5) She recognized the character (mercy) and the power (help) of Jesus; (6) She disregarded the negative response of the leaders surrounding Jesus; (7) She positioned herself in a humble worship posture by kneeling; (8) She clung to her hope; (9) She was willing to take "crumbs" if they came from Jesus; (10) She recognized Him as

---

[171] Bruner, 553.

[172] Lane, 261.

[173] He affirmed that Abraham is the father of both the circumcised and the uncircumcised, Ro 4:9-13; 16-17. See also Ga 3:27-29 and Eph 2:11-22.

[174] See Ga 2; 11-16; and the vision to Peter that he can eat Gentile foods and thus stay and eat with them, Ac 10:9-48. See also the criticism he initially received in Ac 11:1-3 -not a criticism for baptizing Gentiles, but for eating with them. Perhaps some of the factions surrounding the Lord's table included the Jewish/Gentile and the male/female stigmas. See 1 Co 11:7-33 for this passage identified the problem as individualized Christians failing to recognize the church as the unified body of Christ in which differences are not to make a difference (1 Co 11:29-31).

"lord" and "master;" (11) she did not react negatively to the negative attitude of those apostles who were "in-training."

In that situation, the Jewish males did not show great faith, but the Gentile female did. Jesus' response liberated her and her daughter from the Jewish stigmatism of being second-rate persons. Demonstrating positive faith is not restricted to any one ethnic or gender group. Jesus' response foreshadowed the inclusion of both women and Gentiles into Christianity. His response was another example of applying His inauguration speech – releasing the oppressed.

Women today can likewise express their faith and not react negatively to leaders who are prejudiced against them. Instead, women can continue to pray that the attitudes of men about women will follow Jesus' model. Both women and men can pray that all will abandon negative prejudices against women, encourage and accept their positive performances and leadership. Both women and men should also pray that all Christians will invite and include women not only to salvation through God's grace and the Son's sacrifice, but also to services (ministries) through the Spirit's *charismata*. Those answered prayers help the body of Christ today to continue its maturation toward Christlikeness.

Liberated from Being a "Thing" – Less Than an Animal: Luke 13:10-17

It was not only revolutionary for Jesus to help women in a culture that kept women down,[175] but also to do it on the Sabbath that widened the gap between Him and synagogue leaders.[176] However, people who attended the synagogue were delighted which suggested they were uncomfortable that animals were being treated better than women, for an oral law permitted men to untie and lead animals to water on the Sabbath.[177]

Jesus always valued people above property. To treat any part of creation better than people made in the image and likeness of God does not please God.[178] Our contemporary world is saturated with commercials and entertainment that value things more highly than people as evidenced by the steady diet of both products and violence. Pornography is a multi-billion dollar business that values wealth above women and cash above children.

---

[175] Bock, vol. 2, 1215-1216.

[176] Stagg, *Studies*, 94.

[177] Bock, vol. 2, 1218.

[178] Jas 1:26-27.

Jesus liberated this woman not only from her infirmity, but also from her 'inhumanity' by having been treated with less respect, concern, and compassion than donkeys. Jesus not only liberated her disability, but also lifted her dignity by calling her "daughter of Abraham", a relational term not used for women in Judaism.[179] That description elevated women to spiritual equality with men,"sons of Abraham."[180]

While Jesus unleashed the woman from her sickness, He did not unfetter the men from their selfishness. He called them hypocrites, because they were just 'acting' religiously. While they would release a donkey on the Sabbath so it could live well, Jesus released the woman so she could live well. Perhaps some Jewish leaders thought women were property, possessions, and things because of the wording in the tenth commandment that could sound as if a wife is one of the several things a man possesses.[181] Jesus demonstrated that women are above possessions and should be treated as such. This miracle demonstrates that God wants all women to enjoy being treated with dignity, freedom, and worth.[182]

Creative with Faith Expressions: Mark 5:24-34;
Matthew 9:18-26; Luke 8:43-48

This bleeding woman spent her life savings on doctors, but without improvement. While she was at the end of her rope, she perceived that Jesus' touch was a longer "rope." Socially and religiously a woman in her condition was not to be touched by anyone, including her family. She was a misfit who was religiously and socially isolated. Yet she had the courage to express her faith in a way unacceptable to her religious leaders, but acceptable to Jesus—touching and being touched by a man in public. After she touched Jesus' outer garment, instead of criticizing the "unclean" person for touching the "clean" person, Jesus commended her, "Daughter, your faith has healed you." Matthew added, "Take courage,"[183] suggesting she no doubt feared the criticism and rejection of her leaders who were frozen in their traditions.

By calling her "Daughter," Jesus elevated her to the same value level with men in His extended family,[184] which foreshadowed His approval of anyone who will demonstrate faith even if doing so might

---

[179] Evans, 46.

[180] See Mt 3:9; Lk 3:8, 16:24; Jn 8:33-39, 53

[181] Ex 20:17.

[182] Stagg, *World*, 106.

[183] Mt 9:22, NASB and Greek text.

[184] See Mk 3:34-35.

contradict established traditions. Jesus was courageous to go against social and religious traditions which hindered people from becoming what God intends people to be and to do.

While some people quote the passage that a female is a "weaker vessel since she is a woman, . . . ,"[185] that certainly does not refer to inferiority. The same word "weaker," *asthenes*, is also used to refer to God, the Old Testament covenant, Paul, other apostles, and Christians.[186] To be "weak" does not refer to having less courage. In fact, several women demonstrated more courage than men through their interchanges with Jesus. For instance, on the night Jesus was betrayed, His twelve apostles abandoned Him. Three times Peter denied he knew Jesus. It is doubtful that all the apostles witnessed the crucifixion. In those days disciples were vulnerable to share in either the honors or the dishonors their mentors might receive. Close friends and disciples who solidified with a criminal could also be executed or severely punished.[187] In contrast to the probable absence of the apostles (with the exception of one), women appeared at the crucifixion.[188] Some even openly mourned.[189] Doing that put them in harms way, because it could be viewed as an emotional protest, which was unlawful.[190]

Chrysostom, Jerome, and Calvin noted the courage and example of these women.[191] Bruner thinks their example could "serve to recoup the bad notices women have been getting since Eve." He also noted that some in the Church today will allow women to serve men coffee, but not lead and teach. Brunner then stated, "But this will not do. Women have been so singularly honored here, and they are commissioned into such an extraordinary teaching ministry in a moment (28:7), that the power of the passion and resurrection texts, cumulatively gives women full ministry in the church."[192]

In light of women following Jesus to the crucifixion and the tomb, and then going to the tomb the next morning knowing soldiers would be there, is it not somewhat ironical to cite two texts (1 Timothy 2:9-15 and

---

[185] 1 Pe 3:7, NASB.

[186] 1 Co 1:25 for God; Heb 7:18 for the first covenant; 1 Co 9:22 for Paul; 1 Co 4:10 for other apostles; 1 Co 1:27, 8:7, 11:30; 1 Th 5:14 for Christian.

[187] Schotroff, 171-172.

[188] Mt 27:55-56; Mk 15:40-41; Lk 23:27, 49; Jn 19:25. It is possible the apostles were included in the description in Lk 23:49 "all those who knew Him". But that is not clear.

[189] Lk 23:27.

[190] Fitzmyer, 1497.

[191] Bruner, vol. 2, 1065..

[192] *Ibid.*

1 Corinthians 14:34) for preventing women from teaching men anything about Jesus and/or the Bible?

Liberating Women to Do a Deacon's or Minister's Kind of Activities

Our word "minister" comes from the Greek word *diakonos*, which describes a helpful servant. It was used to describe discipleship in general,[193] the work of Paul,[194] activities of Church members,[195] evangelists,[196] preaching and teaching the Word,[197] distribution of food,[198] personal services rendered to another,[199] a deacon,[200] and the use of a *charisma*.[201]

Since Jesus emancipated women for all of the above, there is little biblical support for reserving the role of a minister, pastor, or deacon to males only. While some of the preceding activities discussed in this paper fall under the category of *diakonos*, the following three encounters of women with Jesus are outstanding examples of *diakonos* kind of activities.

A Sinful Woman Serves: Luke 7:36-50

Whenever a celebrity visited a home, the owner would often declare "open house" so anyone could enter and leave at will. Simon, a pharisee, had evidently done just that.

While Jesus and others were reclining to eat, a woman known in the city as a sinner, entered to encounter Jesus. She "washed" His feet with her tears. If the feet of guests were attended to, it was done by a domestic servant.[202] This woman did for Jesus what Jesus Himself would eventually do for His apostles.[203] She then wiped His feet with her hair,

---

[193] Jn 12:26.

[194] Ac 21:19.

[195] 1 Co 16:15.

[196] 2 Ti 4:15.

[197] Ac 6:4.

[198] *Ibid.*, 6:1.

[199] Eph 6:21.

[200] Php 1:1; 1 Ti 3:8.

[201] Ro 12:7; 1 Co 2:5

[202] Morris, 162.

[203] Jn, chapter 13.

the only means available to her.[204] Loose hair hanging down was the decor of a prostitute and/or one who had recently been caught in adultery. If neither of those was her situation, she had voluntarily put her hair down[205] and chose to sacrifice her honor to serve Jesus.[206] She then began to kiss His feet, which was the action of someone, such as a criminal, who had just been forgiven or whose debt had been canceled.[207] She then poured perfume (perhaps her life savings) on Jesus. Simon was upset that Jesus would allow such a sinful woman to touch Him. Jesus replied in a way that explained what she was doing,

> Simon, I have something to tell you . . . . Two men owed money to a certain moneylender. One owed him five hundred denarii, and the other fifty. Neither of them had the money to pay him back, so he canceled the debts of both. Now which of them will love him more? Simon replied, "I suppose the one who had the bigger debt canceled." "You have judged correctly." Jesus then asked Simon, "Do you see this woman?"

That was Simon's problem. He could not see past her sins to see his "sister". He could see only her past, not her personhood; he assumed that she would always be what she had been, a sinful woman. That kind of blindness is still with us. Some people wear perpetual blinders when seeing others. When that happens, we forget the first way to demonstrate living for Jesus is to see people through new eyes.[208]

Jesus then contrasted her ministry to Him with Simon's lack of ministry for Him – no water for His feet, an elementary courtesy of a host; no kiss for his cheek, an elementary greeting; and no oil for his head, a refreshing and cooling welcome. The woman provided substitutes – tears for water, hair for a towel, and perfume for oil. She ministered to Jesus because she loved much, and she loved much because her sins "have been forgiven" (my translation from the Greek perfect passive verb tense which emphasizes a past event with follow-up acts). She did not do what she did in order to get her sins forgiven, but

---

[204] Alfred Plummer, *A Critical and Exegetical Commentary on the Gospel of S. Luke*, 5th ed. (Edinburgh: T & T Clark, 1922), 211.

[205] Witherington III, 56. See also his end note 24, page 164.

[206] Morris, 162.

[207] Joseph A. Fitzmyer, *The Gospel According to Luke* (X-XXIV), The Anchor Bible (Garden Grove, N.Y.: Doubleday & Co., 1985), 686-687; Morris, 162. Stagg, *Studies*, 62-63, Schotroff, 147.

[208] 2 Co 4:15-16. For only as we see people the way God does can we be His authentic representatives on earth. See the rest of 2 Co 5 – verses 17-21.

because Jesus had already forgiven her in a previous encounter. Is it possible that she was that woman caught in the act of adultery (or a similar situation of Jesus' forgiveness), who immediately went home, got her life's savings (perfume), and out of gratitude sacrificed it in grateful worship to Jesus?

While Simon criticized her immorality, Jesus commended her ministry, which demonstrated that a woman could model for a male (Simon) how to minister properly. Should not the Church today adopt Jesus' compliments for women ministering and reject Simon's criticisms of such? And should not male headship initiate freedom for women to blossom with their personhood in whatever ways they have the ability to serve the body of Christ today? (see chapter 7 on headship)

A Friend Serves (Ministers): John 12:1-8

The ministry of Jesus' friend, Mary, was a contrast to Jesus' apostles – particularly Judas.[209] Mary sacrificed over a year's wages to anoint Jesus,[210] but Judas led the complaint committee, which the other apostles joined.[211] Jesus' response that Mary did this to prepare for His own burial[212] communicated several concepts: (1) Mary had more discernment about Jesus' upcoming death than the apostles; (2) Mary was more willing to do an extravagant ministry for what Jesus was facing than they; (3) Mary was more willing to be scandalized (letting her hair down) than they, for all of them would soon shun being scandalized by abandoning Jesus.

Not only did Jesus allow Mary to do a deaconess'/ minister's kind of activity, but He also commanded that her ministry be continually reported, "Truly I say to you, wherever this gospel is preached in the whole world, what this woman has done should also be spoken of in memory of her."[213] How many years do we attend preaching services before hearing a sermon about this woman "minister"? Could it be because men are doing most of the preaching today, and she threatens their manhood? Is it possible that the Church has closed some doors in our era that Jesus opened for women in His era? But isn't this still His era? Do we believe the body (members) should determine the head's

---

[209] Osborne, 268.

[210] One denarius equaled one day's pay for a laborer. Three hundred would equal a year's salary today, working five days a week. Sixty weeks = a year and 2 months, $30,000 - $60,000 in wages or more.

[211] Mt 26:8.

[212] *Ibid.*, 26:12.

[213] *Ibid.*, 26:13.

(Jesus') activities? Or should the head determine and characterize the body's activities, which he so consistently modeled?

Peter's Mother-in-Law Serves (Ministers): Matthew 8:14-15

Rabbis forbade women to do the kind of serving Peter's mother-in-law did, lest women become accustomed to being around men.[214] It was also unlawful for a Jewish man to touch a woman who was not his wife,[215] and to touch anyone with fever.[216]

So by accepting the service of Peter's mother-in-law, Jesus went beyond rabbinic tradition. In so doing, He challenged some male views about what a woman could or could not do. Marshall noted her kind of service was not suggesting domestic work is the only appropriate role for women.[217] If anything, what she did elevated her service to the kind Jesus did in the upper room when He served the meal to His apostles.[218]

Kathleen Corley noted that when a man served food it was often symbolized as leadership,[219] but not so when a woman did it. That she is doing domestic work, and thus was keeping her place as a woman as some suggest, is not a supportable conclusion, because Jesus' apostles served food to the five thousand and four thousand; and seven males served food to the widows in Acts.[220]

The Church as the Extension of Jesus' Speech/Ministry

Jesus was eventually executed for His liberating attitudes, actions, and reactions for oppressed people. But in doing so, He brought newness and freshness to humanity. He is the way, the truth, and the life for all people. And He is the resurrection of new life and new ways for His ongoing body, the Church. Bock is correct, "The Church must face the implications of Jesus' announced relationships to people and reflect the aspects of its mission as they were evidenced in Jesus."[221] He continued,

---

[214] Frederick Dale Bruner, *Matthew* vol. 1: *The Christbook* (Dallas: Word Publishing, 1990), 308.

[215] Witherington III, 67.

[216] Hagner, vol. 33a, 209.

[217] I. Howard Marshall, *Commentary on Luke* (Grand Rapids: Eerdmans, 1978), 195.

[218] Lk 22:25-27.

[219] Kathleen Corley, *Private Women, Public Meals: Social Conflict and Women in the Synoptic Traditions* (Peabody, MA: Hendrickson, 1993), 121. See also Firorenza, 320.

[220] Mt 14:19; Lk 22:25-27; Ac 6:1-7.

[221] Bock, 401.

"The Church is to be the place where such total concern is expressed most visibly. Other human institutions are subsidiary to this institution of God as the vehicle of such concern."[222] That concern certainly involves the liberation of women through the Church's message, ministry, and manners toward women in leadership roles. This may be the last human liberation the Church faces. For as Kirschbaum noted, "The movement of women toward Jesus and Jesus toward women was the most revolutionary event in the history of the Church."[223]

Jesus' liberation put a damper on the honor/shame factors common in His day, for He liberated women from being denied basic freedoms and enjoyable dignity.[224] As the extension of Christ, the Church must never be used to subordinate and exclude anyone on social/cultural bases. For the Church is to be, as Jesus was, "a builder of a new society founded on the principle of fellowship and social harmony."[225] Perhaps Stagg is correct, "Then and now the hardest part of Christianity is to accept all kinds of people that Jesus accepted."[226] Perhaps doing so was in Jesus' mind when He called His disciples to count the cost and to take up the cross daily. While Cook noted, "Christology and liberation are inseparable,"[227] we should also note that the Church should so live that the world's society and the world's scholars would note that theology, pnuematology, soteriology, eschatology, and ecclesiology as well as spirituality, fellowship, benevolence, and evangelism are all linked to liberation. Continuing what Jesus began is a result of the continual incarnation of the Holy Spirit in us. The same Spirit that conceived Jesus also conceived the Church and continues in the Church through Her members for the purpose of characterizing the same nature of Jesus' first century ministry.

---

[222] *Ibid.*, 409.

[223] Charlotte von Kirschbaum, *The Question of Women: The Collected Writings of Charlotte von Kirschaum*, Trans. John Shephard, ed. Eleanor Jackson (Grand Rapids: Eerdmans Publishing, 1996), 86.

[224] Stagg, *World*, 94.

[225] Lesly F. Massey, *Women and the New Testament: An Analysis of Scripture in Light of New Testament Era and Cultures* (Jefferson, NC: McFarland & Company, 1989), 6.

[226] Stagg, *Studies*, 42.

[227] Cook, 137.

Conclusion

From Jesus' encounters with women, many conclusions follow:
1) Jesus did not have prejudices against people based upon any sociological identities.[228]
2) Jesus elevated the status of women and subverted the structures that supported male privileges and superiority.[229]
3) Jesus did not treat women as property of men.[230]
4) Jesus introduced people to new ways to think about and relate to women.[231]
5) Jesus did not do anything to suggest that women were inferior to men, but did many things to contradict the cultural norms against them.[232]
6) Jesus did not communicate a macho male image about women.[233]
7) Some of Jesus' activities and use of women were scandalous in His day.[234]
8) Jesus was driven by God's view of women.[235]
9) Jesus was not tainted by the sexism of His day.[236]
10) Nowhere and in no way was Jesus critical of women as women.[237]
11) Jesus' liberating activities and attitudes about women are for all male disciples to recognize the faith, love, giftedness, knowledge, courage, and ministerial resources of women; which while being restricted by traditions of men, are ready to be released by the truth of the Messiah.

---

[228] Malcom, 53.

[229] Mary Stewart Van Leeuwen, *et al., After Eden: Facing the Challenge of Gender Reconciliation* (Grand Rapids: Eerdmans Publishing, 1993), 8.

[230] Bennett, 28-29.

[231] Hurley, 79.

[232] Osborn, 83.

[233] Bilezikian, *Beyond Sex*, 81.

[234] Ruth R. Barton, *Becoming a Woman of Strength: 14 Life Challenges for Women – and the Men Who Love Them* (Wheaton: Harold Shaw Publishers, 1994), 72.

[235] Stagg, *World*, 130.

[236] Rebecca Merriel Groothuis, Rebecca Merriel, *Women in Conflict: The Cultural War Between Traditionalism and Feminism* (Grand Rapids: Baker Books, 1994) 110-11. See also Osburn, 85.

[237] Stagg, *World*, 277.

12) Jesus never restricted any service of women except choosing one to be one of the twelve apostles. That seems to be because twelve men as the foundation for the "second" Israel would bridge continuity with twelve men who were foundational for the "first" Israel. To exclude women from Church leadership today because Jesus did not choose one to be an apostle is also to exclude any non-Jew such as an American, a German, an Asian, Hispanic, and so on. To restrict leadership in the Church today to only Jewish men would empty most churches of leadership.

13) Since Jesus was right to include the poor, the rich, the sick, the Gentiles, and the Jews, He was also right to include both males and females not only for salvation, but also for service that squares with their *charismata.*

God's goal for individual Christians in the corporate Church is that we be conformed into the likeness of Christ.[238] Many disciplines aid the process of spiritual formation. One is the discipline of seeing people as God does and emancipating them from any internally and externally caused fears and fetters that prevent them from using their abilities in the home, the Church, and the community-at-large as representatives of God

The body of Christ is hindered from becoming like the head when the body is not engaged in the kinds of releasing ministries Jesus demonstrated. To restrict anyone from serving because of sociological differences is to inhibit the spiritual formation of God's new community—individually and corporately.

God's new community, the Church, has been empowered by God's Spirit and commissioned by Christ to represent God in unselfish and unhindered services. That is to live out the gospel – the good news that was announced to Abram—all peoples are to be blessed by God's people (See Paul's reference to the "gospel preached to Abraham" in Galatians 3:8). Anything less than that is just that—something less than good news.

The next chapter will review the Spirit's continuation of Jesus' principles and practices for and with women through the on-going body of Christ, the Church, as recorded in Acts.

---

[238] Lk 6:40; Ro 8:29; 2 Co 3:17-18; Eph 4:11-16.

CHAPTER 4

THE HOLY SPIRIT'S CONTINUATION OF JESUS' MINISTRY WITH, FOR, AND THROUGH WOMEN IN THE EARLY CHURCH

On the night Jesus was betrayed He promised the coming of the Holy Spirit who would remind the apostles what Jesus taught[1] and would guide them into all truth.[2] The book of Acts records the early Church's continuation of what Jesus began.[3] The movements and ministries of the Church in Acts were so Spirit-guided that John Stott refers to the book of Acts as "the continuing words and deeds of Jesus by his Spirit through his apostles."[4]

Because of Spirit's function to lead the first Church in continuing what Jesus began,[5] this chapter will develop the thesis that women's leadership roles in the Church today should correspond with their leadership involvements in the early Church. This chapter will review (1) the purpose of Luke-Acts; (2) the connection of the genesis of the Church in Acts 2 with Jesus' "inauguration speech" in Luke 4:16-27; (3) the significance of Acts 2 to the role of women in the Church; (4) the inclusion and use of women in the early Church.

The Purpose of Luke-Acts

There is no consensus among scholars concerning the purpose of Acts. Hans Conzelmann believed the author wrote primarily an apologetic to the Greco-Roman world on the behalf of a Church that needed to make its peace with the politics of that time.[6] In responding to Conzelmann, I. Howard Marshall viewed Luke, the accepted author of

---

[1] Jn 14:26.

[2] *Ibid.*, 16:13-15.

[3] *Ibid.*, 1:1.

[4] John Stott, *The Spirit, the Church, and the World* (Downer's Grove, IL: InterVarsity Press, 1990), 34.

[5] See the emphasis of the Spirit in chapters 1, 2, 4, 5, 6, 7, 8, 9, 10, 11, 13, 15, 16, 17, 18, 19, 20, 21, 23, 28.

[6] Hans Conzelmann, *The Theology of Luke,* trans. G. Buswell (New York: Harper and Row, 1960). See also Conzelmann in *An Outline of the Theology of the New Testament* trans. John Bowden (New York: Harper and Row, 1969). Conzelmann's influential work saw Luke writing a salvation history packaged in a theological framework but not in a historical accuracy.

Luke-Acts, as both a theologian and a respectable historian.[7] Many others maintain a balance between theology and history in a way that posits Luke's theological emphasis.[8]

Balancing history and theology is appropriate, because all history is interpreted history. Once the bare event is recorded and/or reported, the event is interpreted. That does not necessarily diminish the accuracy of the historical data, but the selectivity reveals the writer's emphasis.

The Connection of the Gospel of Luke with Acts

With the diversity of scholarly opinions, how does one determine the purpose of Acts? Henry Cadbury was the first to argue that Luke and Acts should be studied together since they were the product of a single author.[9] The first verse in Acts should have alerted us to that long before Cadbury's work. "The former book Theophilus, I wrote..." was a common literary device in the first century to identify the second part of one work. Luke-Acts is one writing by one author separated only by the length of the first scroll, and should not be separated in study. To delve into the study of Acts without the consideration of Luke is a methodological flaw.[10]

Consequently, Acts continues the same purpose initially developed in Luke. To uncover the purpose of a synoptic Gospel requires tabulating the major distinctive sections (those sections not found in any other Gospel), and analyzing the correlation of those distinctions.

Luke's differences emphasize the universality of Jesus' Messiahship to all kinds of people by especially spotlighting those who were being

---

[7] Howard Marshall, *Luke: Historian and Theologian* (Exeter: Paternoster Press, 1970). See also Helmut Fender, *St. Luke, Theologian of Redemptive History,* trans. R.H. and Ilse Fuller (Philadelphia: Fortress, 1967).

[8] For instance, see Robert F. O'Toole, *The Unity of Luke's Theology* (Wilmington, DE: Michael Glazier, 1984); Stott; I. Howard Marshall, *Acts of the Apostles: An Introduction and Commentary* (Grand Rapids: Eerdmans, 1980). Frank Stagg, *The Book of Acts: The Early Struggle for an Unhindered Gospel* (Nashville: Broadman Press, 1955).

[9] Henry Cadbury, *The Making of Luke-Acts* (New York: Macmillan, 1928).

[10] Consequently, those who seek to uncover the purpose of Acts by investigating the speeches in isolation from the Gospel of Luke use an approach that is not comprehensive enough. For instance, see Beverly Roberts Gaventa, "Toward a Theology of Acts," *INT* 42 (1988); 146-147. Also see Leon Morris, "Luke and Early Catholicism," *JTSA* 40 (1982): 4-16.

dishonored in the first century.[11] Jesus announced His kind of mission in His inauguration speech recorded in Luke 4:16-27 which committed Himself to fulfill God's call to Israel in Genesis 12:2-3.

What Jesus began to do in the Gospel of Luke, the Church continued throughout the chronicles of Acts. In a faculty address at New Orleans Baptist Theological Seminary, Frank Stagg was the first to identify the purpose of the Luke-Acts as not only the geographical, but also (and primarily) the sociological spread of Christianity as essential to missiological expansion.[12] The universal nature of Luke's Jesus is clearly continued in Acts as seen by the fact that the Church in Acts also crossed every sociological subset that Christ crossed in Luke. Not only does Luke record the Church crossing those lines, but also shared the rationale for doing so.

Perhaps Theophilus asked Luke a question similar to, "Luke, who is correct, the Jews (synagogue) or the Christians (Church)? Who is performing or perverting the will of God, the Jews who say that I need to deny my Gentile ethnicity, be circumcised, become converted to Judaism, and resign my position with the Roman Empire or the Christians who invite anyone to come to God through the Messiah?" Luke does not answer that question briefly, but rather comprehensively. He developed for Theophilus the thesis that "what the Church is doing in accepting and using all kinds is a continuation of what Jesus did, and what Jesus did continued God's purpose for initiating calling a people to be His."

---

[11] Only Luke's Gospel mentions the aged Zechariah and Elizabeth (1:1-25), the shepherds (2), addition to prophecy about John (3:6), acceptance of a tax collector (3:12-14), widow of Nain (7), women traveling with Jesus (8), "good" Samaritan (10), 3 parables explaining Jesus' friendship with the dishonored (15), beggar, Lazarus (16), Zacchaeus, plus forty other Lukan distinctions that stress the broad universality of the Messiah's inclusiveness of people.

[12] Frank Stagg, "The Purpose and Message of Acts," *Rev. Exp.* XLIV (1947): 3-21. Later, Stagg comprehensively developed that thesis in his commentary, *The Book of Acts.* In that commentary, Stagg posited that Luke reached his goal in writing Luke-Acts by the last work in the Luke-Acts Greek manuscript, *akvlutvs* which means unhinderdly. For Stagg, Luke ended with that word to epitomize what he was developing in his two-volume work. See also Stagg's article, "The Unhindered Gospel," *Rev. Exp.* 71 (1974): 451-462. Stagg's point is that Luke was developing how Christianity became unshackled from being a Jewish religion to what God intended. Stagg's purpose for Acts was later supported by W.G. Kummel in *Introduction to the New Testament*, trans. A.J. Mattel Jr. (Nashville: Abingdon Press, 1966), 115. And by Ernst Haenchaen, *The Acts of the Apostles* (Oxford: Basil Blackwell, 1971), 98-103. Leon Morris follows suit in his article, "Luke and Early Catholicism," 4-16. Robert Smith in his article, "The Theology of Acts," *CTM* 42 (1971): 531 says Luke did not intend a third volume but ended with unhindered preaching because that captured and completed Luke's development of Luke-Acts. See also the word "unhindered" in Acts 8:36, 10:47, and 11:17.

The Relationship of Luke 4:16-27 with Acts 2:17-18

God's call to Israel included both privilege (what God would do **for** Israel) and purpose (what God would do **through** Israel) as first enunciated to Abram in Genesis 12:2-3 (see chapter 2). Not only did Jesus incarnate that call in His life, but also the Church in Acts inherited it.[13] By the first century God's people had reduced "all" people to only themselves.[14] Jesus announced a revolutionary reversal to this reductionistic practice in His inauguration speech (Luke 4:16-27), which set the framework for the theology of Luke-Acts. Songer rightly identified two main themes in Jesus' use of the Isaiah passage in that speech: (1) the manifestation and suffering of the Messiah, (2) the fortunes of God's people regardless of their identity.[15]

Jesus' use of the Isaiah 61 passage in Luke 4:16-18 undergirds His subsequent ministry to the disadvantaged. The text clearly deals with the freedom (jubilee) of **all** people from being shackled or excluded because of sociological categories. Sanders views such inclusiveness as, "uncomfortable for any generation of believers to grasp.[16] Harrison correlates Luke 4:16-27 with the inclusive and liberating context of Acts 2:17-18.[17]

Luke 4:16-18 not only looks toward Acts 2:17-18, but also through it to other texts in Acts such as Acts 3:25, the "delocalisation" of God in Acts chapter 7 and 9:15—"this man is my chosen instrument to carry my name before Gentiles and their kings and before the people of Israel"; 10:27—"but God has shown me that I should not call any man impure or unclean"; 13:47—"I have made you a light for the Gentiles,

---

[13] See Ac 3:24-25 and Ga 3:8.

[14] Jerome H. Neyrey, ed., *The Social World of Luke-Acts: Models of Interpretation* (Peabody: Hendrickson Publishers, 1991). See especially the chapter, "Honor and Shame in Luke-Acts: Pivotal Values of the Mediterranean World," 25-65.

[15] Harold S. Songer, "Isaiah in Acts," *Rev. Exp.* 65 (1968): 459-70. See also James A. Sanders, "Isaiah in Luke," *INT.* 36 (1982): 144-155. Sanders calls this one of the most precious passages in the New Testament to discern the hermeneutics applied to interpretation of the Old Testament Scripture, 152. Sanders also relates Jesus saying that no prophet is acceptable in his own country to the fact that Jesus in this inauguration speech was sharing a kind of message that was uncomfortable, for it challenged their traditions, 153.

[16] James A. Sanders, *God Has a Story Too* (Philadelphia: Fortress Press, 1979), 14-26.

[17] Everett F. Harrison, *Acts: The Expanding Church* (Chicago: Moody, 1975), 57.

that you may bring salvation to the ends of the earth" (from Isaiah 49:6 and reflected in Acts 1:8); 15:16-18—"the rebuilding of David's temple," which includes Jewish remnants and Gentiles; and 26:20— the last word in the Greek manuscript, *akolupos,* unhinderingly – free from the shackles of any religious or social traditions that exclude people, which was Luke's intended developmental goal in Luke-Acts

Thus Luke 4:16-27 influenced and shaped the whole of Luke's two-volume work for developing the history and theology of an inclusive community where the gospel is unhindered by prejudices and traditions.

The Inclusion of Women as Part of the Oppressed:
Luke 4:16-27

Allen Black affirmed that the intended ministry to the oppressed in Luke 4:18 is one of several possible reasons for Luke's emphasis about women. However, Black does not believe women were included among the oppressed groups, because they are not "explicitly or implicitly described as oppressed or excluded within Luke-Acts," and "in general are not portrayed in a way that would cause us to see them as oppressed or excluded."[18] However, virtually every encounter Jesus had with people recorded in Luke and the crossing of sociological subsets by the Church in Acts should be viewed through the lens of those people having been oppressed, dishonored, and shamed.[19]

While women were excluded and dishonored in many circles of society throughout various generations and locations, there was a gradual upward trend toward a positive view of women in certain

---

[18] Allen Black, 455.

[19] See especially the helpful insights from Bruce J. Malina and Jerome H. Neyrey in The *Social World of Luke-Acts,* 25-65.

geographical areas.[20] Generally, Roman women could participate in influential roles more frequently than Greek and Jewish women. Brooten, who studied evidence from nineteen Greek and Latin inscriptions, challenged the common concept that Jewish women did not have significance in Judaism. She discovered that some women were called elders and presidents of synagogues.[21] However, Brooten's work is not enough evidence to deny that in Judaism some women in various locations were oppressed as Oepke notes.[22]

While Brooten states there is no archeological evidence to support the evidence of women galleries in the synagogue, which would suggest separation and non-equal involvements, Bristow notes that ancient ruins of Capernaum reveal the pre-existence of a balcony constructed in such a way that those sitting there were hidden from view, which may be a

---

[20] See especially the following sources: William Houghton Leslie, "The Concept of Woman in the Pauline Corpus in Light of the Social and Religious Environment of the First Century" (Ph.D. Diss., Northwestern University; Evelyn and Frank Stagg, *Woman In The World of Jesus*; Alfred Edersheim, *Sketches of Jewish Social Life in the Days of Christ* (Grand Rapids: Eerdmans, 1976); J.P.V.D. Balsdon, *Roman Women: Their History and Habits* (London: The Bodley Heade, 1962); Henri Daniel-Rops, *Daily Life in the Time of Jesus: An Authentic Reconstruction of Biblical Palestine and the Day-to-Day Lives and Customs of its People* (New York: Hawthorn Books, 1962); Bernadette Brooten, "Women Leaders in the Ancient Synagogue: In Scriptural Evidence and Background Issues" *BJS* 36 (1982): 5-33 *Idem*, "Early Christian Women and Their Cultural Context: Issues of Method of Historical Reconstruction," in *Feminist Perspectives on Biblical Scholarship* ed. A. Y. Collins (Chico: Scholars Press, 1985); Leonard Swidler, *Women in Judaism: The Status of Women in Formative Judaism* (Metuchen, N.J.: The Scarecrow Press, 1976); Elizezer L. Sukenek, *Ancient Synagogues in Palestine and Greece* (London: 1984); Joachim Jeremias, *Jerusalem*; Ellen Juhl Christiansen, "Women and Baptism," *ST* 35 (1981): 1-8; Shaye J.D. Cohen, "Women in the Synagogues of Antiquity," *CJ* 34 (1980): 23-29. Ross Kraemer, "Hellenistic Jewish Women: The Epigraphical Evidence," *SBLSB* (1986): 183-200; For one excellent source of the study of the Greek view of women in the philosophies prior to the rise of Stoicism, see Byrne L. Bullough, *The Subordinate Sex* (Baltimore: Penguin Books, 973): 50-76; Albert Oepke's article, *gunh* in *TDNT* vol. I (1964): 776-789; Dorothy Irvin, "The Ministry of Women in the Early Church: The Archeological Evidence," *DDSR* 45 (1980): 76-86; Ben Witherington III. *Women and the Genesis of Christianity* (New York: Cambridge University Press, 1990).

[21] Bernadette J. Brooten, *Women Leaders*. The inscriptions revealed that women wore the tiles of heads of synagogues, leaders, elders, mothers of the synagogue, and priestesses. Those inscriptions were from Italy, Asia Minor, Egypt, and Palestine, and dated from 27 B.C. to the A.D. Sixth Century.

[22] Oepke, 777.

diaspora counterpart to the court of women in the Jerusalem temple.[23] Women were generally among the less accepted groups in Israel, as well as were the Samaritans, Gentiles, and various occupations and the poor.[24]

Scholarly Neglect of Acts for Affirming the Significance of Women's Role in Today's Church

Acts is to the early formation of the Church what Genesis is to the early formation of Israel. If Acts provides foundational teaching for the nature of the Church, the role of apostles, the inclusion of Gentiles, the expansion of Christianity, the Church's role in benevolence, witnessing, and soteriology, then Acts is also the foundational teachings for the inclusion or non-inclusion of women functions in the Church.

For instance, James Dunn who notes that too much attention has been given to I Corinthians 11:2-16; 14:34-35; and I Timothy 2:11-12 on the one hand, and Galatians 3:28 on the other hand with too little attention given to other texts on the other hand, does not include Acts passages, except the role of women prophetesses in 21:9.[25] George Knight III, whose position about the role of women is influential, reduces the significance of Acts to pairing some passages about women with other scriptural references.[26]

Since Acts is foundational for the development of the early Church, one would expect it to be a primary background study for leadership issues in today's Church. But that has not often been the case. A study prepared by the Committee on Pastoral Research and Practices and approved for publication by the Administrative Committee of the

---

[23] John Temple Bristow, *What Paul Really Said About Women* (San Francisco: Harper and Row, 1988), 49.

[24] Richard J. Cassidy, *Society and Politics in the Acts of Apostles* (Maryknoll, N.Y.: Orbis Books, 1987), 3. See also Neyrey's position that Luke-Acts has significance for our situation today because of its concern with the rich and poor, roles of women, and the exclusiveness of outsiders in *The Social World of Luke-Acts*, 10.

[25] James D.G.Dunn, *Unity and Diversity in the New Testament: An Inquiry into the Character of Earliest Christianity* (Philadelphia: Trinity Press International, 1990), 130.

[26] George W. Knight III, *The New Testament Teaching on the Role and Relationship of Men and Women* (Grand Rapids: Baker Book House, 1977); See also his neglect of Acts in "The New Testament Teaching of the Role Relationship of Male and Female," *JETS* 18 (1975): 81-91; and his by-pass of Acts 2:17-19 in his "The Ordination of Women: No," *CT* 25 (1981): 260-63.

National Conference of Catholic Bishops overlooked Acts.[27] When addressing the ordination issue facing the Episcopal Church in the United States, Longstaff does not consider the Acts 2:17-18 passage.[28] Cerling virtually ignores Acts in his article dealing with women ministries in the New Testament Church.[29] An essential source for serious studies of Acts is the comprehensive listing of articles in the *Theologische Arundschau*. However, the listing reveals only a few articles dealing with women in Acts.[30] Reviewing 38 years of *New Testament Abstracts*, I found only four abstracted articles that dealt with Acts 2:17-18, with none of those opting for women leaders today.

The Significance of Acts 2 to the Role of Women in the Early Church

Acts 2 is formative for understanding the role of women in not only the early Church, but also today's Church. The events on Pentecost not only inaugurated the Church era, but also provided various doctrines and models for the transtemporal Church such as the essentiality of the Spirit (2:1-4), the centrality of Christ in preaching (2:22-36), the terms of salvation (2:37-41), commitments of early Christians (2:42), the benevolence of early Christians (2:43-45), and their balanced life (2:46-47).

The coming of the Spirit on Pentecost transformed that day from being only an annual event for Jewish people to also an eschatological event for all people in fulfillment of such Old Testament passages as Ezekiel 36:26-27, Psalm 16:8-11, and Joel 2:28-32.

In spite of the few who received the Spirit in 2:1-4, it is clear that the Holy Spirit was to be available to "All people" (2:17) i.e., to all different sociological categories.[31] While literally "all flesh," (all people)

---

[27] "Theological Reflections on the Ordination of Women," *JES* 10 (1973): 695-99. See also Bruce D. Chilton, Jr., "Opening the Book: Biblical Warrants for the Ordination of Women," *MCM* 20 (1977); M.E. Thrall, *The Ordination of Women to the Priesthood: A Study of the Biblical Evidence* (London: SCM Press, 1958); Swarte Gifford, ed., *The Defense of Women's Rights to Ordination in the Methodist Episcopal Church* (New Garland Publishing, 1988).

[28] Thomas R. W. Longstaff, "The Ordination of Women: A Biblical Perspective," *ATR* 57 (1975): 316-327.

[29] C.E. Cerling, Jr., "Women Ministers in the New Testament Church," *JETS* 19 (1976): 209-215.

[30] Eckard Plumacher, "Acta-forschung 1974-1982," *Theologische Rundschau* 49 (1984). This listing has been updated beyond 1982 with even fewer articles concerning women in Acts.

[31] John Stott, 74.

did not receive the Spirit on that day, Bruce notes that those who did were the first fruits of a great harvest of others to follow.[32] *Thus Joel's prophecy pointed to a new kind of community in which those previously excluded would be included not only for salvation, but also for service.*

Today some eliminate women from a teaching role in the Church today by restricting their prophecy role announced in Acts 2:17-18 to a non-repeatable foundational function of the Church that ceased with the death of the apostles and the first century prophets.[33] However, restricting the function of New Testament prophecy to only the formative years of the Church (even if that were an accurate limitation) does not eliminate other kinds of speaking by the same people who were prophesying. If females cannot teach or preach today because prophecy ended, then neither can males today, for they were also included in the same passage. Hans Kung notes a variety of words (about thirty) in the New Testament that describes the activity of preaching. He then notes that the variety of different kinds of preaching allows any one to proclaim the gospel message.[34] Thus we must be cautious that we do not deny **any** kind of speaking because of the potential cessation of a different kind.

The Involvement of Women in Acts

Acts matches the number of times women are mentioned in the Gospel of Luke, (33 times in each). Their variety of involvements in Acts shows a liberation of the oppressed (Luke 4:16-17), the Church's early continuation of Jesus' ministry, and the application of God's intention for the Church's use of women as prophesied by Joel (Acts 2:17-18). Harnack believed the equalizing of men and women in Acts produced a kind of religious independence among women that aided the Christian mission. Thus no one who reads the New Testament attentively can fail to notice that in the apostolic age women played an important role for spreading the Christian community.[35] Following are some of the specific roles of women in the Church in Acts:

---

[32] F.F. Bruce, "Luke's Presentation of the Spirit in Acts," *CTR* 5 (1990): 20.

[33] See George W. Knight III, "The Number and Function of Permanent Office in the New Testament Church," *Presbyterian* I (1975): 111-116; See also Jack Cottrell, "Priscilla, Phoebe, and Company."

[34] Hans Kung, *The Church*, (Garden City, N.Y.: ImageBooks, 1976), 479

[35] Adolph Von Harnack. *The Mission and Expansion of Christianity in the First Three Centuries,* vol. II, trans. and ed., James Moffatt (New York: Williams and Norgate, 1908): 64-65.

Women as Prayer Partners

Women were linked with men in prayer meetings (1:4). From that pre-Pentecostal experience, it is unlikely that women were excluded from subsequent times the disciples met to pray (Acts 2:42; 4:23-31). Women were certainly present in the meeting in Mary's house (Acts 12:12-18). The Church at Philippi began from a nucleus of women praying (Acts 16:13). Including women in special prayer gatherings involved them in one of the four foundational commitments that characterized the Church in Acts – "devoting themselves to the apostles teaching, and to fellowship, to the breaking of bread, and to prayer" (Acts 2:42).

Women as Equal Members in the Congregations

In several situations, women were included in conversions (Acts 5:14; 8:12; 16:15; 17:4; 12:34). Although a woman's name is not mentioned until Acts 5, it is likely women were baptized on Pentecost, for women were among the 120 anticipating this day (Acts 1:12-14), and were included in the announcement of salvation and service (Acts 2:17-21).[36]

Decision-Making Women

Women may have participated in the selection of the apostle, Matthias, (Acts 1:12-26) and in choosing the seven leaders in 6:1-6, since they were among those gathered. Sapphira was a co-decision maker with her husband, Ananias, as seen by Peter's questions, "How could you agree…" (Acts 5:9). Lydia was a businesswoman who owned her own house (Acts 16:14). Priscilla was a decision-maker with her husband, for "they" (not just he) were tentmakers (Acts 18:2-3).

It seems unlikely that women who were decision-makers in some of the cities Paul visited would have joined a community of believers in which their abilities would have been buried. That women were significant decision makers in some cities is clear by the fact that on occasions the Jews enlisted influential decision-making women to help eject Paul and his team from the area (Acts 13:50).

After Paul spoke to the council in Athens, a woman, Damaris, was converted which may suggest she was a member of Areopagus, an

---

[36] There is a possibility that women were baptizing women and may have done so on the day of Pentecost. The likelihood of that is tied to the fact that women proselytes entering Judaism were immersed out of the sight of the men, because baptism was done in an unclothed condition. Thus, if women were baptizing women, that may have been the earliest function of women "deacons" whether they were called that or not. See Ellen Juhl Christiansen, "Women and Baptism," 1-8.

influential group of civic movers and shakers in Athens. The openness of the Athenians to the involvement of women, along with the structure of the Greek language in Acts 17:34, allows for such a conclusion.

House-Church Hostesses

Mary's house was a gathering place for Christians (Acts 12:12). The openness of women to host house churches may have been a major factor for the apostles' teaching and evangelizing "from house to house" (5:22) and "breaking bread" in the homes (2:46). The church at Philippi may have begun in Lydia's house (16:15). A church met in the house of Priscilla and Aquila (Romans 16:5; 1 Corinthians 16:19).[37] A church in Colosse met in Nympha's house (Colossians 4:11).

The fact that Christians were meeting in house churches is further evidenced by Saul going from "house to house" (Acts 8:3) to stop Christianity. When Christians could no longer meet in the synagogues, they established house churches (18:4-7).

As Learners

Women were learners in the early Church as seen in several places where they were present when Christian teaching was done — in the synagogues (Acts 17:4, 12), in communities devoid of synagogues (Acts 8:12; 16:13; 17:34), and in houses (10:27; 1:14, 16:31-34; 18:8). Women were included among the Bereans who were studying Scripture (17:10-12).

As Benevolent Sharers with the Needy

Quite early, those who were able shared their possessions with the needy. That women participated in this is inferred by Luke reporting that "all the believers . . . gave to anyone as he had need" (2:44). Later Sapphira participated in selling property for benevolent work, which seemed to be a normal activity of women (5:1-11). When the Antioch church sent gifts to Judea, Luke records, "the disciples, each according to his ability, decided to provide help . . . " (11:29). That certainly included women. Perhaps the generosity of the church at Philippi was initiated, or at least supported, by the nucleus of women who began that church (See Philippians 4:14-16).

Tabitha, also called Dorcas, was spotlighted for her benevolent work (Acts 9:34-39), and may have had the charisma of mercy and generosity (Romans 12:8). She was described as a disciple (learner-

---

[37] Harnack considers the possibility that women served as presidents of the Church that met in their houses, 67.

follower, 9:39) whom some consider to have been a proto-type of a deaconess.[38]

As Proclaimers of the Word

Hans Kung affirms that preaching the Word was entrusted to all, not to just a few.[39] Women were prophesying in a church that Paul established (1 Corinthians 11:5; Acts 18:1-18).

When persecution against Christians broke out in Jerusalem, those who were scattered preached the word wherever they went (Acts 8:4), and the scattered included both the men and women (verse 3). Later Paul admitted that his attempt to destroy the Church included the arrest and imprisonment (and probably the execution) of both men and women (Acts 9:1; 22:4, and inferred in 26:9-11). Saul may have included the persecution of women as well as men because they were also proclaiming the Word wherever they went, including the house churches where some may have been key speakers. If women were simply benevolent workers and non-speaking servants, the Jewish leaders would probably not have threatened them, for Jewish rulers did not command the apostles to quit doing good deeds or performing miracles, but to quit speaking about Jesus (Acts 4:17; 5:40).

Aquila and Priscilla model a Christian couple (Acts 18:2, 26; Romans 16:3-5; 1 Corinthians 16:19; 2 Timothy 4:19) who can work together not only in a secular profession (Acts 18:3), but also in the Christian endeavor of teaching people (Acts 18:24-26), and co-hosting house churches (Romans 16:3-4). No wonder Luke employs identical descriptions for each.[40] Both Christian males and Priscilla were referred to as *sunergoi* (fellow workers) indicating the early Church did not discredit the contribution of women in ministry. However, we do not

---

[38] Ben Witherington III, *Women in Genesis,* 223.

[39] Hans Kung, The *Church,* 479. See also Gilbert Bilezikian, *Beyond Sex Roles,* 124.

[40] Both received gratitude from the Gentile churches; both risked their lives for Paul, and both were called fellow workers (*sunergoi*). It is possible that the term *sunergoi* can be paralleled with *diakonoi*, for Apollos is referred to as both in 1 Co 3:5, 9, in what appears to be an interchangeable usage. *Diakonoi* is a significant reading of *sunergoi* in 1 Th 3:2. It is clear that Priscilla and Aquila were both referred to by this term. That term was used to refer to several different males including those who had significant speaking roles (Urbanus, Ro 16:9; Timothy, Ro 16:21; Apollos and Paul, 1 Co 3:9; Titus, 2 Co 8:23; Epaphroditus, Php 2:25; Aristarchus and Justus, Col 4:10, 11; Clement among others, Php. 4:3).

have enough data to concur with Harnack that Priscilla was the leading figure of the two.[41]

The conclusion of some that Priscilla's co-teaching activity with Apollos was insignificant, because it was not public teaching (which supposedly is more authoritative) is without warrant. What is clear is that Apollos needed some advanced teaching, and Priscilla shared in giving it.[42]

Paul wrote that both single women and men Christians have undivided concern about the affairs of the Lord (I Corinthians 7:32-35). It seems likely that both single women and men were involved in significant teaching-leadership functions in the church at Corinth.[43]

Phoebe is not mentioned in Acts; however, due to the proximity of Cenchrea to Corinth, she may have been converted as a result of Paul's activities in Corinth (Acts 18:1-18). While we should not read more than necessary into Paul describing her as a *prostatis* and *diakonos*, there is no reason to deny that she was significantly involved as a leader with potential speaking functions in the Cenchrean congregation (Romans 16:1-2).

Nearly three decades passed between Peter's announcement that the Christian era would include female prophets (Acts 2:17-18) and Paul's visit to Philip and his four prophetess daughters (Acts 21:9). These four virgins may have had the *charismata* of both celibacy (1 Corinthians 7:7) and prophecy (1 Corinthians 12:10, Romans 12:6). Luke mentioned these four in a matter-of-fact kind of reporting, not as an exceptional situation. 1 Corinthians 7:7 and 11:2-16 do not allow us to view those four as exceptions in the early Church. Mentioning their virginity may have been Luke's way of emphasizing that a woman does not have to be paired with a man to have significant leadership ministry and influence in the early Church.

Hans Kung attributed the early spread of the Christian message to the fact that all according to their gifts proclaimed it, for all were filled with the Holy Spirit.[44] Thus the early Church reversed the reductionistic Jewish practice of not using women. This incipient reversal deserves to continue in the Church today.

---

[41] Harnack, 66. See also William Ramsay, *St. Paul The Traveller And The Roman Citizen.* 3d ed. (London: Hodder & Stoughton, 1897), 268-269. Elisabeth Schussler Fiorenze, "Women in the Pre-Pauline Churches," *USQR* 33 (1978): 156.

[42] Ben Witherington III, *Women in Genesis,* 220.

[43] Following Brooten's evidence of women leaders in synagogues, it is possible that some women were leaders in some of the synagogues in the diaspora, and thus provided a model for women being leaders in the early Church. See J. Massyn Gberde Ford, "Biblical Material Relevant to the Ordination of Women." *JES* 10 (1973): 664-669.

[44] Kung, *The Church,* 479.

Inclusion of Males and Females in Leadership as One Essential for Spiritual Formation

All people either progress or regress in their individual spiritual development through their relationships with others,[45] self, and God. Denying men or women the freedom to use their gifts hinders not only individual progress toward maturity, but also the Church's for the following reasons:

1) It violates the mutuality of male and female in God's original intention for His community on earth as seen in Genesis 1 and 2.

2) The body of Christ cannot mature when not in conformity with the head of the body, Jesus (Ephesians 4:11-16).

3) Jesus included and used women and men in identical ways, except for women being one of the twelve apostles; however, later a woman was perhaps referred to as an apostle (Romans 16:7).

4) As God's new community, the Church should demonstrate in every culture the mutuality and equality of all humans (1 Corinthians 10:32; 2 Corinthians 5:16-17; Galatians 3:28; Ephesians 3:10; Ephesians 2:11-22).

5) God's redemptive act in Jesus restores individuals not only to Himself, but also to one another (Ephesians 2:19-22 and all the "one anothers in the epistles).

6) God's goal for both individuals and the Church is that they mature into Christlikeness (Romans 8:29).

7) God's *charismata* are not gender specific (I Corinthians 12-14; Romans 12:4-6; I Peter 4:10).

8) The Church will not mature fully if the gifts of persons are squelched, for to do so is to not utilize gifts according to God's spiritual formational purposes (Ephesians 4:11-16).

9) The Church will not mature when some members feel superior, while others feel inferior (1 Corinthians 12:12-31).

10) The Church is the ongoing incarnation of Christ's universality, and is to invite all people not only to salvation, but also to service without regard to gender, economical, race, and national identities (Matthew 28:18-20; Acts 2:17-18).

---

[45] See Erik Erikson. *Identity, Youth and Crisis*; James W. Fowler. *Stages of Faith: The Psychology of Human Development and the Quest for Meaning* (San Francisco: HarperSanFrancisco, 1981).

11) For the Church to use only two passages to keep women in silent chambers (1 Corinthians 14:34; I Timothy 2:11-12) is to overlook God's holistic view and use of women throughout both the Old and the New Testaments (see chapter 6 for a look into those two passages).

12) It is an inadequate hermeneutic that separates only one category of humans from Galatians 3:28 and then restrict that category from any leadership function in the Church. Those three categories are racial—national or ethnical, economical—class or status, and gender—male or female. Since the Church does not keep any nationality nor economical status from leadership roles, she should not restrict the third category — women (see discussion on Galatians 3:28 in chapter 5).

13) To maintain a traditional prejudice against using any category of people in any gifted service hinders fulfilling the great commandment of John 13:34-35, the great commission of Matthew 28:18-20, and the many "one anothers".

14) Since the Church is built upon the foundation of the apostles and prophets (Eph. 2:20), and women were female prophets in the early Church, then it is hermeneutically inadequate to keep women from leadership roles today.

15) The body of Christ will not mature properly by **verbally** committed to the oneness of God — one body, one Spirit, one hope, one Lord, one faith, one baptism, one God "and Father of all, who is over all, and through all and in all" (Ephesians 4:4-6) while **functioning** hindering the equal service of all members.

In the future the irony of ironies for historians who review the 20th century may note that the sports industry did more for the recognizing and using the gifts and abilities of black people than did the Church. And a parallel irony of ironies may be that historians may note that during the 21st century politicians and entrepreneurs did more for recognizing and using the gifts and abilities of women than did preachers and elders; and that companies did more for liberating and using women for the industry than did the Church for the Immanuel.

Summary

1. The apostolic Church followed Christ's example by including women in the ministry of the new community.

2. Women and men were involved in various ministries in the early Church as recorded in Acts.

3. Women were probably among those who received the Spirit in Acts 2:1-3 and were certainly targeted for speaking roles in the early Church (Acts 2:17-18).
4. Women and men served in a variety of roles that brought persecution to them.
5. The involvement of women and men in Acts is both descriptive and prescriptive. It is descriptive in that it depicts the authentic history of the early Church, but is also prescriptive in that it serves as the model for the Church throughout the new covenant era.
6. Luke revealed that wherever the gospel was preached, women were some of the first and most fruitful converts to the Christian faith.[48]
7. There is to be a continuity of the Church today with the Church in Acts concerning how people in different groups are viewed and used.[46]
8. Ministry is no longer to be restricted to only one segment of the Church.[47]
9. The Christian Church introduced new relationships and structures where men and women can work together with the spirit of fraternal love and respect for one another's dignity, distinctiveness, and giftedness. For an incisive work that develops this, see Sarah Sumner's deep and important work.[48]

The next chapter relates the significance of baptism and charisma to the role of women and men in the Church.

---

[46] See A.J.M. Wedderburn, "A New Testament Church Today," *SJT* 31 (1967): 517-532.

[47] S.R. Philsy, "Diakonia of Women in the New Testament Church," *IJT* 32 (1983): 117.

[48] Sarah Sumner. *Men and Women in the Church* (Downer's Grove, IL: InterVarsity Press, 2003).

CHAPTER 5

BAPTISM AND *CHARISMA*: TWO DYNAMICS EMPOWERING WOMEN FOR LEADERSHIP ROLES IN THE CHURCH

After reviewing the heavenly Father's intention for women, the incarnated Son continuing the Father's intention, and the Holy Spirit empowering the early Church to perpetuate Jesus' ministry to and through women as well as men, this chapter will relate the enlistment of baptism to ministry and the empowerment of the Spirit's *charismata* for all Christians regardless of their biological or sociological identities. This chapter will develop the thesis that women can be leaders because of being enlisted into God's new community by baptism and equipped for ministry by charisma

The Need For Liberation

Jewish reductionism marginalized many categories of people into second-rate persons "such as women, poor, uneducated, sick, lame, blind, deformed, lepers, tax collectors, panders, prostitutes, shepherds, seamen, servants, slaves, peddlers of fruit and garlic."[1]

The stigmatisms of honor and shame were dominant in the first century Mediterranean world. Honor was the positive value placed on people based upon how society appreciated them, and was usually related to a person's power, achievements, and superior status. While honor included males and females, a woman's honor was granted only when she remained under a male as her protector.[2] Thus in many cultures women were excluded from having significant roles in the public arena, for that would humiliate the honor of men. While men were honored for being involved in the public arena, women were shamed, but honored for her domestic arena.[3] Male honor was symbolized in the testicles, which stood for courage, authority, the refusal to submit to humiliation, and engaging in activities to defend his reputation; however, female honor was symbolized by the hymen, which stood for her exclusiveness, shyness, restraint, and timidity.[4]

---

[1] Rosemary Radford Ruether, *Women and Redemption: A Theological History* (Minneapolis: Fortress Press, 1998), 16-17.

[2] Jerome H. Neyrey, ed., *The Social World*, 41-42.

[3] *Ibid.*, 42.

[4] *Ibid.*, See also Richard Rohrbaugh, ed., The *Social Sciences and New Testament Interpretations* (Peabody, MA: Hendrickson Publishers, 1996), 20-22, 31-37; John J. Pilch and Bruce Malina, eds., Biblical *Social Values and Their Meaning: A Handbook* (Peabody, MA: Henrickson Publishers, 1993), 95-104.

God's liberation ministry was first introduced when He promised that the woman's offspring would crush the head of Satan.[5] The crescendo of freedom for the Hebrew people was the exodus, followed by liberations during periods of the Judges, Kings, and the Maccabeans.[6] Luise Schotroff believes the exodus demonstrates God's concern for any one being oppressed.[7]

The New Community: A Reality

Jesus the Inaugurator

Jesus came into a world sociologically divided into categories of superiority and inferiority maintained by the concepts of honor and shame. The three broad sociological categories were racial (Jew and Gentile), economical (slave and free), and gender (male and female). Jesus' life and ministry fulfilled four purposes: (1) to reveal what God is like. He was God's personal exegesis.[8] To see Jesus was to see God[9] because He modeled the dominant characteristic of God—love;[10] (2) to reveal how to live as a human in the midst of a dehumanized world; (3) to restore people to their original created nature who could then function in mutual partnership; (4) to recruit those restored to continue what He began through their lives and ministries. The third and fourth purposes characterize the new community Jesus intended when He said, "I will build my church,"[11] and for which He prayed, "My prayer is not for them alone. I pray also for those who will believe in me through their message, that all of them may be one, Father, just as you are in me and I am in you. May they also be in us so that the world may believe that you have sent me."[12]

---

[5] Ge 3:15. A Messianic text that foreshadows the life, death, and resurrection of Jesus.

[6] It is interesting that the time the Hebrews were in Egypt (approximately 400 years) parallels the total time they were later oppressed by the Babylonians, Persians, and Greeks. Indeed the Passover and Hanukah celebrate liberations.

[7] Luise Schotroff, *Let The Oppressed Go Free: Feminist Perspectives on the New Testament*, trans. Annemarie S. Kidder (Louisville, KY: Westminster/John Knox Press, 1993), 24.

[8] Jn 1:18.

[9] *Ibid.*, 14:9.

[10] *Ibid.*, 3:16, 2 Pe 3:9.

[11] Mt 16:18.

[12] Jn 17:20-21.

This new community was described as branches drawing life, vitality, character, and conduct from Him, the vine;[13] as sheep following the shepherd; as the body of Christ maturing into the likeness of its head; as the temple housing the presence of God's Spirit; as children imitating the Father; as the bride submitting to the husband—Christ; and over 100 other images each of which emphasizes at least one aspect of how God's will can be done on earth as the Church crosses sociological barriers[14] to make disciples *panta to ethne* — all categories of people.[15]

Baptism into the New Community

While there are diverse understandings and applications about the mode of baptism (immersion, sprinkling, pouring, etc.), the candidates for baptism (infants or adults), and the connection of baptism to salvation (essential for or expressive of), I will address only the role of baptism for transferring all categories of people into God's new community—the Church as the new creation and simultaneously ordaining them into ministry.

Baptism as *Sacramentum*

Sacramentum described the military oath taking in the Roman military. I enlisted in the military during the Korean conflict. Prior to raising my hand and taking the oath, I was a "Mr"; but following the oath taking, I was instantly transferred from "Mr." civilian to "Private" military. The oath taking in the current military is that positional change from civilian to military life. And so it was in the Roman Empire.

While some today use the word *sacrament* differently, the original use was the oath of allegiance from a new soldier.[16] During Christianity's, second century, the Church adopted the word *sacramentum* to describe becoming a soldier of Christ. The word *pagani* (the word from which our word "pagan" came) was also adopted from that military/civilian culture, for prior to taking the *sacramentum* a

---

[13] *Ibid.,* 15:1-8; 10:1-10; Eph 1:22-23; 4:11-13; 1 Co 3:16; Eph 2:22; *Ibid.,* 5:1-2; 5:21-31.

[14] Ac 1:8. The four-fold description of Jerusalem, Judea, Samaria and ends of the earth is not just geography, but also and probably is primarily sociological.

[15] Mt 28:18-20.

[16] Hendrick Kraemer, A *Theology of the Laity* (Philadelphia: The Westminster Press 1958), 106. See also Arthur Darby Nock, *Early Gentile Christianity and Its Hellenistic Background* (New York: Harper & Row Publishers, 1964), 141 and Weber, Hans-Ruedi. *Salty Christians* (New York: The Seabury Press, 1969), 25.

person was a *pagani*, meaning a civilian.[17] In early Christianity, baptism was viewed as the pivotal transfer act described by Paul, "For He delivered us from the domain of darkness, and transferred us to the kingdom of His beloved Son."[18] Baptism was a person's pledge of allegiance to enter the *militia Christou*[19] by deserting the old life as a worldly civilian. Paul linked the soldier image to the new Christian[20] wearing the uniform of a Christian soldier[21] and the full armor for spiritual warfare.[22] There were to be no sociological barriers keeping people from taking that *sacramentum*. Thus Jews and Gentiles, males and females, slaves and free persons could and did become co-enlistees in Christ's army (*militia Christou*).

Baptism as Incorporation into Unity amid Diversity

Through the baptismal pledge of allegiance, a person is initiated into God's new community in which the barriers between groups are to be eliminated.[23] Peter affirmed this integration when he declared the good news was not only for the Jews, but also for those who were far off — *makran*,[24] a term used to describe Gentiles.[25] Scroggs correctly states, "any value judgements based on the distinctions in human society are nullified by baptism."[26] Alan Richardson put it this way, "It is through baptism that the new creation of the end-time comes into being."[27] Thus

---

[17] Weber, 12.

[18] Col 1:13, NASB. Connect this to Col 2:11-12 where Paul describes baptism as a circumcision and a resurrection with Christ in this life for this life (Col 3:1-4:6).

[19] Kraemer, 106; Nock, 141. See also 1 Pe 3:12 for baptism as a person answering God's call – a pledge or faith commitment which one can desert (1 Ti 5:12).

[20] 2 Ti 2:3-4.

[21] Eph 6:11-20. See also Ga 3:27.

[22] 1 Ti 1:18; 6:12; 2 Ti 4:7. See also 2 Co 10:3.

[23] Robin Scoggs, "Paul and the Eschatological Woman," *JAAR* XL (September 1972): 292.

[24] Ac 2:39.

[25] See makran for "Gentiles" in Ac 22:21 and Eph 2:13, 17.

[26] Scroggs, 293.

[27] Alan Richardson. *An Introduction to the Theology of the New Testament* (London: SCM Press, 1958), 354.

the kind of relationships a Christian will enjoy in heaven are to be lived on earth fulfilling the model prayer, "Thy will be done on earth as it is in heaven." What Christ did for all humanity on Calvary is appropriated in baptism for each individual, regardless of sociological differences.[28]

Baptism in the New Testament is never only in water, but also in the Holy Spirit.

To be baptized in the Spirit is to be incorporated into one body together with all others baptized, for we were all (*pantes*) baptized by one Spirit into *(eis)* one body. The *eis* describes a movement from without to within – whether Jews or Greeks, males or females, slaves or free persons – we will all (*pantes*) given one Spirit to drink.[29]

The use of *eis* (into) affirms an εκ (out of) movement which Paul developed in the Galatian letter showing that Christians had been transferred out of condemnation into salvation, out of legalism into "lovalism", out of being non-children of God into being children of God, out of being non-heirs into being joint-heirs, out of being non-free into freedom, out of being a society of inequality into being a society of *koinonia* – an interdependence of commonality with mutuality and equality. The pivotal point of the εκ/εις movement and the resulting mutuality are recorded in Galatians 3:26-28:

> For you are all sons of God through trust in
> Christ Jesus, for as many as were baptized
> into Christ have put on Christ. There is not
> Jew nor Greek, there is not slave nor free,
> there is not male and female for you are all
> one in Christ Jesus. (My translation)

Several concepts in this passage are clear: (1) in baptism a person is incorporated into (εις) Christ; (2) the three pairings represent the most critical sociological divisions in the first century fed by hostility, exclusiveness, superiority/inferiority, and honor/shame labels; (3) this three-fold pairing is Paul's summative position about the new sociological reality of being united to Christ, i.e., the horizontal connections being vertically connected to Christ; (4) the unity amid diversity in God's new society, the Church; (5) the phrase "you are all one" parallels Paul's words in Ephesians 2:12-22 that Christ made the two one . . . destroyed the dividing wall of hostility . . . one new person out of two thus making peace . . . one body . . . to reconcile both . . . you (plural) are a dwelling in which God lives by His Spirit;[30] (6) to be one in Christ is to be united to a diversity of people in the same Church.

---

[28] *Ibid.*, 341.

[29] 1 Co 12:13 my translation

[30] Eph 2:14-22.

To refer to males and females as "sons" is not a gender description, but rather a common idiomatic term[31] that described one person sharing the likeness (son) of another person or thing.[32] To put on Christ may be a reference to converts taking off their clothes before baptism, then being clothed with a clean robe.[33] To put on Christ is to take on His characteristics, virtues, intentions, and spiritual armor.[34] Martyn argued that the new clothing has less to do with cleansing and more to do with equipping the baptized to participate in warfare.[35] Bruce connected putting on Christ to being "vitalized by the life of the risen Christ and energized by His Spirit."[36] In this context, putting on Christ certainly refers to taking on His non-prejudicial attitudes, actions, and reactions that eliminate favoritism. "In Christ" is the position/place/person where the baptized discovers the corporate life.[37] Dunn related baptism to the *sacramentum* concept when he wrote that it is the formal act of transferring from one lordship (sin and law) to Christ.[38]

The three distinctive pairings in Galatians 3:28 not only reflect a Jewish benediction,[39] but also Greek sayings.[40] Therefore, Paul introduced the integrative nature of God's new community to both Jewish and Greek cultures.

---

[31] James D.G. Dunn. *The Epistle to the Galatians*, Black's New Testament Commentary, reprint (Peabody, MA: Hendrickson Publisher, 1993), 201.

[32] See Barnabas being called son of encouragement (Acts 4:36) and James and John being referred to as sons of thunder (Mk 3:17). So "sons" of God refer to sharing a likeness with God regardless of gender.

[33] F.F. Bruce, The *Epistle to the Galatians: A Commentary on the Greek Text*, The New International Greek Testament Commentary (Grand Rapids: William B. Eerdmans Publishing, 1982), 186.

[34] Richard N. Longenecker. *Galatians*, Word Biblical Commentary, vol. 41 (Dallas: Word Books Publishers, 1990), 156.

[35] Louis J. Martyn. *Galatians: A New Translation with Introduction and Commentary*, The Anchor Bible (New York: Doubleday, 1997), 377.

[36] Bruce, *Galatians*, 184.

[37] *Ibid.*, 376.

[38] Dunn, *Galatians*, 203.

[39] See the reference in Longenecher, 157; Bruce, *Galatians*, 187; and Ruth A Tucker and Walter L Liefeld, *Daughters of the Church: Women and Ministry from New Testament Times to the Present* (Grand Rapids: Zondervan Publishing, 1987), 61.

[40] Ben Witherington, III. "Rite & Rights for Women – Galatians 3.28," *NTS* 27 (1981): 594.

While people distinctions are not obliterated by baptism into Christ,[41] they are transcended and should not be used as a basis for denying entrance into or status within the Christian community.[42] Paul's statement is an "affirmation of the ontological equality of these pairs,[43] which introduces the basis for a new social ethic in the Church."[44] Thus Galatians 3:28 is revolutionary, for these three pairings represent the three deepest divisions, which split the society of the ancient world.[45] Paul argued that these distinctions are to have no place in the thought or practice of those in Christ. To use any ethnic, economic, or gender distinctions to make a difference in treating or utilizing people is to misunderstand the nature of Christ and the Church.[46] Therefore, the new community is to demonstrate a new kind of humanity in relationships[47]—united persons who prior to being in Christ were terribly divided.[48] Consequently, any protection of only pre-selected members and any prejudices against others are to be rejected.[49]

While the actual distinctive sociological realties are not removed, they are no longer to have significance in relationships.[50] Gentiles do not become Jews,[51] or females males,[52] but in Christ people are lifted to full personhood.[53] Caird noted that in Christ God judged the old order that

---

[41] *Ibid.,* Bruce, *Galatians,* 189.

[42] Witherington III, "Rights," 594.

[43] *Ibid.,* 600 and Bruce, *Galatians,* 189.

[44] Longenecker, 159.

[45] G.B. Caird, "Paul and Women's Liberty," *BJRL* 54 (1972): 273-274.

[46] Gerald L. Borchert, "A Key to Pauline Thinking – Galatians 3:23-29: Faith and the New Humanity," *Rev Exp* 91 (1994): 149.

[47] *Ibid.,* 148; Caird, 274.

[48] Wayne Litke, "Beyond Creation: Galatians 3:28, Genesis and the Hermaphrodite Myth" *SRSR* 24 (1995): 176-177.

[49] James D and Evelyn Whitehead, The *Emerging Laity: Returning Leadership to the Community of Faith.* Image books ed. (New York: Doubleday, 1988), 160.

[50] Dunn, *Galatians,* 201.

[51] See Acts 15:1-21, Galatians 3:25-28, Romans 3:29-30.

[52] Witherington III, "Rite," 599.

[53] Lawrence O. Richards and Clyde Hoeldtke, A *Theology of Church Leadership* (Grand Rapids: Zondervan Publishing House, 1980), 18.

was so prevalent in relationships throughout the Roman Empire and found it wanting.[54] Since people differences share equal value in the equipment for ministry.

Baptism as Ordination into Ministry

It was God's original intention that males and females be co-partners while doing His will on earth,[55] as a kingdom of priests.[56] Various factors reduced that universal access to ministry; therefore, God reestablished His intention for the Church: "You are a chosen people, a royal priesthood, a holy nation, a people belonging to God, that you may declare the praises of Him who called you out of darkness into His marvelous light."[57] All Christians have God's treasure in their earthly bodies to show that the power is from Him when they serve Christ. [58]All Christians are God's workmanship, His new creation for good works.[59]

Baptism is directly related to ministry. Hans Kung argued that it is by baptism that all believers are consecrated as priests and no person is to control the ministry of others.[60] Richardson maintains that baptism is the "ordination" to ministry.[61] Anne Rowthorn quoted Aiden Kavanaugh, "Christians do not ordain to priesthood. They baptize into it."[62] Whitehead anchored baptism to the call to ministry.[63] Greg Ogden believes the Church needs to reclaim baptism as ordination to ministry, for it is not just an invitation into the body of Christ, but also "an opportunity for the gathered people of God to reconnect themselves to living out the implications of their baptismal vows."[64]

---

[54] Caird, 274.

[55] Ge 1:26-28.

[56] Ex 19:6.

[57] 1 Pe 2:9.

[58] 2 Co 4:5-7.

[59] Eph 2:10.

[60] Hans Kung, The *Church*, 477.

[61] Richardson, 301, 331, 350-351.

[62] Anne Rowthorn, *The Liberation of the Laity* (Wilton, CT: Morehouse-Barlow, 1986), 16.

[63] Whitehead, 158.

[64] Greg Ogden, *The New Reformation: Returning the Ministry to the People of God* (Grand Rapids: Zondervan Publishing House, 1990), 212-213.

Baptism as ordination to ministry is rooted in Jesus' own baptism, which was the launching event for His ministry (see chapter 3). Our baptism is also our commitment (vow – change of allegiance) through which we non-verbally declare, "I pledge allegiance to the Christ of the United Kingdom of the world – one family under God, indivisible, with liberty and justice for all."

Galatians 3:28 describes the result of being baptized into Christ with no member having a more privileged position than any other due to a sociological difference.[65] While the pairing of male and female is linked with και (and) instead of *oude (*nor) which connects the other two pairings, there is no substantial significance to that change.[66] Nor is there substantial evidence that Paul restricted the equality of the pairs to only salvation or inheritance.

To be saved from sin is to be saved for service. To be in the Messiah is to be in His ministry. As all have equal access to baptism, all simultaneously have equal access to ministry. All are free to use their gifts without being restricted by gender, race, or economical status.[67] The concept of mutuality is not an invention of liberals nor a borrowing from cultural theories of equalitarianism,[68] but results from being transferred out of the kingdom of darkness into the kingdom of God's Son through the *sacramentum* of baptism. All baptized Christians are called through baptism to become ministers of Christ's saving and uniting purpose.[69] Ministry is then a shared imperative across the pairings; regardless of which identity in those pairings a person may be belong.[70]

William Ramsey (an historian) shared a cogent concept, "A nation cannot permanently remain on a level above the level of its women." He further stated that to raise the level of women is a primary condition of national health, and the Church must work for the equality of the sexes.[71] Ramsay encouraged the Church to raise the standard of how she thinks

---

[65] Witherington III, "Rite," 599.

[66] Bruce, *Galatians*, 189.

[67] Virginia Ramey Mollenkott, *Women, Men & the Bible* (Nashville: Abingdon Press, 1977), 84-85.

[68] Whitehead, 156.

[69] Weber, 17.

[70] Whitehead, 159.

[71] Wm. Ramsay, *A Historical Commentary on St. Paul's Epistle to the Galatians,* 2d ed. (London: Hodder and Stoughton, 1900), 390.

about and treats all people distinctions. If the Church does not do that for women, then "no amount of excellence in abstract principles and truths will make that religion a practical power for steadily elevating the race which clings to it."[72] Witherington suggests Galatians 3:28 may be the "emancipation proclamation for women" which legitimized their place and ministry in the Church.[73]

Instead of tying Galatians 3:28 to only salvation as some do, Clark Pinnock states, "God justifies and saves individuals only to give them a vocation in the service of the kingdom."[74] It seems likely the reason some do not want to link Galatians 3:28 with an equality for ministry is because of the male and female pairing. FF Bruce is helpful here:

> No more restriction is implied in Paul's equalizing of
> the status of male and female in Christ than in His
> equalizing of the status of Jew and Gentile, or of slave
> and free person. . . . If a Gentile may exercise spiritual
> leadership in the Church as freely as a Jew . . . , why
> not a woman as freely as a man? . . . Paul states the
> basic principle here; if restrictions are placed on it
> elsewhere in the Pauline corpus, as in 1 Cor.14:34f . . .
> or 1 Tim. 2:11f, they are to be understood in relation to
> Galatians 3:28 and not *visa versa*.[75]

Dunn's comment also deserves careful reflection and application:

> Not a leveling and abolishing of all racial, social or
> gender differences, but as an integration of just such
> differences into a common participation in Christ,
> wherein they enhance (rather than detract from) the
> unity of the body, and enrich the mutual
> interdependence and service of its members. In other
> words, it is a oneness, because such differences cease to
> be a barrier and cause of pride or regret or
> embarrassment and become a means to display the
> diverse richness of God's creation and grace, both in the
> acceptance of the "all" and in the gifting of each.[76]

While baptism into Christ integrates each person into God's new community and into mutual ministry, Jewett observes that applying this is not easy in our sinful world; however, it will be an easy lifestyle in heaven – our future hope, and the Church should strive to realize that

---

[72] *Ibid.,* 388.

[73] Witherington III, "Rite," 600.

[74] Clark H. Pinnock, *Flame of Fire: A Theology of the Holy Spirit* (Downers Grove, IL: InterVarsity Press, 1996), 141.

[75] Bruce, 190.

[76] Dunn, *Galatians,* 208.

future hope more completely and perfectly in our time and locations.[77] John challenged us to that when he wrote that we should begin to become here what we will be in heaven, "For we shall see him as he is. Everyone who has this hope in him purifies himself, just as he is pure."[78]

Let us then be baptized not only for affirming the erasing of our sins, but also for engaging our services; not just to enter the gates of heaven, but also to walk the streets of earth as Christ's continuing body; not only to fellowship with the saints, but also to be friends with non-Christians; not only to be mercifully reconciled, but also to be ministers of reconciliation; not only because we have heard the good news, but also to be heralds of that message; not only to receive the Holy Spirit, but also to replicate the Spirit both in our attitudes and activities by touching all kinds of people in all kinds of ways with all kinds of talents and *charisma* from all kinds of members of the Church. In doing so we will partially fulfill Jesus' prayer in John 17.

Jesus' ministry foreshadowed that both men and women would participate in the *sacramentum*—incorporation into oneness and ordination to ministry when He liberated women to be His disciples and affirmed them in many different kinds of ministries including evangelizing and teaching men (see chapter 3). Prior to announcing the good news on the day of Pentecost, Peter proclaimed that the Christian era would include both men and women as prophets (see chapter 4). Paul not only evangelized women as well as men, but also affirmed women as evangelists, prophetesses, and teachers and did not link a specific *charisma* to any specific gender or restrict any *charisma* from either gender.

As baptism is our enlistment into "God's colony in man's world,"[79] *charisma* is our equipment that defines our specific ministry.

To that we now turn with positive insight from Witherington, "So long as one member does not think its place or function is more important or more equal than others, then Christians can function with sexual differences and functional divisions of labor."[80]

---

[77] Paul K. Jewett, Man as Male and Female: A Study in Sexual Relationships from a Theological Point of View (Grand Rapids: Eerdmans Publishing, 1975), 171.

[78] 1 Jn 3:2-3.

[79] The title of George Webber's splendid book about renewal (Nashville: Abingdon Press, 1960), "We are a colony of heaven" is Moffatt's translation of "Our citizenship is in heaven" (Php 3:20); and is the topic of Stanley Haverwas and William H. Willimon's book, *Resident Aliens: A Provocative Christian Assessment of Culture and Ministry for People Who Know that Something is Wrong* (Nashville: Abingdon Press, 1989).

[80] Witherington IIII, "Rite," 600.

Charisma and the New Community

Charisma – What is it?

Charisma comes from *charis*,[81] the Greek word for grace, which is
an action related word. At times the Greek language added *"ma"* το a
noun of activity indicating a result of the corresponding action.
Charis+ma is the result from active grace – a grace-gift. Anyone
receiving God's grace simultaneously receives *charisma*. *Charisma* is
used thirteen times in the New Testament[82] and is interchangeable with
dorea, another word for gift, as seen below:

The Gift	as *charisma*	as *dorea*
Reconciliation . . .	Romans 5:15 . . .	Ephesians 4:7 . . .
A ministry . . .	1 Timothy 4:14; 2 Timothy 1:6 . . .	Ephesians 3:7 . . .
Eternal life . . .	Romans 6:23. . .	John 4:10 . . .
Grace involvement . . .	Romans 12:6 . . .	2 Corinthians 9:15 . . .

Thus charisma does not have greater significance nor does it grant
someone a higher status than dorea.

The Universality of *Charisma*

Charisma shares universality in two ways, (1) some *charismata*
(plural for charisma) are given to all Christians such as eternal life,[83]
encouragement,[84] justification,[85] the propensity for either marriage or
celibacy,[86] answered prayers,[87] and a ministry,[88] (2) all Christians have
individual (specialized) *charisma*.[89]

---

[81] S. Schatz Mann, *A Pauline Theology of Charismata* (Peabody, MA:
Hendrickson, 1987), 2. See also J.D.G. Dunn, *Jesus and the Spirit* (London: SCM
Press, 1975), 253.

[82] Ro 1:11; 5:15; 16, 6:23; 11:29; 12:6; 1 Co 1:7; 7:7; 12:4, 9, 28, 30, 31; 2
Co 1:11; 1 Ti 4:14; 2 Ti 1:6; 1 Pe 4:10.

[83] Ro 6:23.

[84] *Ibid.*, 1:11.

[85] *Ibid.*, 5:15-16.

[86] 1 Co 7:7.

[87] 2 Co 1:11.

[88] 1 Ti 4:14.

[89] Ro 12:5-6; 1 Pe 4:10.

Charisma and the Nature of the Church

As there is no Christian without *charisma*, so there is no non-charismatic congregation. Dunn noted, "Paul evidently did not conceive of a congregation made up of charismatics and non-charismatics: all are charismatics, for that is what being a member of the body in Christ means."[90] Nardoni wrote, "being charismatic by origin and nature, the Church is a spiritual and supernatural entity, independent of any human, ecclesiastical organization and, therefore, free from any human law."[91] The Church is not a humanly designed organization, but rather a supernaturally created organism – the ongoing body of Christ conceived with the same Spirit who conceived Jesus,[92] and equipped Him with ministering gifts.[93] As the fullness of deity was incarnated in Jesus' first century body[94] to enable Him to do a diversity of ministries, that fullness continues to be incarnated in His trans-temporal and trans-cultural body – the Church[95] which participates in Jesus' character through the Spirit and in His diverse ministries through the *charismata*.

The diversity of gifts comes from the sameness of source:

Diversity of Gifts	From sameness of source
Different kinds of gifts	The same Spirit (Holy Spirit)
Different kinds of ministries	The same Lord (Jesus)
Different kinds of operations	The same God[96] (the Father)

The same Godhead (Father, Son, Holy Spirit) produces various kinds of equipment for the diverse kinds of ministries Jesus would do if He were here in person, and He is.[97] Each person is gifted with both universal and individual *charismata* so together all the different ways

---

[90] J.D.G. Dunn, *Jesus and the Spirit*, 734

[91] E. Nardoni, "Charisma in the Early Church Since Rudoph Sohm: An Ecumenical Challenge," *TS* (1993): 647.

[92] Compare Mt 1:20 ("for the child in her having been conceived out of the Spirit is Holy" (my translation) with Ac 2:38 "...and you will receive the gift of the Holy Spirit."

[93] Jesus was anointed with the Holy Spirit and power to do ministry (Ac 10:37-38), and so is the Christian "anointed" with individual charisma.

[94] Col 1:19.

[95] Eph 1:22-23.

[96] 1 Co 12:4-6.

[97] 1 Co 12:27; Ro 12:5 - see presence of Christ/God in our persons in Jn 14:16-23; 15:1-8, 16; 17:21-23, 26; Ro 8:9-10; 1 Co 3:16, 6:19; Ga 2:20; Eph 2:22; 1 Jn 3:24.

Christ ministered in His first century body, His twenty-first century body can minister in Christ. Although no one Christian has all the gifts,[98] the universal Church lacks none.

Paul wrote that we have *charismata* according to the grace having been given to us.[99]

"According to the grace having been given to us" was a Pauline phrase that identified different gifts[100] for different ministries. Therefore, people could serve side by side with unity amid diversity, for both unity and diversity result from God's grace.

Ministerial *Charisma* and Membership Diversity

Throughout the New Testament not one *charisma* is reserved for any one category of members – gender, education, ethnic, powerful or weak, culturally honored or shamed, and so on. All spiritual gifts are given without sociological restrictions attached to them.[101] Thus every Christian has a part in the ministry of the body of Christ.[102] It is only when all members are liberated to use their *charismata* in cooperation and coordination with all other members that the Church can fully mature into Christlikeness.[103] Schweizer maintained that neither status as a layman nor any office in the Church restricts a person from using *charisma* in ministry.[104] Thus "all believers share fundamental equality to be God's ministers. Not even the head can say to the feet that it has no need of them."[105] Simply stated, "nobody is a nobody in Christ's body." No gifted person should feel or be programmed to feel inferior,[106] nor superior.[107] Gifted members are to enhance unity not to express

---

[98] Ro 12:4 and 1 Co 12:29-30. See also Paul's discussion of different gifts for different people in 1 Co 3:5-16.

[99] *Ibid.*, 12:6.

[100] See identical Greek words in Ro 12:6 and 1 Co 3:10; notice the context of both have to do with unity amid the diversity of gifts.

[101] Howard A. Snyder, *A Kingdom Manifesto*, reprint (Eugene OR: Wipe & Stock Publishers, 1997), 116.

[102] Richardson, 305.

[103] Eph 4:11-16.

[104] Eduard Schwizer, *Church Order in the New Testament*, trans. Frank Clarke (London: SCM Press, 1959), 191.

[105] Kung, 473.

[106] 1 Co 12:14-17.

[107] *Ibid.*, 12:21-24.

divisiveness.[108] The health of Christ's body requires indispensable corporeality of mutual support without any one member having too little or too much dependency upon any other member.[109]

The Usages of *Charisma*

The expressions of *charisma* are for the good of the diverse community;[110] for equipping each other in the body;[111] for enhancing spiritual formation toward Christ likeness;[112] for maturing members;[113] for building up the church[114] with edification, encouragement, and consolation;[115] for drawing non-Christians to Christ;[116] for ministering to outsiders with compassion and grace;[117] and for serving in and through the structures of the church and her surrounding culture.[118]

The Dispenser of *Charisma*

The total Godhead gives to each person as He determines,[119] for "God has arranged the parts in the body, everyone of them, just as He wanted them to be,[120] and has planted in each person the exact measure of faith needed for using the *charisma* given.[121] Thus it is inappropriate for anyone to keep another person from using his/her *charisma*.

---

[108] *Ibid.*, 12:25.

[109] Dunn, *Galatians*, 733.

[110] 1 Co 12:7.

[111] Eph 4:11-12.

[112] *Ibid.*, 4:13.

[113] *Ibid.*, 4:14-16.

[114] 1 Co 14:12.

[115] *Ibid.*, 14:3.

[116] *Ibid.*, 14:24-25.

[117] Ga 6:10.

[118] Richardson, 302.

[119] 1 Co 12:7,11.

[120] *Ibid.*, 12:18.

[121] Ro 12:3. Faith in this verse is in the context of using charisms without superiority or inferiority complex.

Freedom with *Charisma*

A regular part of congregational ministry is to call forth the gifts of the Spirit from all members and to provide opportunities for their use.[122] Snyder noted, "an effective church will welcome and encourage, and also discipline and guide the gifts of women and men."[123]

Liberating the use of *charisma* includes freeing people from thinking that God equips people to use their gift in only religious settings. The Whiteheads argue, "describing a boundary between the holy and secular now serves less to focus our attention on God . . . and to restrict God's presence. God's presence in the Church, in the sacraments, and in the sanctuary ought not to suggest an absence or deprivation of God beyond their locales."[124] Findley Edge correctly observed, "it is in the world where the witness for God is most desperately needed – the shop, service station, office, on the farm. It is humanly impossible for the minister to be in all these places. But there are Christian laymen in these places."[125] Ann Rowthorn called on the church to encourage and release the members to view their careers as having sacred dignity and as a locality for the exercise of *charisma*, for it is in those kinds of places that Jesus would frequent.[126] Moltmann called for liberation when he wrote, "Everyone must be accepted with his gifts and tasks, his weaknesses and handicaps. . . . The charismatic congregation gives everyone the room he needs to be free. . . ."[127] But does that include the liberation of women as well? We will turn to that next.

Charisma and the Female Gender

Many today restrict leadership and speaking gifts to only the male gender. George Knight III allows women to use their leadership gifts only with other women. He believes that if Phoebe were a deacon, she was not in leadership because that is reserved for male elders, rulers, and servers.[128] However, the granting of *charisma* in the New Testament was

---

[122] Ogden, 129.

[123] Snyder, *Manifesto,* 117.

[124] Whitehead, 159.

[125] Findley B. Edge, *A Quest for Vitality in Religion* (Nashville: Broadman Press, 1963), 103.

[126] Rowthorn, 5, 87-91.

[127] Jurgen Moltmann, *The Church in the Power of the Spirit: A Contribution to Messianic Ecclessiology,* trans. Margaret Kohl (Minneapolis: Fortress Press, 1993), 343.

[128] George W. Knight III, "The Ordination of Women," 19.

neither gender specific for the recipient of the gift or for the recipient of the ministry from the gifted person. Paul called Phoebe a *diakonos*, the same word for a church leader in 1 Timothy 3:8,[129] and a *prostates*. The twin word for *prostates* is *proistemi* which is listed as a leadership *charisma* in Romans 12:8.[130]

If women were to be denied any specific *charisma*, Paul had many opportunities to state it, but did not. The silent passages of 1 Corinthians 14:34-35 and 1Timothy 2:9-15 are not universally restrictive because God used women leaders in the Old Testament (chapter 2), Jesus used women teaching men (chapter 3), and women prophetesses functioned in the early Church (chapters 4 and 6).

Grenz believes denying women the use of their gifts not only acts unjustly toward women, but also opposes the work of the Holy Spirit.[131] He quoted Margaret Howe's observation that if gifts "are distributed by *God*, what higher authority does the Church have for denying the women their expression?"[132] Kraemer notes, "the place and rights of women in the Church are treated on the basis of non-Christian and sub-Christian ideas."[133] Gordon Fee wrote, "to deny women to minister and teach in the Church is to deny the clear gifts of God Himself."[134]

The Roman Catholic theologian, Kung, called for revising whatever is used to deny ordaining women and stated, "there should be an upgrading of women's position in the Church; full participation of women in the life of the Church, on the basis of equal rights; . . . training and enlistment of women for an active share in responsibilities at the different levels; promotion of theological studies for women and also of a corresponding theological teaching activity."[135]

---

[129] Ro 16:1-2.

[130] See Ro 12:8 translated as govern (my Greek translation); leads (NASB); leadership (NIV); authority (TEV and TCNT); presides (Weymouth); leader (NEB, CEV); put in charge (The Message). However, see Bo Reicke's discussion in the *TDNT* that proistnmi primarily emphasizes pastoral care and not rank or authority. He also linked prostatis in Ro 16:2 with proistnmi, (the gift) in Ro 12:8. Bo Reicke, "proistnmi" in *Theological Dictionary of the New Testament*, vol. VI, 700-703.

[131] Stanley J. Grenz and Denise Muir Kjesbo, *Women in the Church: A Biblical Theology of Women in Ministry* (Downers Grove, IL: InterVarsity Press, 1995), 16.

[132] *Ibid.*, 191.

[133] Kraemer, 70.

[134] Gordon D. Fee, "Issues in Evangelical Hermeneutics, Part III: The Great Watershed – Intentionality & Particularity/Eternality: I Timothy 2:8-15 as a Test Case," *Crux* 26 (1990): 37.

[135] Hans Kung, *Truthfulness: The Future of the Church* (New York: Sheed and Ward, 1968), 174-175.

Equality in distributing gifts to both genders leads to an equality in using those gifts. Denying women the use of any gift which they have is to reduce the morality of Christian love to the immorality of victimization "which divides the body of Christ into super and subordinate parts and reverses Paul's direction to honor the less honorable parts."[136]

Fiddes wrote that women "should have the same opportunities as men to use their God-given gifts within the Christian ministry."[137] To not do so is to continue the clergy/laity distinction, which was institutionalized by Catholicism. That institutional thinking continues today despite the availability of all *charismata* to both genders.[138] Protecting the demarcation between clergy and laity or between male and female maintains an "unequal society" in the Church,[139] reverses Jesus' own announced ministerial intention of releasing the oppressed,[140] and "represents an estrangement from the dominate thought of the New Testament that the whole Church regardless of sex is διακονια (ministry)."[141]

Women's gifts complement the ministry of men in the body of Christ. Allowing women to serve with their gifts helps the Church to mature, to follow the modeling of Jesus with women, to affirm His comments that leadership and greatness are packaged in service—not in control, status, and hindrances,[142] and to build on the foundation of the apostolic Church in Acts.

To affirm giftedness and to give opportunities for ministries do not suggest that women should copycat the way men do ministries. Erik Erikson keenly maintained that a woman's holistic nature is integrated to her inner-space, which is designed to conceive and nurture new life.[143] This does not mean, however, that women are doomed (Erikson's word) to have children in order to be whole. But since a woman is never not a

---

[136] Elizabeth Virgina Emrey, "Paul's Ethics and Feminism in Light of 1 Corinthians," D.Min. diss., (School of Theology at Claremont, 1980), 169-172.

[137] P.S. Fiddes, "'Woman's Head is Man': A Doctrinal Reflection Upon a Paul Text," BQ 31 (1986): 370.

[138] Lawrence O. Richards and Gib Martin, *A Theology of Personal Ministry: Spiritual Giftedness in the Local Church* (Grand Rapids: Zondervan Publishing House, 1981), 103.

[139] Rowthorn, 8.

[140] Lk 4:18-19.

[141] Kraemer, 142.

[142] Molly Marshall-Green, "When Keeping Silent Will No Longer Do: A Theological Agenda for the Contemporary Church," Rev *Exp* 83 (1986): 29.

[143] Erik Erikson, 284.

woman, she should bring her femininity of caring, nurturing, and preserving life to whatever she does. Those attitudes, perceptions, and modes of activities are to be integrated with her womanly "inner space" design.

Erikson affirmed that women share with men an equality of intellectual capacity for work and leadership, but the influence of women will not be fully actualized until it reflects without apology the uniqueness of her "inner space."[144] For a woman to copycat a man in the way she uses her *charismata* may result in her losing emancipation to be who she is – a woman, as well as a Christian. Erikson also notes, "a truly emancipated woman . . . would refuse to accept comparisons with more active male proclivities . . . even when . . . it has, or precisely when, it has become quite clear that she can match man's performance and competence in most spheres of achievement. *True equality can only mean the right to be uniquely creative*[145] (italics mine). Erikson continues with the following:

> Do we and can we really know what will happen to science or any other field if and when women are truly represented in it? . . . she may . . . balance man's indiscriminate endeavor to perfect his dominion . . . at the cost of hazarding the annihilation of the specifics with the determination to emphasize such varieties of caring and care taking. . . .
>
> We may hope, therefore, that there is something in woman's specific creativity which has waited only for a clarification of her relationship to masculinity...in order to assume her share of leadership in those fateful human affairs which so far have been left entirely in the hands of gifted and driven men, and often of men whose geniuses of leadership eventually has yielded to ruthless self/aggrandizement.[146]

The above from Erikson can be applied to various ministries in and through the Church.

Summary

1. By baptism into Christ, each person is enlisted into God's new community.
2. This new community is to function without any cultural honor and shame concepts; without favoritism lifting up some; without prejudices putting down others.

---

[144] *Ibid.* 290.

[145] *Ibid.,* 290-291.

[146] *Ibid.,* 292-293

3. The *sacramentum* incorporates the diversity of people into a relationship of oneness – a new kind of humanity.
4. The *sacramentum* ordains all people (without distinctions) into ministry.
5. Any *charisma* from God's Spirit is available to anyone as the Holy Spirit wills.
6. *Charisma* is for ministry within the body of Christ that helps develop the body's maturity into Christlikeness.
7. *Charisma* is also for sharing Christ's kind of life through a ministry to meet people needs outside the body, wherever God's people are and through whatever tasks they may be engaged.
8. All God's people are ordained by baptism and equipped by *charisma* to function as God's priesthood — Christ's extended body on earth.
9. To prevent anyone from using *charisma* interferes with God's strategy for community living.

Conclusion

Individual members and the corporate Church are hindered from maturing into Christ likeness when any one is either prevented from becoming a member or from using any *charisma* due to a sociological distinction.

The Church that does not mature is unhealthy, weak in ministry, and deficient as God's *Christos Victor* against Satan.

Denying any Christian the use of any *charisma* withdraws God's quality of life from both the church and secular communities. Community life can more easily become anti-community, i.e., living with competition without the interdependence of caring, loyalty, integrity, virtue, unity, peace, and mutual respect with and for one another. Thus the culture more easily becomes more violent, individualistic, relativistic, and utilitarianistic.

Little research has been done to reveal the negative affects to both sacred and secular communities when the Church refuses to release all God's empowered laity into communities with His equipped *charismata*.

The next chapter will investigate the meaning of the two silent passages and how they fit into the holistic biblical use of women.

CHAPTER 6

REVISITING THE "SILENT PASSAGES" OF 1 CORINTHIANS 14:34-35 AND 1 TIMOTHY 2:9-15: WOMEN MUZZLED OR UNMUZZLED?

After navigating over the territory of God's use of women in leadership roles in the Old Testament, Jesus' inclusion of women in ministry, the Spirit's guidance of the early Church's inclusion of women in leadership and speaking roles, and the relationship of baptism and *charisma* to non-gender specific ministries, this chapter will investigate the two New Testament passages that are commonly used for preventing women from speaking ministries in the Church.

The Silent Treatment

Some traditions in both the historical and contemporary Church have placed a muzzle over the mouth of women. Disagreements about women speaking or remaining silent vary in the following representative ways:

1. The location: any place or only in a formal assembly of the Church.
2. The content: any biblical content or only false doctrine.
3. The type of speaking: teaching, prophecy, singing, or asking questions.
4. The speakers: women by gender or wives by marriage.
5. The audience: any one or males by gender or husbands by marriage.

Approaching the Silent Passages

If a person without any background in Christianity and preconceived ideas about women speaking were given an assignment to read the Bible consecutively from Genesis through Revelation for the purpose of discovering the nature of women's role in God's religion, that person would no doubt be surprised to come to 1 Corinthians 14:34 and then later to 1 Timothy 2:12—the only two silent passages that seemingly muzzle women. Surely the neutral reader would question how those two texts fit into the rest of biblical teaching.

God created both male and female in His image to function as co-partners in doing His will.[1] Eve was not created as an inferior person because she was Adam's help (*ezer*), for this Hebrew word describes

---

[1] Ge 1:26-28.

[2] Ex 18:4; Dt 33:7,26, 29; Ps 33:20; 70:5,;115: 9, 10, 11; 121:1, 2; 146:5.

God several times in the Old Testament.[2] Women in the Old Testament saved both males and the entire Hebrew nation.[3] One was the military, civil, and religious leader for the Hebrew nation.[4] Some were female prophets.[5]

During the intertestamental period, several Greek philosophers popularized a negative view about women. The following is a brief sampling of Aristotle's view, which spread widely partly by the military conquests by one of his esteemed students, Alexander the Great:

> Woman is to man as the slave to the master, the manual to the mental worker, the Barbarian to the Greek. Woman is an unfinished man, left standing on the lower step of the scale of development. The male is by nature superior, and the female inferior; the one rules and the other is ruled. Woman is weak of will, and therefore incapable of independence of character or position, her best position is a quiet home life in which, while ruled by man in her external relations, she may be in domestic affairs supreme. . . . The courage of a man and that of a woman are not . . . the same: the courage of a man is shown in commanding; that of a woman in obeying . . . as the poet says, "Silence is a woman's glory."[6]

With the input of that kind of thinking, men in the Greco-Roman and Jewish world eventually belittled women and restricted their involvements in both political and religious circles.[7] However, Jesus modeled a different value of women and liberated them to significant

---

[3] Midwives, Moses' mother, Abigail, Esther.

[4] Deborah.

[5] Miriam, Deborah, Huldah, Isaiah's wife.

[6] Taken from several of Aristotle's writings as researched by Will Durant, *The Story of Philosophy* (New York: Simon and Schuster, 1961), 83-84. Other such views were held by Socrates, Xenophon, Plato, and Demosthenes.

[7] For a sampling see Joachim Jeremias, *Jerusalem*; Jerome H. Neyrey, ed., *The Social World*; Richard Rohrbaugh, ed., *The Social Sciences*; Evelyn and Frank Stagg, *Woman in the World*; Tal Ilan, *Jewish Women in Greco-Roman Palestine* (Peabody, MA: Hendrickson Publishers, 1996); Ben Witherington III, *Genesis*.

[8] Lk 4:16-30. For a broad look at Jesus' view of women see Ben Witherington III, *Women in the Ministry of Jesus: A Study of Jesus' attitudes to Women and Their Roles as Reflected in His Early Life* (Cambridge: Cambridge University Press, 1984).

[9] Ac 2:17-18.

roles,[8] and the early Church continued the liberation Jesus began.[9]

Many contemporary scholars agree. Werner Kummel viewed baptism as the rite of admission into the community of the Church in which in which cooperation and ministry can flourish without regards to differences of gender.[10] Alan Richardson wrote that every member of the Church receives his own *phanerosis tou pneumatos*—"manifestation of the Spirit" for doing ministry.[11] Leaders are not to be controllers of the gifts, but be catalysts for motivating people to serve.[12] Snyder noted the norm for Church leadership is not gender, but the Spirit's giftedness.[13] Witherington believes the issue of gifts is not how or whether a person ministers, but rather what gifts are received.[14] The differences in ministry are not to be related to gender, but to the respective gifts.[15] Each person needs to develop whatever gift is given "without undue concern about whether society brands those gifts as 'masculine' or 'feminine.'[16] Any expression of *charismata (gifts)* should take precedence over tradition,[17] for "who knows the needs of the body best is the Spirit who in consequence, distributes His gifts as He sees fit."[18] Therefore, the Church should provide avenues for the use of as many gifts as the Spirit bestows,[19] for the use of gifts is one essential for Church renewal and maturity.[20]

As God's community became institutionalized, clergy gradually

---

[10] Werner Georg Kummel, *The Theology of the New Testament: According to its Major Witnesses Jesus – Paul – John*, trans. John E. Steely (Nashville: Abingdon Press, 1973), 131, 207, 209.

[11] Richardson, 304.

[12] Pinnock, 140-141.

[13] Howard A. Snyder, *The Community of the King* (Downers Grove, IL: Inter-Varsity Press, 1977), 131, 146.

[14] Ben Witherington III, *Women and the Genesis*, 182.

[15] Whitehead, 159.

[16] Mollenkott, 82.

[17] Marshall-Green, 30.

[18] Jerome Murphy-O'Connor "1 Corinthians 11:2-16 Once Again," *CBQ* 50 (1988): 188.

[19] Snyder, *Community*, 61.

[20] Snyder, 116.

distanced themselves from laity; baptism and *charisma* were disconnected from ministry; and leadership roles for women were neglected and rejected. The ministry of all members was a tenet of the Reformation that was not carried out well. Today many are calling the Church to fulfill that tenet which includes unmuzzling women for ministry, including speaking roles. However, doing that requires objective analysis of the two silent passages, which are speed bumps slowing the liberation of women.[21]

The Muzzle in 1 Corinthians 14:34-35

> Women should remain silent in the churches. They
> are not allowed to speak, but must be in submission, as
> the Law says. If they want to inquire about something,
> they should ask their own husbands at home; for it is
> disgraceful for a woman to speak in the church.

Disagreements about these two verses include the following:
1. The textual beginning of the section.
2. The identity of women.
3. The role of women.
4. The meaning of "remaining silent."
5. The kind of speaking being prohibited.
6. The meaning and object of "submission."
7. The identity of "the law."
8. The reason for speaking being called disgraceful.
9. The immediate context.
10. The author of the two verses.

Textual Integrity

In order to solve the apparent contradictions between preventing women from speaking in 14:34-35 and allowing them to pray and

---

[21] A sampling of those are S. Scott Bartchy, Vickie Becker, Gilbert Bilezikian, Emil Brunner, Findley Edge, Douglas and Rebecca Groothuis, Roberta Hestenes, Gretchen Hull, Hendrik Kraemer, Richard and Catherine Kroeger, Hans Kung, Alvera and Berkeley Michelsen, Greg Ogden, Clark Pinnock, Lawrence Richards, Alan Richardson, Anne Rowthorn, David Scholer, Krister Stendahl, Frank and Evelyn Stagg, Knofel and Julia Staton, Sarah Sumner, Don Thorsen, Elton Trueblood, James and Evelyn Whitehead, Leland Wilshire, and Ben Witherington III. All of these are evangelical Christians, thus the idea that egalitarians do not believe in the authority of the Scripture is without warrant. Differences lie in hermeneutics and exegesis, not in heresy and enmity.

prophesy in 11:5, some have suggested that 14:34-35 is an interpolation and thus not Paul's.[22] However, there are no extant manuscripts that omit the text;[23] therefore, without objective textual evidence to the contrary it is prudent to accept these verses as Pauline.

Original Location

A few manuscripts locate verses 34-35 after verse 40, but the evidence is weak for that being the original location, which would also be extremely awkward reading. Perhaps a scribe in a scriptorium placed the two verses behind verse 40 to "catch up" with something missed earlier when copying dictation. I see no literary reason for verses 34-35 not having been originally positioned in their present textual context.

The Textual Beginning of this Section

To which issue does "as in all the congregations of the saints" (33b) relate? The two possibilities are: (1) verse 33b is a continuation of 33a, "for God is not a God of disorder, but of peace as in all the congregations of the saints"; (2) verse 33b introduces the issue in 34, "as in all the congregations of the saints women should remain silent in the churches..." The first option seems to be the better one, partly because of the repetition of *ekklesiais*, translated as " the congregations" (33b) and "the churches."(34) The first option is better than the second one also because it links the speaking issue to the immediate context of disorder in the assembly. Paul brackets (and thus links) the issue of women speaking with the issue of disorder,[24] which fits his literary style, for he injects similar kinds of bracketing and linkage elsewhere in 1 Corinthians.[25]

---

[22] Hans Conzelmann, *1 Corinthians: A Commentary*, trans. James W. Leitch (Philadelphia: Fortress Pres, 1975), 246; Gordon Fee, *The First Epistle to the Corinthians*, International Commentary on the New Testament (Grand Rapids: Eerdmans Publishing, 1987); Schweizer also shifts the authorship to someone else. Eduard Schweizer, "The Source of Worship: An Exposition of 1 Corinthians 14," *INT* XIII (1959): 402; F.F. Bruce, *1 and 2 Corinthians*, New Century Bible (London: Oliphants, 1971), 135-136; M.E. Thrall, *1 and 2 Corinthians*, The Cambridge Bible. reprint (Cambridge: Cambridge University Press, 1965), 102; C. Holladay. *The First Letter of Paul to the Corinthians* (Austin, TX: Sweet, 1979), 188-190.

[23] Curt Niccum specifically disagrees with Conzelmann and Fee on this issue in the article, "The Voice Of The Manuscripts On The Silence Of Women: The External Evidence For 1 Cor. 14.34-35," NTS 43 (1997): 242-255.

[24] "Disorder" in verse 33 and "orderly way" in verse 40.

[25] See 2:6 with 16; 5:5 with 13; 11:20-22 with 34; 12:7 with 11; 14:1 with 12; 15:37 with 49.

The Situation Being Addressed

While most believe Paul prohibited women from doing some kind of speaking, Odell-Scott argues that Paul was quoting the Corinthians in their letter to him, which he refuted in verse 36 (See 7:1 for a reference to that letter). With this view, Paul was not prohibiting women from speaking, but was correcting the Corinthian's prohibition. Odell-Scott arrives at this by interpreting Paul's use of ε (which is not translated) to introduce a refutation.[26] However, his position does not have internal support, because the formula Paul used to introduce other topics from the Corinthian letter sent to him is missing here.[27]

My positions concerning the previous issues are (a) the text is Pauline, (b) its original location is the same as in our text, (c) the sentence begins with verse 34, not with 33b, (d) consequently, Paul addressed women interrupting a gathered worship service.

The Contexts of The Passage

The Holistic Context

From Genesis to this passage, women were not prohibited from speaking because of their gender.[28] Holistically, it is inappropriate to use either this text or the 1 Timothy 2:12-15 passage to negate women from doing what they had been historically doing.

The "Umbrella" Context

The theme of 1 Corinthians under which every passage in the letter relates is division in the Corinthian church, which was continuing to confuse the members and hinder their edification. Members were divided over many issues: (1) which leader to follow and the role of baptism,[29] (2) incest in the church and a previous letter Paul sent,[30] (3)

---

[26] David W. Odell-Scott, "Let the Women Speak in Church: an Equalitarian Interpretation of I Cor. 14:33b-36," Bib *Theal B* VII 13 (1983): 90-93. Odell-Scott gives other examples of Paul using the e elsewhere in 1 Cor. to negate an earlier statement.

[27] The formula is peri de ("but concerning" or "now for" See 7:1; 25; 8:1; 12:1; 16:1; 16:12.

[28] Paul prohibited a demonized girl from continuing to interfere with his witness, but not because she was female (Ac 16:16-18). John criticized the Thyatira church for tolerating Jezebel's immorality and false teaching. Gender was not the issue.

[29] Chapters 1-4.

[30] Chapter 5 – see especially 5:9-12 for the confusion over a previous letter.

lawsuits,[31] (4) marital intimacy and celibacy,[32] (5) participation in amoral (neutral) practices,[33] (6) the decorum of women and men in public worship,[34] (7) practices during the *agape* feast, (8) the nature and purpose of the Lord's supper,[35] (9) gifts,[36] (10) the resurrection of Christians,[37] (11) the collection for the poor saints in Judea.[38]

The cause for so much divisiveness and confusion was immaturity among members.[39] One solution for immaturity is *agape* - love. Every description of *agape* in chapter 13 relates to a characteristic missing in their relationships with one another, which hindered their peace, unity, and maturational process.[40] Love helps to mature, but when absent keeps immaturity stymied at best or regressed at worst.[41] 1 Corinthians 14:34-35 describes another immature activity, which contributed to disorder and confusion related to the speaking gifts.

The Immediate Literary Context

Verses 34-40 is the last section Paul wrote dealing with the purposes and benefits of *charismata*, especially the speaking gifts. No gift was primarily for benefiting the gifted person,[42] but for the edification, encouragement, and conciliation of the entire body.[43] Verses 34-35 follow immediately on the heels of some members exercising their speaking gifts that interrupted others.[44] Consequently, emotionalism was hindering edification, eruption was hindering evangelism, confusion was hindering conciliation, and disorder was hindering discipling. The kind of speaking women were doing in verse 34 added to the disruption as

---

[31] Chapter 6.

[32] Chapter 7.

[33] Chapters 8-10.

[34] 11:3-16.

[35] 11:17-34.

[36] 12-14.

[37] 15.

[38] 16:1-9.

[39] 3:1-4.

[40] 13:4-7.

[41] 13:1-3; 8:1-2.

[42] 14:4.

[43] 14:3.

[44] 14:26-32.

seen by the statement immediately preceding, "For God is not a God of disorder but peace, as in all the congregations of the saints"; and by a subsequent statement to which Paul's corrective directed, "But everything should be done in a fitting and orderly way."[45] Consequently, understanding 14:34-35 should not be divorced from the context of people stepping on one another's words.

The Speaking

Following are some suggestions identifying the kind of speaking women were

doing in 34-35.

1. Teaching and prophesying.[46] There are several weaknesses with this position: (a) words Paul used elsewhere for teaching or prophesying do not appear here.[47] (b) elsewhere women were not prevented from teaching or prophesying. (c) Paul already dealt with the way teaching or prophecy was disruptive in verses 26-33. (d) this suggestion does not relate well to verse 35. (e) prophecy was clearly an option for women in the New Testament Church.[48] (f) the suggestion does not square with what women were doing in the Corinthian church as recorded in 1 Corinthians 11:5.

2. Women were visiting among themselves.[49] This position has two weaknesses: (a) the words *eis allelos* (one another) are not used. (b) This suggestion ignores verse 35.

3. Paul's use of *lalein (to speak)* suggests that women were chattering, babbling, or talking nonsense.[50] However, *lalein* in the New Testament was never restricted to that kind of speaking, and certainly not in this chapter.[51] This suggestion also fails to relate to verse 35.

---

[45] 14:33 and 40.

[46] John Calvin, *Commentary on the Epistle of Paul the Apostle to the Corinthians*, vol. 1, trans. John Pringle, reprint (Grand Rapids: Baker Book House, 1993), 467-468.

[47] His use of "women" and "prophesy" in 1 Co 11:5 and his teaching in 1 Ti 2:12.

[48] See Ac 2:17-18, 21:9.

[49] Catherine and Richard Kroeger, "Strange Tongues or Plain Talk," *Daughters of Sarah* 12 (1986): 13.

[50] *Ibid.,* 10. The Kroegers' idea that Paul instructed women to keep silent so outsiders would not associate them with the cults that practiced babblings is a terribly weak argument.

[51] See 14:2, 3, 4, 5, 6, 9, 10, 13, 18-19, 21, 23, 27-28, 29, 39.

4. Usurpative speaking, i.e., women were not being disorderly but insubordinate.[52] This suggestion does not relate the verses to its immediate preceding literary context nor to verse 35, and places too much emphasis on "submission" with a narrow identity of "the Law."

5. Evaluating prophecies. This position also has several weaknesses: (a) it is not hermeneutically valid to lay the situation in 1 Timothy 2:12 over 1 Corinthians 14:34 as Carson does.[53] (b) this suggestion does not relate to the immediate literary context of confusion and discord. (c) denying women the function of questioning prophecies weakens the role of women prophets in 1 Corinthians 11:5-6. That is, women prophets would not be able to do what prophets *per se* were instructed to do.[54] (d) all Christians have the responsibility to admonish (*nouthetein*) one another.[55] To keep women from doing any of the "one anothers" sets up a double standard that is not supported in the New Testament. (e) denying women prophets to evaluate restricts their use of the *charisma* of wisdom, word of knowledge, or distinguishing of spirits[56], which one or more may have received. (f) Paul did not use the word for weighing (*diakrinetosan*) in verse 34 which he used in verse 29.

6. Contradicting their husbands.[57] This perspective would prohibit women with the gift of prophecy from using it equally with male prophets. To base this suggestion on the use of the word submission is questionable.

7. Speaking in tongues.[58] There are several problems with this suggestion: (a) Paul already dealt with that issue in 14:2-25. (b) elsewhere when Paul discussed speaking in tongues, he linked λαλεο

---

[52] H. Wayne House, "A Biblical View of Women in Ministry. Part 3 (of 5 parts): "The Speaking of Women and the Prohibition of the Law," *Bib Sac* 145 (1988): 307.

[53] D.A. Carson, "Silence in the Churches: On the Role of Women in 1 Corinthians 14:33b-36," in *Recovering Biblical Manhood & Womanhood: A Response to Evangelical Feminism*, eds. John Piper and Wayne Grudem (Wheaton: Crossway Books, 1991), 151.

[54] 14:29-32.

[55] Ro 15:14.

[56] 1 Co 12:8-10.

[57] See William F. Orr and James Arthur Walther, *1 Corinthians: A New Translation: Introduction with a Study of the Life of Paul, Notes , and Commentary*. The Anchor Bible (Garden City, NY: Doubleday & Company, 1976), 313.

[58] *Ibid.,* 312. Joseph Dillow, *Speaking in Tongues: Seven Crucial Questions* (Grand Rapids: Zondervan Publishing House, 1975), 170.

(speaking) with *glossa* (tongue).[59] (c) this position denies women the use of the tongues *charisma,* which is not a gender specific *charisma.*

8. Asking questions loudly concerning what others were saying in verses 26-31. This is the best option because it integrates well the preceding verses, the confusing situation at hand, and the instructions to women in verse 35. Women were probably separated from men in the assembly and could not hear well what was being said because of the confusion caused by other people speaking simultaneously.[60]

Although Keener does not think evidence supports a separation of males from females in the assembly,[61] ancient ruins of a synagogue in Capernaum reveal the pre-existence of a balcony constructed in such a way that those sitting there were hidden from view.[62] The synagogue system began during the Babylonian exile as a way for Judaism to flourish without the temple. Separation of women from men in the diaspora synagogues would have paralleled the same practice in the Jerusalem temple area.[63] It has been estimated that there were 480 synagogues in Jerusalem existing simultaneously with the temple.[64] It is likely that the required separation of the genders in the temple area would also have been required in the synagogues, especially in Jerusalem. It is equally unlikely that the Great Synagogue in Jerusalem, which set policies for the worldwide synagogues, would have eliminated the separation of the genders outside Jerusalem, particularly when diaspora Jews would return to the Jerusalem temple for various festivals. The Jewish scholar, Alfred Edersheim, argues that all synagogues established space for women with a boarded off partition. He also noted that when the number of Jews in an area did not warrant a separate building, a large room in a private house was used to serve as a

---

[59] See 14:2, 4, 5, 6, 13, 18; as do other New Testament writers, Ac 2:4; 10:46; 19:6; Mk 16:17.

[60] F.F. Bruce, *Corinthians,* 135; See also F. W. Grosheide, *Commentary on the First Epistle to the Corinthians.* The New International Commentary on the New Testament (Grand Rapids: Wm. B. Eerdmans Publishing Company, 1968), 342, 342; Roger L. Omanson, "The Role of Women in the New Testament Church." *Rev Exp* 83 (1986): 21; Boyce W. Balckwelder, *Light from the Greek New Testament,* (Anderson, IN: Warner Press, 1958), 56.

[61] Craig Keener, *Paul, Women & Wives: Marriage and Women's Ministry in the Letters of Paul* (Peabody, MA: Hendrickson Publishers, 1992), 376.

[62] Bristow, 49.

[63] George Foot Moore, *Judaism in the First Centuries of the Christian Era: The Age of Tannam,* reprint (Peabody, MA: Hendrickson Publishers, 1997), 290.

[64] Charles Guignebert, *The Jewish World in the Time of Jesus.* (New Hyde Park, N.Y.: University Books, 1959), 77.

synagogue, but with women separated from men.[65] Emil Schurer noted, "the separation of the sexes must be assumed as self-evident."[66]

After the church in Corinth was expelled from the synagogue, it began to meet in a house next door. Keeping the genders separated would probably have continued in the house church to not offend Jewish visitors, particularly those who had already been exposed to Christian teachings when the church first met in the synagogue. One example of the house church relating well to Jews is Crispus, a synagogue ruler, who was converted when the church assembly moved from the synagogue to a house.[67] By the time Paul wrote 1 Corinthians (around two years later), the meeting may have moved to a larger two-storied house, such as the one in Troas,[68] or to a lecture hall such as in Ephesus.[69] A larger meeting would have distanced men and women farther from each other, which would necessitate women speaking up more loudly with their clarifying questions.

The Identity of the Women

Maier identified *ai gunaikes* (the women) as any female;[70] others identified them as wives.[71] When Paul used *gunaikes* (women) and *andras* (men/husbands) in close literary proximity, he usually referred to wives and husbands. To translate *gunaikes* as women in verse 34 while translating *andras* as husbands in verse 35 is unfortunate, because it blurs the identity of the women in verse 34.[72] If *tous idios andras* are "their own husbands" in 35, then the women in verse 34 are wives. Paul used the same Greek words not only here, but also elsewhere in the

---

[65] Alfred Edersheim, *Sketchers of Jewish Social Life in the Days of Christ* (Grand Rapids: Wm. B. Eerdmans Publishing Company, 1976), 258-261.

[66] Emil Schurer, *A History of the Jewish People,* second division, vol. II, revised, trans. Sophia Taylor and Peter Christie (Peabody: MA: Hendrickson Publishers, 1995), 75-76 n. 109.

[67] Ac 18:4-8. See Paul's practical theology for cross-cultural evangelism in 1 Co 9:19-23.

[68] Ac 20:6-8.

[69] Eph 19:8-10.

[70] Maier translates v. 35 as men folk instead of husbands. Walter A. Maier, "An Exegetical Study of 1 Corinthians 14.33b-38," *CTQ* 55 (1991), 91.

[71] Keener, 376; Omanson, 21; Orr and Walther, 312; C.K. Barrett, *The First Epistle to the Corinthians*, Harper's New Testament Commentaries (New York: Harper & Row Publishers, 1968), 331.

[72] NIV, NASB, NASB updated, KJV, NKJV, TEV, LEV, NEB, RSV, NRSV. *The Message* is consistent "wives...husbands," as well as C.B. Williams' translation, *The New Testament*.

Corinthian correspondence to identify a wife/husband relationship,[73] and there is no reason to assume he changed the meaning of those words here.

The Meaning of Silent

Paul used the Greek word for silent, *sigao*, not only in verse 34, but also in 28 and 30. With each of those usages there is a specific qualifier that restricts a certain kind of speaking, but does not require total silence. In 28, the restriction is not to speak in tongues without a translator; in 30, the restriction is not to speak while others are speaking; in 34, the restriction is qualified by verse 35 – ask husbands at home to keep them from asking questions during the assembly that would add to the chaos described in 27-31. For to do so would hinder Paul's concern that "All of these must be done for the strengthening of the church."[74]

The Meaning of Submission and the Law

Commentators disagree about how "submission" and "the Law" are related in verse 34. For Fee, the two concepts are difficult to fit into any kind of Pauline context.[75] Barrett identified "the Law" as Genesis 3:16;[76] however, *nomos* (Law) is not directly tied to Genesis 3:16 anywhere else in the Bible. Some linked "the Law" to only the creation of the male and female in Genesis 1:26-27;[77] however, *nomos* is not elsewhere directly linked to those creation verses. The concepts of "Law" and "submission" might refer to the husband/wife relationship. Perhaps the wives were directing their questions to other husbands, but not to their own.

Before drawing conclusions about this issue, we need to analyze the meaning of submission and the relationship of that meaning to "the Law" and to the immediate situation being reported. Gerhard Delling gives evidence that *upotasso* (submission) does not immediately carry with it the thought of obedience. Its general use in the New Testament is "the readiness to renounce one's own will for the sake of others, i.e.,

---

[73] See 1 Co 7:2.

[74] 1 Co 14:26; see also verses 3 and 12.

[75] Fee, Corinthians, 708.

[76] Barrett, 330 as well as several others.

[77] Bruce, *Corinthians*, but does not explain how that connection fits this context; Ed Boschman, however, links law with the creation in order to argue that God assigned various ministries in that creative act and did not assign speaking ministries to women, "Women's Role in Ministry in the Church," *DIR* 18 (1889): 47; Knight takes a similar view; George W. Knight, *The Pastoral Epistles: A Commentary on the Greek Text,* The New International Greek Testament Commentary (Grand Rapids: William B. Eerdmans Publishing, 1992), 140.

αγαπη (love), to give precedence to others...." It is to voluntarily "lose or surrender one's own right or will..." rather than meaning so much to "obey...or to do the will of someone."[78] It characterizes unselfish service to others without regard to self-advantage.

To submit is to express love– agape style that fulfills "the Law" of the Old Testament. Jesus taught that the entire Old Testament Law system is summed up when one does for another what "you would have them do to you."[79] The entire Old Testament Law system hangs on the love commandment.[80] Paul also taught that love is the summation and fulfillment of the law.[81] James identified love as the "royal law found in Scripture."[82] The law system was characterized in the Old Testament as God's "covenant of love."[83] Submission and its connection to the "law of love" fit the context of Paul's instructions in 34-35. Women were to conduct themselves in the assembly with some of the characteristics of agape listed in the preceding chapter – patient, not rude, and not insisting on their own way. Those agape attitudes were to be expressed by women who would surrender their right to ask questions in the assembly for the sake of order, and thus would be serving others. They were to be submissive **to the structure and purpose of the assembly** by waiting to ask their husbands at home. It would also demonstrate their submissiveness to their own husbands by not distracting them from learning or speaking by yelling out questions to them. This submissive act of agape on their part squares with the reason Paul wrote the agape chapter (13) in the middle of his teaching about gifts (12, 14). Chapter13 is not an interruption or digression from the topic of gifts, but outlines characteristic attitudes for expressing *charismata* actions, for both agape and *charisma* are always service oriented.

The Reason for Disgraceful Speaking

The disgrace mentioned in verse 35 is not related to women speaking *per se*, but doing so in a manner that contributed to disorder (the immediate context) and to divisiveness and confusion (the umbrella context). Submissiveness expressed with agape fulfills the intention of God, which is to enhance a community with harmony, peace, and mutual benefits. Consequently, women (wives) were to submit to the purpose of the assembly by contributing to the order, peace, clarity, learning, and unity of the gathered community.

---

[78] Gehard Delling, "upotassv" *TDNT,* vol. VIII, 40-45.

[79] Mt 7:12.

[80] *Ibid.,* 22:36-40.

[81] Ro 13:8-10; Ga 5:14.

[82] Jas 2:8.

[83] Dt 7:9-12; 1 Ki 8:23; 2 Ch 6:14; Ne 1:5, 9:32.

Summary and Application of 14:34-35

Paul does not prohibit women from using their speaking *charismata* when so endowed. Women (wives) as well as men (husbands) were to combine their "communication of content" (understandable substance) with their "character of conduct" (submissiveness of love). 1 Corinthians 14:34-35 corrects a **specific** situation in that **particular** congregation **with a general principle** adaptable for all Christians to demonstrate a submissive spirit for the good of others so encouragement, conciliation, edification, and learning can happen in any congregation within any culture during any era. Such submissiveness for the benefit of the assembly today would include the prohibition of interrupting worship by yelling out questions, contradictions, name-calling; stomping out of an assembly; taking over the platform; making corrections; and introducing arguments.

The Muzzle In 1 Timothy 2:9-15

This passage is the most forceful text many use to deny women speaking leadership roles in the Church. Witherington suggests it is a modification of the argument in 1 Corinthians 14:33b-34.[84]

Several different conclusions exist include the "umbrella" context of 1 Timothy; the location of the speaking; the cultural issue; the identity of the women; the meaning of silence, submission, and authority; the relationship of teaching to authority; the reason for mentioning Adam and Eve; the meaning of being saved through childbearing; and the relationship of verse 15 to verse 12.

The Contexts

The Cultural Context

Some suggest Gnosticism had a significant presence in the Ephesian culture and had captured the interest and teaching of women.[85] However, the long-standing idea that many of the terms in the New Testament were written to counter Gnosticism is no longer acceptable. Instead, it is more likely that Gnosticism began using terms that were popular in Christianity in order to make more headway in a culture that had been

---

[84] Witherington III, *Genesis,* 191.

[85] Richard Clark Kroeger and Catherine Clark Kroeger, *I Suffer Not a Woman: Rethinking 1 Timothy 2:11-15 in Light of Ancient Evidence* (Grand Rapids: Baker Books, 1992), 60, 72-73, 117-125, 145, 170; Bruce Barron, "Putting Women in Their Place: 1 Timothy 2 and Evangelical Views of Women in Church Leadership," *JETS* 33 (1990): 451-459. M. Low, "Can Women Teach? A Consideration of Arguments From 1 Tim 2:11-15," TTS [Singapore] 3 (1994): 99-123.

significantly attracted to Christianity. While there may have been some Gnostic ideas floating around in the latter part of the first century that helped crystallize the later formation of Gnosticism, there was not a Gnostic system until after the second century.[86]

Some suggest local women caved into a feministic culture fueled by many female goddesses in Ephesus. That is certainly possible; however, Baugh argued against Ephesus being a center of feminism.[87] Ephesus had its share of pagan cults and philosophies,[88] but not with an intensity different from other cities of its size. The speaking activity of women in Ephesus does not seem to be related to the influence of either Gnosticism or the cults, but to a cultural characteristic of independence, which was common in Greek culture and mirrors the umbrella context of 1 Timothy.

The "Umbrella" Context

Many identify false teaching as the big picture (umbrella context) of 1 Timothy.[89] However, false teaching does not fit every section in this epistle. When a section does not fit the "false teaching" theme, some label that section as either a digression or puzzling.[90] However, those "digressions" or "puzzling" passages suggest a different "umbrella" under which every passage falls.

---

[86] See Nock, xiii-xvii.

[87] S.M. Baugh, "A Foreign World: Ephesus in the First Century," in *Women in the Church: A Fresh Analysis of 1 Timothy 2:9-15*, eds., Andreas J. Kostenberger, Thomas R. Schreiner, and H. Scott Baldwin (Grand Rapids: Baker Books, 1995), 13-52. From examining 4,000 extant primary documents, Baugh argued that there were no females on the 450-member political ruling council; that males only ratified decisions of the ruling council; female dominance in the culture was absent; and the majority of priests even in the cults of goddesses were male. Baugh, however, is weak in linking limitation of women's freedom with slaves who have no freedom. For the most authoritative research on slaves in the Roman Empire reveals much freedom. See S. Scott Bartchy, *First-Century slavery and 1 Corinthians 7:21*, dissertation series, number eleven (Missoula, MT: Society of Biblical Literature, 1973).

[88] Artemis, Demeter Ge, Meter. And had lecture halls for the teaching of philosophers.

[89] Gordon D. Fee, *1 and 2 Timothy, Titus*, New International Biblical Commentary (Peabody, MA: Hendrickson Publisher, 1988); Philip H. Towner, *1-2 Timothy & Titus*, The IVP New Testament Commentary Series (Downers Grove, IL: InterVarsity Press, 1994); Knight III, *Pastorals*, 110-111; Douglas Moo, "What Does It Mean Not To Teach or Have Authority Over Men?" in *Recovering Biblical Manhood & Womanhood: A Response to Evangelical Feminism*, eds. John Piper and Wayne Grudem (Wheaton: Crossway Books, 1991, 180-181.

[90] See Fee, *Timothy-Titus*, 50, 132, 114, 136, and others.

The overarching issue Paul addressed in 1 Timothy is more likely super-independence that was being demonstrated in a variety of ways by church members reflecting the Greek culture of that day. Under the umbrella of super-independence, no section in 1 Timothy is a digression or puzzling.[91] Intense independence was driving the kind of teaching women were doing in this section.

The Immediate Literary Context

The immediate preceding context of 2:1-8 helps identify the persons in 2:9-15. Prior to 2:8, Paul addressed men with the Greek word *anthropos*.[92] Paul then switched to *aner* in verse 8. Elsewhere in 1 Timothy, *anthropos* was used to refer to the male gender,[93] or to people without being gender specific, while *aner* to husbands.[94] Paul followed that same pattern in the other Pastoral Epistles.[95] Without exception, Paul, Peter, and John used *aner* for husbands, as did Jesus. Each New Testament writer/speaker shifted from *anthropos* to *aner* when the topic shifted from the male gender (or generic people) to husbands. Although *aner* is not used exclusively to identify husbands, every time it is used the topic is husband. My contention is that Paul shifted from men (males or generic people) to husbands specifically by shifting from *anthropos* to *aner* in 2:8 and 2:12. The women in 2:9-15 would then be wives.

---

[91] Aspects of independence being addressed are men teaching *independently* from apostolic truths (1:3-11); using legalistic measurements for accepting or non-accepting people independently from mercy (1:12-20); living independently from political authority (2:1-7); men or husbands arbitrarily reacting independently from prayer and gentleness (2:8); women (wives) dressing independently from modesty (2:9-10); women (wives) teaching independently from men (husbands 2:11-15); men seeking to become elders or deacons independently from godly characteristics (3:1-16); some teaching "morality" independently from apostolic example and truth (thanksgiving & revelational resources (4:1-16); treatment of older and younger people independently of agape love (5:1-3); family members using their financial resources independently from providing for aged parents, especially widowed mothers (5:4-8, 16); putting widows on the list independently of character and need (5:9-15); reacting to elders independently from respect and support (5:17-20); responding to people independently from eliminating favoritism (5:21-25); slave and masters relating to each other independently from the characteristics of love (6:1-2); teaching independently from healthy (sound) doctrine (6:3-5); use of money independently from having only one master (6:6-19).

[92] 2:1, 4, 5.

[93] 4:10; 5:24; 6:5, 9, 11, 16.

[94] 3:2, 12; 5:9.

[95] Paul used *aner* in 2 Ti where a husband is not discussed, but he made the distinction in the parallel passage in Titus. See *anthropos* as the male gender (or all people) in Titus 1:4; 2:11; 3:2, 8, 10 and svhr as husbands in 1:6.

Comparing 1 Timothy 2:8-15 with 1 Peter 3:1-7 strengthens this position. The terminology and the words of 1 Timothy 2:8-14 are strikingly similar to 1 Peter 3:1-7 but in an inverted order.[96]

1 Peter	1 Timothy 2
Dress (v.3)	Dress (v.9)
Behavior (v. 4)	Behavior (v. 10)
Submissiveness (v.5)	Submissiveness (v.11)
Style of Communication (v.1, 2)	Style of Communication (v.12)
Appeal to an Old Testament wife (v.6)	Appeal to an Old Testament wife (v.13)
A quiet spirit (v.4)	A quiet spirit (v.11, 12)

Several identical Greek words appear in both passages such as *proseuche, andros, gune, esuchia, kosmos, chrusios, imation, theos.*[97] Paul seemed to have intentionally sandwiched *aner* between *anthropos* in 1Timothy 2:4 and 4:10 to signal a husband/wife relationship.[98] He also sandwiched the activity of wives between two leadership roles (kings in 2:2 and elders in 3:2) to signal the inappropriateness of a super-independent attitude/activity (*authentein*—authority in 2:12, which violates the biblical concept of great leadership.[99]

Not all, however, view the shift of the Greek words as supporting the identity of women as wives. Fee's position that the absence of the Greek definite article with *gune* (woman/wife) cancels the meaning

.

---

[96] Knofel Staton, Paul and Jesus Agree: You Don't Have to Stay the Way You Are (Cincinnati: Standard Publishing, 1976), 90. Before I was aware that others had made the connection, I noticed the comparison in 1975 and wrote my observation to S. Scott Bartchy: (Ph.D. Harvard) who was teaching theology at Tubingen University. Dr. Bartchy replied that in his judgment I had made a significant connection. Dr. Bartchy is presently professor at U.C.L.A.

[97] For a detailed side by side comparison of the two passages see Gordon P. Hugenberger, "Women in Church Office: Hermeneutics or Exegesis? A Survey of approaches to 1 Tim 2:8-15," *JETS* 35 (1995): 355-356.

[98] Paul used *aner*50 times and *gune*54 times in his writings. Outside 1 Tim 2:8-15, every other time he used two words in close proximity he referred to a husband/wife situation.

[99] See what constitutes "great" leadership in Mt 20:25-28; Lk22: 24-27.

being a wife[100] is weak because the use or non-use of the article is not consistent when *gune* clearly refers to a wife in other texts. Hugenberger's rationale for identifying the women as wives is stronger than Fee's.[101]

The Specific Characters and Content of 2:9-15

Some writers identify the women more specifically than being simply generic women. For instance, Fee views them as being the younger widows in chapter five, and suggests they are teaching false doctrine because they are weak-willed and loaded down with sins.[102] Scanzoni and Hardesty identify them as those who grabbed authority from others and began to teach without having the *charisma* for doing so.[103] Others view them as exercising authority over men.[104] Padgett thinks they were recent converts who were prime targets for false teachers.[105] Barnett believes they were trying to be like elders.[106] Nolland believes they wanted the kind of false teachings they had received to

---

[100] Fee, *1 Tim – Titus*. Fee argues that without the definite article *gune* is not a wife, but he understands the word to be wives without the definite article in 3:11. The use and non-use of the definite article is not consistent for a wife or for a husband in the New Testament. For instance there is no article (or personal pronoun) when *gune* is clearly a wife in Mk 10:2; 12:19; Lk 14:20; 20: 28; 29, 30; Ac 21:5; 1 Co 7:2, 27, 29; 9:5; 1 Ti 3:2, 12; 1 Pe 3:1. There is no article with *andros* when it is clearly a husband in Lk 2:36; Ro 7:2; 1 Co 7:10, 13; 1 Ti 3:2, 12; 5:9; Tit 1:6. Schreiner also makes this argument about the article against wives; Thomas R. Schreiner, "An Interpretation of 1 Timothy 2:9-15: a Dialogue with Scholarship," in *Women in the Church*, 115-116. Others who identify the subject as women and not wives are Moo, "1 Timothy 2:11-15: Meaning and Significance," TJ 1 (1980), 63; *Pastorals*, 63; Paul W. Barnett, "Wives and Women's Ministry (1 Ti 2:11-15) *EQ* 61 (1989): 222-23; Ann L. Bowman, "Women in Ministry: an Exegetical Study of 1 Timothy 2:11-15," BIB *SAC* 149 (1992): 198-199; George Knight III, *Pastorals*, 140; and a host of others.

[101] Hugenberger argues keenly for wives and husbands and lists several scholars who share the same view, 350-351 n. 39-40.

[102] Fee in *1 Timothy - Titus,* 70 and *Crux* 32-34.

[103] Scanzoni and Hardesty, 101.

[104] Hurley, 202; Homer A. Kent Jr. *The Pastoral Epistles,* revised ed. (Chicago: Moody, 1982), 107-109; J.N.D. Kelly, *A Commentary on the Pastoral Epistles* (New York: Harper & Row, 1963), 68.

[105] Alan Padgett, "Wealthy Women at Ephesus 1 Timothy 2:8-15 in Social Context," *INT* 41 (1987): 23-24.

[106] Barnett, 230-231.

become a part of the church's doctrine.[107] Others thought these women were simply teaching false doctrines, but without necessarily wanting them to be accepted in the church's teachings.[108]

The text does not specifically support any of the above identities, for there is no hint they were widows, recent converts, or teachers of false doctrine. Paul already addressed false teaching in chapter one and clearly targeted false teachers in chapter four. Consequently, the "muzzling" of women relates to some other issue. Witherington correctly notes that if the speaking content was false teaching, then "abuse of the gift of teaching does not rule out the privilege of correct teaching and does not extend beyond the abuse."[109]

The Location of Women Teaching

Many commentators link the location where women were teaching in 2:12 to e*n panti topos* (in every place or everywhere) in 2:8 and seek to identify a **specific** location. Fee thinks the location is the assembly of God's people because women were learning.[110] This is a weak rationale because it suggests that an assembly is the **only** place where learning happens. Such a concept contradicts women asking their husbands questions at home for the purpose of learning (1 Corinthians 14:34-35).

---

[107] John Nolland, "Women in the Public Life of the Church," CRUX 19 (1983): 18.

[108] Timothy Harris, "Why Did Paul Mention Eve's Deception? A Critique of P.W. Barnett's Interpretation of 1 Timothy 2," EQ 62 (1990): 34-50; Kroeger, *I Suffer Not*, 62-66. Stanley J. Grenz and Denise Muir Kjesbo, *Women in the Church: A Biblical Theology of Women in Ministry* (Downer Grove, IL: InterVarsity Press, 1995), 132; Aida Besancon Spencer, "Eve at Ephesus," JETS 17 (1974): 215-222; David Scholer, "Women in the Church's Ministry: Does 1 Timothy 2:9-15 Help or Hinder Them?" *Daughters of Sarah* 16 (1990): 8-9; Austin H. Stouffer, "The Ordination of Women: Yes," CT XV (Feb. 20, 1981): 15; Gloria Redekop, "Let the Women Learn: I Timothy 2:8-15 Reconsidered," SRSR 19 (1990): 236-237; Ben Wiebe, "Two Texts on Women (1 Tim 2:11-15; Gal 3:26-29): A Test of Interpretation" *HOR BIB TH* 16 (1994): 55.

[109] Witherington III, *Genesis* 194. Redekop also argued that once women learned sound doctrine, they could teach, 245.

[110] Fee, *Timothy - Titus*, 71-73 and "Issues," 33.

Others suggest the location is where Christian worship happens,[111] any place the Gospel is preached,[112] or any public gathering.[113]

There are several weaknesses in restricting the location to the gathering of God's people: (1) the text does not identify the specific location; (2) to specify the identity by the words *en panti topos* (in every place or everywhere—v.8) is exegetically and hermeneutically unsound. To do so would suggest that men (or probably husbands) should pray only in the gathered meetings which contradicts the various non-assembly places where Jesus prayed, and His instructions about prayer;[114] (3) other issues in 1Timothy are not linked to any specified location. For instance, is false teaching forbidden only in assemblies, but not in other places? Do we pray for kings only in the assemblies? Do elders function only in the assemblies? Do children financially provide for their widowed mothers only in the assembly, and so on? (4) Paul wrote *en panti topos* four other times, none of which is restricted to an assembly for worshipping or teaching;[115] (5) the use of *topos* for identifying a Christian assembly is extremely rare.[116] Whatever is wrong about women teaching in one place is surely wrong in any other locale.

The Sequential Content

2:9-10

In the same way also wives are to adorn
themselves with respectable apparel with modesty and
decency not with an elaborate hairstyle and gold or
pearls or very expensive clothing, but with what is
fitting for wives who are themselves professing piety
through good deeds (personal translation).

---

[111] E.K. Simpson, *The Pastoral Epistles: The Greek Text with Introduction and Commentary* (Grand Rapids: Wm. B. Eerdmans Publishing, 1954), 47; Donald Guthrie, *The Pastoral Epistles: An Introduction and Commentary*. The Tyndale New Testament Commentaries (Grand Rapids: William B. Eerdmans Publishing, 1990), 84; H. W. House, 110; Ann Bowman, 200; Barnett, 225; Schreiner, 113;Knight III, *Pastorals*, 128; Towner, 69.

[112] Kelly, 65.

[113] Schreiner, 117; Moo, "I Timothy 2:11-15, 62; and "What Does It Mean Not to Teach or Have Authority Over Men" in Piper and Grudem's *Recovering*, 118; B. W. Power, "Women in the Church: The Application of 1 Tim 2:8-15," Interchange 17 (1975): 55-59.

[114] Mt 6:5-6.

[115] Ro 9:26; 1 Co 1:2; 2Co 2:14; 1Th 1:8.

[116] Only once is topos so used (1 Co 14:16). See other usages (in addition to *en panti topon*). Ro 12:19; 15:23; 2 Co 2:14; Eph 4:27; He 8:7; 11:8; 12:17; 2 Pe 1:19; Re 2:5; 6:14; 12:6, 8, 14; 16:16; 18:17; 20:11.

The NIV does not translate the first word, *osautos* ("likewise" or ""in the same way"), which directly connects verse nine with verse eight. Some link *osauto*s in verse 9 with *boulomai* (I want) in verse 8.[117] That linkage is unlikely for every other place *osautos* is used in the New Testament it connects similar actions or manners not just desires.[118] "Likewise" at the beginning of verse nine is not suggesting women should **pray as men were** as suggested by the Kroegers,[119] for prayer is not the topic of verses 9-10. Instead, "in the same way" or "likewise" connects **the manner men (husbands)** were communicating with God **with the manner women (wives)** were communicating with men (husbands). The effectiveness of both kinds of communication does not come primarily from the **outer actions**, but from the **inner attitudes**. The inner attitude from the men (husbands) is to be peaceful – without anger (v.8); the inner attitude from women (wives) is also to be peaceful—with a gentle spirit (v.10). Elsewhere Paul used *osautos* (likewise or in this way) to connect inner attitudes.[120]

Some commentators believe women were distracting men from worshipping by the way they looked.[121] Moo links a woman's extravagant dress to false teaching.[122] Others identify her decorum with prostitutes,[123] but there is no supporting evidence for such analogies. In fact, braided hair symbolized a wife's commitment to her husband.[124] Sometimes wealthy women married to poor husbands would wear extravagant clothing and jewels,[125] without suggesting promiscuity or insubordination. Without relating extravagant dress to wealthy woman, Fee states that dressing up and insubordination go hand in hand.[126] However, cultural evidence does not support that position either.

---

[117] Simpson, 46; Schreiner, 114; Moo, in *Recovering,* 182.

[118] Mt 20:5; 21:30, 36; Mk 12:21; 14:31; Lk 13:5; 20:31; 22:20; Ro 8:26; 1 Co 11:25; 1 Ti 3:8, 11; 5:25; Tit 2:3,6.

[119] The Kroegers, *I Suffer Not,* 74.

[120] In Tit 2:3, the disposition of old women is to be the same (wsautws) as old men —pleasant. A Greek synonym also connects the same kind of inner source in 1 Pe 3:7.

[121] Guthrie, 85; Towner, 71; Kelly, 66.

[122] Moo, in *Recovering*, 182.

[123] P.B. Payne, "Libertarian Women in Ephesus: A Response to Douglas J. Moo's Article '1 Timothy 2:11-15: Meaning and Significance,'" *TJ* 2 (1981): 185-190; Knight III, *Pastorals*, 135-136.

[124] J.P.V.D. Balsdon, A woman with fashioned hair was a symbol of the honor due to a married woman, 255.

[125] *Ibid.,* 264.

[126] Fee, "Issues," 33.

The woman's decorum in this text is not related to her being promiscuous, but to how she was communicating with her husband. Comparing this section with 1 Peter 3:1-8 is a more likely rationale for understanding what may have been going on. The wife may have been linking up her exterior attractiveness with her verbal communication to more effectively influence her husband instead of demonstrating the quiet, peaceful, and inner disposition characterized by the nine different words in this section.[127] Paul masterfully bracketed the wife's relationship with her husband by the same Greek word, *sophrosunes* (propriety) at the beginning (9) and at the ending (15) of this section. Placing that word at both ends characterizes the entirety of 9-15, which focuses more upon the **interior character** of the woman than upon exterior **decorum** and speech. The wife was to be frame her communication with her character not clothing, patience not pearls, helpfulness not hair, inner disposition not outer decorum.

2:11-12

11.Let a wife learn in quietness in all subjection. 12. But I do not permit a wife to teach standoffishly from a husband. But she is to be in quietness (my translation).

For reasons stated earlier (the shift from *anthropos* to *aner*), this passage more likely deals with a husband/wife relationship. But if it refers to just a male/female relationship, the thrust of the passage remains the same, with the specific application being different. The women referred to were evidently engaged in two activities – learning and teaching, which are connected in the New Testament.[128] So it is not surprising that their teaching (12) follows their learning in (11). However, the way a wife teaches should mirror the way she learns, for both her learning and teaching are connected to *esuchia* (quietness, 11-12). Scholars differ about whether or not a woman is to teach after she learns. Moo suggests she is to be verbally still.[129] Towner believes she is not even to enter into public discussions about the teachings of others.[130] Knight believes her learning was not to gain the privilege of speaking.[131]

---

[127] qeosebeian (piety), nsuxia (silent—quiet disposition), upotagn (subjection), auqentein (independently), piatein (faith, trust), agapn (love), swjrosunns (respectable).

[128] Mt 28:5-7; Jn 4:19-26, 28-30, 39; 2 Ti 2:1-2.

[129] Douglas J. Moo, "1 Timothy 2:11-15,," 64.

[130] Towner, 77.

[131] Knight III, *Pastorals*, 140.

Boschman muzzles her completely by stating that Paul gives her an "absolute gag order not to teach."[132] Payne contradicts Moo's definition (and thus all the others above), by showing that both the lexicon evidence and Paul's use of *esuchia* (silent) elsewhere refer to a quiet sweet manner, not to a silenced mouth.[133] Several others believe this Greek word stresses the peaceful, gentle, and quiet disposition of women.[134] Internal evidence also supports that *esuchia* (translated in the NIV as "quietness" in v.11 but as "silent" in v.12) does not suggest a total lack of verbalization because of its use in 2:2 which is paralleled with being tranquil (*eremos* for "peaceful" and *esuchios* for "quiet"— v.2). The Greek word *escuchios* in v.2 (quiet) and *esuchia* in v.11 (quietness) are twin words that appear in only four other texts in the New Testament, none of which refers to being verbally muzzled. In other texts, the same word used in verse 11 described someone having a peaceful, settled down, calmed down, contemplative, and sweet disposition.[135]

Throughout the rest of 1 Timothy, Paul used the particle *en* (in or with) to describe the environment or surroundings that engulfed or characterized a situation[136] and used it similarly here. Thus to do something "in quietness" (11 and 12) means to function within an internal environment characterized by tranquility, and then to externally act (or speak) with that characteristic. To be in quietness is paralleled with being in full submission (v.11b – literally *pase* means "all" not "full").

Being in "all subjection" refers to the women (wives) expressing a submissive attitude and character. But to whom? Some suggest their submission is to their **husbands**.[137] Schreiner believes it is to **the men** who had authority in the church.[138] Some are close to making *upotage*

---

[132] Boschman, 48.

[133] Payne, 169-170.

[134] Fee, *Timothy - Titus*, 72; Nolland, 18; Keener, 108; N.J. Hommes, "Let Women Be Silent in Church: A Message Concerning the Worship Service and the Decorum to be Observed by Women," CTJ 4 (1969), 15.

[135] 2 Th 3:12; 1 Ti 2:2; 1 Pe 3:4, and Ac 22:2. A superficial look at Ac 22:2 might cause one to think the text is describing the absence of sound, but it is introducing a contrast.... 21:33-35 – "uproar violence, mob, kept shouting."

[136] The other environments Paul connected with *ev* are Ephesus (1:2,3), faith (1:4; 2:7; 3:15; 3:9, 4:11), unbelief (1:13), Christ (1:14), authority (2:2), piety, every place (2:8), transgression (2:14), love (3:15), holiness (3:15), clean conscience (3:9), house of God (3:15), latter times (4:1), hypocrisy (4:2), conduct (4:11), purity (4:11, 5:2).

[137] Fee, *Timothy-Titus*, 72. But here Fee is inconsistent for he rejects the woman being the wife.

[138] Schreiner, "An Interpretation," 124; see also Knight III, *Pastorals*, 139.

(subjection) identical with the Greek word *upakoe* (obedience); however, these are two different words with 2 different meanings, and the word for obedience is not used here and is not even related to the same Greek word-family with subjection. The Greek word for subjection (*upotage*) is a form of the Greek word for submission (*upotasso*), and appears in the New Testament in only two other places outside of 1 Timothy.[139] Elsewhere when Paul uses *upotasso* (submission) in the context of *gune* (woman/wife) and *aner* (man//husband) in close proximity, the topic is a husband/wife situation.[140] There is no substantive reason Paul did not do so here.

To live in all subjection means to voluntarily act for the benefit of another. To do so is to humbly demonstrate surrendering one's will for the needs of others as Jesus did. Doing so is to make all decisions and deeds with "a tactical yielding."[141] To learn in all subjection is to transfer the reason for learning from benefiting only self to building up others. In Christ we learn not just for facts, but also for formation – ours and others; we learn not only for the purpose of retaining, but also for the purpose of sharing; we learn to be better representatives of Christ and ambassadors of God; we learn to be better able to communicate the gospel; we learn so *charisma* can help us be more effective.[142] **All** Christians share ministry responsibilities–men and women alike.[143] Paul instructed Timothy to continue what he had learned in order to help equip others.[144] Learning God's Word and ways for the benefit of self only can result in having a big head and a small heart; being correct without compassion; being right without proper relationships. Knowledge alone puffs up, but love connected to it builds up.[145] To learn in quietness and in submission is to learn "in love" for the purpose of communicating with love what is learned so the entire body may be built up.[146] Whatever is learned from God's Word is to be both lived and "lipped" by men and women alike.[147]

---

[139] 2Co 9:13 and Ga 2:5.

[140] 1 Co 14:34-35; Eph 5:21-33; Col 3:18-19; 1 Pe 3:1-7.

[141] Gerhard Delling's understanding of the use of upotaah in Ga 5:2 which relates to learning here, for Ga 5:2 discusses reaction to the Gospel. See his article, "uptagh" in *TDNT*, vol. VIII, 46.

[142] Eph 4:11-16.

[143] 1 Pe 2:5, 9-10; see Kung, *Church*, 476-488.

[144] 1 Ti 4:6, 11, 14-16; 2 Ti 1:6-7; 2:1-2; 3:24-26.

[145] 1 Co 8:1.

[146] Eph 4:15-16.

[147] Php 4:9.

Some believe this section prohibits women from teaching **biblical content**,[148] but the text does not state the content of teaching. Some suggest Paul prohibited women teaching only **false doctrine**,[149] but the text does not suggest that. Kelly believes Paul prohibited women addressing the congregation in a **wrong location**—a worship assembly,[150] but the text does not address the place. Schreiner believes the text prohibited women teaching *per se,* because women were less prone to see the importance of doctrine and thus more likely to be gullible and deceived,[151] But God choosing women to be prophets does not support that concept. Moo believes women teaching men "denigrates marriage,"[152] but God advised Abraham to listen to his wife.[153] Bowman suggests God's curse will come upon the earth if women teach,[154] but God, Jesus and Paul's use of women do not affirm that. For Knight, women are not to teach because only men are to lead worship services,[155] but nowhere does the Bible affirm that position. Moo's argument that teaching is restricted to elders[156] is without scriptural support. Barnett believes men only are to teach because of their "primacy and resistance to transgression."[157] Schreiner suggests that teaching is always authoritative and is the responsibility of only elders.[158] Moo also opposes women teaching because Jesus never put women in positions of authority.[159] All the above suggestions sink with biblical data. For instance, being less prone to doctrinal formations, more gullible, and less resistant to temptations are not gender specific.

To suggest that women function as prophets, but not as teachers because prophecy does not require preparation or learning, does not transmit Christian tradition or expound Scripture, does not overturn male

---

[148] Schreiner, "An Interpretation," 127; Knight III, *Pastorals*, 141, and others.

[149] Fee, "Issues," 33; and *Timothy - Titus,* 73; Towner, 75-76; Knight III, *Pastorals*, 10-11.

[150] Kelly, 68.

[151] Schreiner, "An Interpretation," 144-145.

[152] Moo, "I Timothy," 83.

[153] Ge 21:12.

[154] Bowman, 206.

[155] Knight III, *Pastorals,* 128.

[156] Moo, "I Timothy,"

[157] Barnett, 234.

[158] Schreiner, "An Interpretation," 128.

[159] Moo, "I Timothy," 75-76.

headship, and is not as authoritative as teaching[160] is not biblically supportable.[161]

Neither the **content** nor **locality** of teaching is addressed, but the **demeanor** is. Paul prohibited a wife διδασκειν (to teach) ουδε (or) αυθεντειν (to have authority over – NIV translations). Some suggest that "to teach or to have authority over" are two distinct activities;[162] however, the connecting word ουδε can also introduce a descriptive amplification,[163] i.e., the word following ουδε adds a description to the kind of person, place, thing, or activity mentioned by the preceding word.[164] With this use, the kind of teaching being described or amplified is an *authentein* (an authoritative) kind.

Using the *Thesaurus Linguae Graecae* database at the University of California Irvine (with sixty-three million words in ancient Greek literature written by 3,000 authors), Leland Wilshire discovered that during the time Paul wrote *authentein* (and its cognates) was almost exclusively used to describe murder and limiting another person's rights by doing or perpetuating a crime, or by doing violence to the person. In his second article, Wilshire cautiously agrees with the Kroegers' subsidiary idea that *authentein* in 1Timothy 2:12 suggests that Ephesian women "who have been embroiled in various religious conflicts between Christianity and the cults in Ephesus should stand aloof from the

---

[160] *Ibid.,* 75 see also Schreiner, "An Interpretation," 129-130.

[161] See the role of prophets in the Old Testament and such New Testament texts as Mt 16:13-14; Eph 2:20, 4:11-12; 1 Co 14:1, 3, 12; 2 Pe 1:16-21. Both teaching and prophecy are listed as charisma without gender restrictions in Ro 12:6-7 and 1 Co 12:27. Peter evidently summarized both as simply speaking the utterances of God in 1 Pe 4:10.

[162] Moo, "1 Timothy," 65-68; "What does it Mean," 187; Knight III, "The Ordination," 16-19; *Idem.,* "AUENTEW" in reference to women in 1 Timothy 2:12, NTS 30 (1984): 143-154; Knight rejects the meaning of "to domineer," and murder; Witherington, *Genesis,* 194.

[163] See Kroeger, *I Suffer Not,* for another way ouse is used, 189-191.

[164] Some examples of amplification use: 1 Co 15:50 – perishable flesh and blood; Php 2:16 – the running kind of toiling; 1 Th 5:5 – night kind of darkness; Ga 4:14 – loathing kind of disguising. See the following for explanatory use of oude, i.e., what follows oude explains what is before oude; Ro 2:28 – Jew, that is, circumcised; Ro 3:10 – none, that is, not one; Ro 8:7 does not subject, that is, not able to; Ro 9:7 – explaining 9:6; 1 Co 2:6 of this age, that is, the ruler of this age; 1 Co 5:1 of such a fornication, that is, not among pagan's kind; 1 Co 14:21 perhaps "we" refers to the churches here; Ga 1:1 not sent by men, that is, through men; Ga 1:12 did not receive, that is not taught it....; Ga 6:13 explains 6:12;

conflict."[165] That is, their teaching should not instigate violence or be a launching pad to oppress others, but instead be a "launching pad for service and the development of Christian character" by bringing "compassion and the presence of Christ to each location and each situation."[166] This concept of *authentein* was more common in the first century than the concept of simply domineering or having authority over another. The problem of super-independence runs throughout 1 Timothy and squares with instructing women to do what they do in quietness and in subjection and is further characterized by the other seven words listed in footnote 128.

Although *authentein* gradually evolved to describe one person having domination over another, that was not the usual meaning when Paul wrote. If Paul wanted to write a word to stress authority, he probably would have used *ezousia* which he did twenty-six times in seven different letters. Paul probably used *authentein* (the only use in the New Testament) to introduce a different nuance from *ezousia* (the common word for authority in the New Testament). *Authentein* communicates a more independent intensity than *ezousia*, for a person cannot demonstrate more independence from another than to murder, to instigate an activity that might lead to violence, or to separate from the other person.

After connecting all the dots it seems that Paul used *authentein* to prohibit wives teaching their husbands in an **independent or autocratic manner**. Perriman defines it as acting "independently or according to one's own purpose," which would sever (or at least seriously weaken) the wife/husband relationship.[167] This kind of prohibition squares with other Pauline passages that emphasize husbands and wives are to relate to each other with love, harmony, peace, unity, and partnership.

2: 13-15

> For Adam was first formed, then Eve. And
> Adam was not deceived but the wife when she was
> deceived came to be in transgression. But wives
> shall be whole through child bearing if they remain
> in faith and love and holiness with propriety.
> (translation mine)

---

[165] LeLand Wilshire, "The TLG Computer and Further Reference to AUOENTEP in 1 Ti 2:12," *NTS* 34 (1988): 120-134; *idem*, "1 Timothy 2:12 Revisted: A Reply to Paul W. Barnett and Timothy J. Harris," *EQ* 65 (1993): 43-55.

[166] *Ibid.*, 54. A reference to Kroegers, *I Suffer Not*, 104, 180.

[167] Andrew Perriman. *Speaking of Women: interpreting Paul* (Leicester, England: Apollos, 1998), 143, 150, 153-156.

A wife who acts or teaches her husband independently or autocratically fits the negative example of Adam and Eve who were not just the first male and female, but also the first husband and wife. Eve's deception happened in the context of independence– a dissociated attitude and activity from the partnership she enjoyed with Adam. To mention deception in the context of independence may suggest that resistance to temptation is weakened when faced alone. There is spiritual strength in companionship as noted by the writer of Ecclesiastes, "Two are better than one . . . if one can overpower him who is alone, two can resist him. A cord of three strands is not quickly torn apart."[168]

Listing Adam first in the order of creation records only God's historical sequence, not a rationale for suggesting male superiority.[169] The word "first" introduces the idea that something else will follow— companionship and unity with Eve – the two became one. The *gar* (for) beginning verse 13 does not introduce either **the cause** of women being more easily deceived than men, or the prohibition against them teaching men,[170] but **the aloneness** of Adam who was created to live with interdependence, not independence.

A woman being saved (*sozo*) is not a reference to the eschatological event.[171] The Greek word translated saved also carries the meanings of being delivered, being made whole, complete, and well—all of which relates to an inner unity. Being saved in this text probably describes a wife's wholeness that helps to contribute community or oneness in and for her family. A united husband and wife help bring wholeness to all family members.[172] A disunited family brings disintegration, disconnectedness, individualism and autocratic ways that can weaken and destroy any community.

Verse 15 supports the conclusion that the women in 2:9-14 are wives, for Paul is certainly not suggesting that all women become mothers. However, a wife who becomes a mother enhances the development of her children by her harmonious relationship with her husband. She acts **inter**dependently with her husband as she raises children and thus contributes to the healthy spiritual development of the next generation. It is possible that the words "if they remain in faith and love and holiness with propriety" refer to the **children** who are nurtured

---

[168] Ecc 4:9,12 (NASB).

[169] Kelly, 68, and many others.

[170] As suggested by Keener, 117; Simpson, 47; Nolland, 19.

[171] As suggested by Bowman, 207-208; Moo, "1 Timothy," 70-71; Fee, "Issues," 34.

[172] For a Pauline parallel to this see Eph 5:28 – the husband who loves his wife loves his own body; the one who cares for his wife cares for his own body.

within a united family, for Paul changed from the singular "**she** will be saved" (the mother-wife) to the plural "if **they** remain"—the children.

Based upon the holistic biblical teaching about men and women, the use of women throughout biblical history, and the inter-play of words used in this section, the entirety of 2:8-15 seems to be dealing with a harmonious husband/wife relationship. That relationship not only advances the development of church members toward Christlikeness, but also the children of biological families who hopefully will become subsequent leaders in the family of the church.

Temporal or Trans-Temporal: Cultural or Trans-Cultural

How binding the teaching of 2:8-15 is depends upon the meaning of the texts and how that meaning fits the holistic teaching of men and women or husbands and wives throughout the rest of the Bible. It is trans-culturally (for all areas) and trans-temporally (for all times) binding if the restriction of women teaching men rests upon a chain-of-command relationship intended when God created them.[173] Packer believes since we do not know how Paul would apply this teaching today, we should give him "the benefit of that doubt and retain his restriction on women exercising authority on Christ's behalf over men in the church."[174] But that position negates the accepted and approved roles of women teaching and prophesying elsewhere in the Bible. Packer's remark also assumes that certain *charismata* are gender specific.

If this text addresses women teaching only false doctrine, it is also trans-culturally and trans-temporally binding, but only when false teaching is the content. Otherwise, this passage does not prevent women teaching men correct doctrine.[175]

---

[173] Andreas J. Kostenberger. "'The Crux of the Matter': Paul's Pastoral Pronouncements Regarding Women's Roles in 1 Timothy 2:9-15," *Faith & Mission* 14 (1996): 34-35; Moo, "1 Timothy," 82; Bruce K. Waltke, "1 Timothy 2:8-15: Unique or Normative?" *CRUX* 28 (1992): 23.

[174] J I Packer, "Let's Stop Making Women Presbyters", CT 35 (February 11, 1991): 20.

[175] Fee, "Issues," 35; Padgett, 30-31; Leonard, 320; Scholer, 7-12; Harris, 347; Spencer, 219-220.

Preventing **anyone** teaching in an independent/autocratic manner that severs unity is trans-culturally and trans-temporally binding,[176] and more specifically in this context when wives are teaching in a way that disconnects them from their husbands, for unity in the family demonstrated by mutual submission and love between a husband and a wife is universally applicable. Such unity is the human foundation for having and maintaining harmony in the extended spiritual family, the church. That is why all the issues, principles, attitudes, and activities of unity in the congregation developed in Paul's Ephesian letter were to be first applied in the wife/husband relationship to each other. See the relationship of Ephesians 5:21-33 with 1:9-10 (God's plan for unity); with 2:11-18, (God's means for unity); with 2:19-23, (the results of God's means); with 3:10 (who should demonstrate unity); with 4:1-3 (attitudes of unity); with 4:4-6 (basis of unity); with 4:7-16 (gifts for unity); with 4:20-24 (new creation for unity); with 4:25-5:2 (activities of unity); with 5:3-17 (examples of individualism which oppose unity). Whenever there is unity within the body of Christ which springs from unity within individual families making up the body, then the answer to Paul's prayer in Ephesians 3:14-19 will be experienced, and the awesomeness of what God can and will do in 3:20-21 will be observable. The issue in 1Timothy 2:9-15 (as well as the rest of 1Timothy) directly continues Paul's previous letter to the same church about unity, and subsequently to and for us all today.

Conclusion

The two "muzzling" passages are not normative passages by which all other passages about the role and use of women throughout the Bible are evaluated, but vice versa. The restrictions of women speaking in 1 Corinthians 14:34-35 and 1Timothy 2:9-15 were to specific situations for the purpose of preventing women (wives) from acting independently by insisting on their own way in a manner that does not contribute to the order, peace, harmony, and connectedness of the members of Christ's body to one another. To act independently weakens interpersonal relationships, violates *koinonia* (fellowship), and hinders spiritual formation towards Christlikeness for both the violator of harmony and those hurt by disharmony.

---

[176] God's *mysterion* (plan) is to unite us not dwindle us (Eph 1:9-10), thus we need to be eager to maintain the unity of the Spirit in the bond of peace (Eph 4:3) by using our gifts to tighten our bond to each other, not weaken it (1 Co 12-14). Anyone who continues being divisive needs to be disciplined (Tit 3:10) for the good of the individual and the community. Unity in the family demonstrated by mutual submission and love is universally applicable and is foundational for maintaining unity in the extended spiritual family, the Church. That is the reason all principles about unity in the church as recorded in Ephesians was first applied to the wife/husband relationship. See Eph 5:21ff.

Wartenberg-Potter correctly noted that imposing women's silence has been a way to oppress and trivialize them.[177] That kind of oppression and trivialization continues when any Christian, regardless of sociological identity, is denied using *charisma* or when any person uses *charisma* in an independent and autocratic way or according to one's own purpose.

To deny any ministerial function that fulfills a person's *charisma* is to weaken the priesthood of all believers. The Church stands aloof from God's original intention for all members in His community to be equal partners in ministry when she excludes people who have the same gifts from using them. Church renewal cannot happen until congregations liberate **all** members to any leadership or speaking roles whom the Spirit so equips with *charisma*. Perhaps during the new millennium we will see a fresh manifestation of the ministry of all believers demonstrated by mutual and loving submission to one another regardless of race, gender, and economical status.

Mutual submission and love surely involve including women to be leaders as God did, to be both learners and teachers as Jesus allowed, and to be involved in multiple ministries (including speaking as prophets) as the early

Church did. It is not easy, but essential, for us to wrestle with the question, "is it possible to reach the maturity level God desires for us if we exclude **any** gifted person from ministry?" Surely encouraging and including **all** God's family (the members in the body of Christ, the rooms in the temple of the Holy Spirit, the flames in God's light, the branches on the vine, the children of the Father, and the grains of His salt) to use their gifts enhances our progress toward God's goal for us to "be conformed to the likeness of his Son" (Romans 8:29). This goal is stated in many different ways that include being "renewed in knowledge in the image of Christ" (Colossians 3:10); becoming "mature, attaining to the whole measure of the fullness of Christ" (Ephesians 4:13); being held together, growing, and building ourselves up in love "as each part does its work" (Ephesians 4:16); being "made new in the attitude of your minds"; putting "off the old self"; putting "on the new self created to be like God" (Ephesians 4:22-24); and being "imitators of God" (Ephesians 5:1).

Reaching this multi-stated goal of God for us as individuals and for the Church as a whole requires that we permit the Spirit to liberate us to reflect the Lord's glory (character) by continuously being transformed into his likeness (2 Corinthians 3:17-18). Then we can and will approve God's will and be pleasing to Him as we release **every** Christian to use

---

[177] Christopher Duraisingh, ed., *Women's Perspective: Articulating the Liberating Power of the Gospel*, Gospel and Cultures Pamplet 14 (Geneva: WCC Publications, 1996), 2.

his/her gifts in ministry (Romans 12:2-6). To do so escalates the spiritual formation of individual congregations into God's mature body that can and will adequately and accurately be His representatives and ambassadors who reflect His life in our day, as Jesus did in His day. To that level of maturity and expression of mission all of us have been called.

Let us therefore help one another grow up into the freshness of His truth and not just grow old into the frozenness of our traditions.

CHAPTER 7

RETHINKING HEADSHIP IN LIGHT OF THE TRIAD IN 1 CORINTHIANS 11:3

After reviewing God's intention for women in creation; His use of women in speaking and leadership roles in the Old Testament; Jesus teaching woman and not only permitting, but also commanding women to verbally share with men what they learned; the early Church applying Joel's prophecy for women prophets; the relationship of baptism and charisma to non-gender specific ministries; and the two silent passages not muzzling women from speaking/teaching men; the question is, how does all of that relate to "The head of the woman is man" in 1 Corinthians 11:3? This chapter will consider First Corinthians 11:3 in its literary and cultural contexts; the meaning of *kephale* (head) as used in secular Greek literature, *The Septuagint*, and the New Testament; the function of "head" in the triad; and how that relates to the holistic issue Paul addresses in the First Corinthian correspondence, the specific issues in 11:3-16, and women in leadership roles in the congregation.

The Contexts

Considering both the literary and cultural context is essential to correctly understanding and applying any biblical text.

The Literary Context

Paul positioned 1 Corinthians 11:3-16 immediately after three chapters applying neutral moral issues in ways that will not influence weaker Christians to sin.[1] Chapters 11 through 14 shift the focus to Christians gathered for worship. The guidelines for conduct within the assembly (chapters 11-14) are relationally the same as outside the assembly (chapters 8-10: (1) to not be a stumbling block to the weak;[2] (2) to use liberty in a way that contributes to saving and serving people;[3] (3) to not use freedom in a way that hinders a person maturing

---

[1] See the focus for decision-making in 8:9-13; the apostolic example in 9:19-27: an exception in 10:25-30; and the goal for living with liberty in 10:31-11:1.

[2] 8:9.

[3] 9:19-22.

spiritually;[4] (4) to do all for the glory of God,[5] i.e., characterizing God; (5) being sensitive to the culture.[6]

Chapter eleven comes on the heels of some Christians taking liberties with amoral issues without considering how those liberties affected others with different traditions. Evidently some women and men in chapter eleven were doing the same by liberalizing their decorum when praying and prophesying.[7] The issue here, as it was in chapters 8-10 is for Christians to consider the maturity of others and their own maturity or lack of it,[8] for all problems in that church were rooted in some members being immature[9] and thus needing to develop/express *agape* love.[10] Some people may have thought their decorum was irrelevant since they were now Christians.[11] Both women and men seem to be insensitive about how their decorum could affect others.[12]

The sections following 11:3-16 also deal with conduct in the gathered assembly in a way that demonstrates sensitivity to others – to not be factious; to not humiliate; to rightly discern needs of others; to function with unity amid diversity; to not be disruptive, and to do everything decently.[13]

The Cultural Context

This is a complex passage due to different possible word meanings such as the following: (1) man as male or husband? (2) woman as a female or a wife; (3) head as authority over, source-origin, or initiator; (4) covered and uncovered as veil or hairstyle; (5) glory as praise or character; (6) angels as heavenly or earthly messengers; (7) sign of authority as being the woman herself, or her husband;

---

[4] 9:27-10:14 – especially, "if you think you are standing firm, be careful that you don't fall."

[5] 10:31.

[6] 9:20-22 and 10:33-11:1.

[7] Murphy-O'Connor, "1 Corinthians 11:2-16," Once Again," *CBQ* 50 (1988): 265-269.

[8] Antoinette Wire is not treating the text comprehensively by stating that the issue is not the other person's weakness, but one's own strength.

[9] 1 Co 3:1-3.

[10] *Ibid.,* 13.

[11] See 1 Co 1:7; 12:7 and Gordon Fee, *First Corinthians*, 498. Richards and Hoeldtke suggested women may have resented "the traditional symbols of their femaleness," 118. See also Orr and Walter, 264.

[12] See 1 Co 11:4, 7, 14; Murphy-O'Connor, *CBQ*, 50, 264-274; Fee, 505-506, 514-515; Staton, *First Corinthians*, 198-199.

[13] 11:18, 23, 33; 12:12-26; 13:5; 14:26-35, 40.

Craig Blomberg believes this is "probably the most complex, controversial, and opaque of any text of comparable length in the New Testament."[14] Fiorenza suggests, "it is very doubtful whether we will be able to reconstruct the correct meaning of the passage."[15] Consequently, Christians need to be gracious with those who hold different views by not allowing a specific position to serve as a litmus test of orthodoxy and/or of fellowship with other Christians.

Most scholars agree that at least part of this passage deals with the current cultural issue of men and women covering/uncovering their heads while praying and/or prophesying in the gathered assembly.[16]

While women speaking publicly contradicted Jewish[17] custom, that was evidently not a problem in the Corinthian congregation; however, covering/uncovering the head was not only a social issue,[18] but also may have been a spiritual one.[19]

Some believe covering and uncovering refer to wearing or not wearing a veil;[20] however, that is probably not the issue for the following reasons: (1) there is no evidence that men (even homosexuals) wore veils; (2) the word for veil, *kalumma*, is not in this passage; (3) hair quickly becomes the focus;[21] (4) hair is identified as the covering (verse 15); (5) the Greek word for uncovered, *akatakalupos*, literally means "hang down loose" and described a woman's hair that was not bound on

---

[14] Blomberg, 214.

[15] Fiorenza, 153.

[16] The idea that both praying and prophesying were being done in private in untenable for two reasons: (1) prophesying is a *charisma* to be done publicly; (2) the decorum would not have been a problem if done in privacy; see Fiddes, 370; Grosheide opts for a private setting, 251, 342; C.K. Barrett offers a significant counter against a private environment, "If Paul had thought it wrong for them to do this, he would certainly not have wasted his time in discussing what…they should do with their heads," 250.

[17] Murphy-O'Connor *CBQ* 42, 497.

[18] Nolland, 22.

[19] Particularly in dishonoring the "head" and possibly trying to be the other gender sexually, i.e., men trying to look and function as women, and women trying to look and function as men – thus denying their gender nature.

[20] Barrett, 20-21; Fee, 496, 528-529; Keener, 27-30; Thrall, 78; and several others.

[21] Verses 5b, 6, 14, 15.

top of her head,[22] but was hanging down loose; (6) if the issue is the veil, it is difficult to understand the discussion about hair length.[23]

A woman in that era let her hair grow long to bind it on top as an outward show of modesty, marriage, and faithfulness to her husband.[24] Prior to marriage, she would gather her hair at the back of her head, tie it with a ribbon or fasten it with a pin, and then let it fall back over the neck like a ponytail. But for her wedding, and subsequently as a wife, she wore her hair on top of her head. To gather the hair on top was a "symbol of the honour due to a married woman." In fact, the glory of a woman "was her storied hair."[25] Several extant sculptures depict women wearing a bun of hair on top of their head.[26] Knowing that hair positioned on top symbolized a faithful married woman helps to identify who is the immediate "head" she would either honor or dishonor.

There are several possible reasons why a married woman would wear her hair down and loose: (1) she may have wanted to express a degree of autonomy without being sexually unfaithful to her husband;[27] (2) she may have thought that hair cultural standards were irrelevant for a Christian living in a kind of realized eschatological state;[28] (3) she may have been signaling that she was sexually available to other men;[29] (4) she may have been recently converted from one of the cults in Corinth in which being a temple prostitute with loose hair was common. "Prostitutes were also attached to most of the temples of oriental divinities."[30] The temple of Aphrodite in Corinth had 1,000 such "worship leaders" on duty; (5) she may have wanted to demonstrate that members in the Christian community are not to judge or be judged by outward appearances.

---

[22] This use is ancient, going back as far as Leviticus in the LXX, 10:6, 13:45 and Nu 5:18.

[23] Several understand that hairstyle is the issue Murphy-O'Connor, *CBQ* 42, 483 - 489; Blomberg, 211; and several others.

[24] Judy Brown, 250.

[25] Balsdon, 182, 255. See also Blomberg, 211. Orr and Walther, 264.

[26] Anderson and Zinsser, 1. See pictures of sculpture with a variety of topped styles between pages 240 and 241 in Balsdon.

[27] Nolland, 23.

[28] Murphy-O'Conner, *CBQ* 42, 490.

[29] About prostitutes in that era, Balsdon states "prostitutes were to be encountered....and were no more difficult to recognize in Roman antiquity than in the modern world...their faces were heavily made up, they wore no bands in the hair...," 224.

[30] *Ibid.*

However, while God transcends culture, His church lives in and relates to its immediate culture, which Paul signaled earlier, "To the church of God **in Corinth**."[31] (bold print mine) Because of the cultural issue, Paul wrote "it is just as though her head were shaved . . . a disgrace." There are several possible reasons for linking shaving women to disgrace: (1) a" punishment" for women caught in prostitution;[32] (2) lesbians wore a "mannish" hair style in the cults;[33] (3) an attempt to change their sexual identity from femaleness to maleness by adopting a man's hairstyle;[34] (4) rather than hairstyle being an immoral disgrace, it may have been only a natural disgrace.[35]

Paul also instructed men to wear their hair in a male fashion.[36] (4, 7, 14). Some may have been growing long flowing hair for some of the same reasons women were changing their style: (1) independence from the culture; (2) living eschatalogically; (3) recently converted from homosexuality, but not looking like it; (4) trying to break down gender distinctions.[37] (5) wanting to demonstrate the Christians are not to be judged by outward appearances.

Although some of the reasons for bucking culture are not immoral, Christians need to be sensitive to how their actions are viewed by culture. Blomberg noted, "In any culture believers must strenuously avoid whatever forms or dress or grooming that potentially communicates . . .sexual misconduct . . . Behavior, mannerisms, clothing, or hairstyle that suggest that a person is sexually unfaithful to his or her spouse, promiscuous, homosexual, or the devotees of some non-Christian religions or cultic or occult sects are entirely inappropriate for Christians."[38]

While the "disgrace" for a man with long flowing hair may have been due to a sexual reversal attempt or to homosexuality, hair length

---

[31] 1 Co 1:2.

[32] According to Edersheim, it was the custom to shave a woman who was guilty of adultery, 154. See also Grosheide, 254; and Judy Brown, 250.

[33] Fee, 511, n. 81; See also Tucker and Liefeld, 77.

[34] Grosheide, 254; Fee, 510-511; Hering, 105.

[35] 1 Co 11:14-15.

[36] See 1 Co 6:9-11; Blomberg, 210; Murphy-O'Connor, *CBQ* 42, 485-487 – long hair on men was associated with homosexuals by Greeks, Jews, Romans, and pagan philosophies.

[37] Judy Brown, 251; Fee, 505; Murphy-O'Connor, *CBQ* 42, 485-499; *Idem.,* 50, 269.

[38] Blomberg, 215.

may also have been only a cultural standard, "does not the very nature of things teach you that if a man has long hair, it is a disgrace to him."[39]

But how does all of that affect the relationship of a person to his/her corresponding head? The dishonored head refers first to the person's own physical head, i.e., to dishonor self. To dress in a way that intentionally or unintentionally links a Christian to immorality, homosexuality, lesbianism, or cults is self-debasement. To do so cheapens self in the eyes of others because of cultural expectations and acceptance as suggested in verses 14 and 15, "Women should be women and men should be men, and the difference should be obvious."[40]

However, there is another "head" that is dishonored by inappropriate decorum—that other "head" in the triad.[41]

The "Heads" and "Non-Heads" of the Triad

But I want you to understand that Christ is the head of every man, and the man is the head of a woman, and God is the head of Christ (11:3).

It is imperative to consider the meaning of "head" (*kephale*), the relationship of head to its corresponding non-head, and the implications of that relationship to the role of women in the church.

The "community" within the trinity is a model for the relationships of people to each other within the family and the church. The sets of relationships in the triad pairings need to viewed side by side, because the character/nature of the interrelationship of one set affects the next ones.

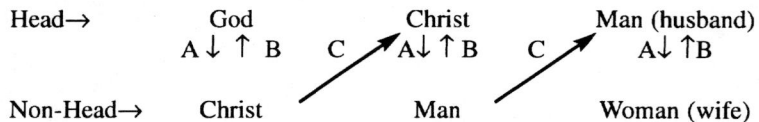

Head→   God   Christ   Man (husband)
          A↓ ↑ B   C ↗A↓ ↑B   C ↗   A↓ ↑B

Non-Head→ Christ   Man   Woman (wife)

The descending "A" arrows depict the relationship initiated by the "head." The ascending "B" arrows depict the relational response from the non-head back to the head. The diagonal "C" arrows depict the "non-head" in one set becoming the "head" in a different set.

The "head" in each set initiates the relational characteristics (**arrows A**) which are assimilated and continued by the "non-head's"

---

[39] 1 Co 11:14. Men normally wore short hair during this period. Murphy-O'Connor, *CBI 42, 486.*

[40] Murphy-O'Connor, *1 Corinthians*, 106-107.

[41] Hering considers both heads – his own/her own and the corresponding head in the triad. 103-105.

reciprocity to its corresponding head (**arrows B**), and then the relational characteristics are transferred to another set of relationships because the "non-head" in the preceding set simultaneously functions as "head" in the subsequent set (**arrows C**).

There are different opinions concerning the meaning of head in this passage. Many depend upon only the lexicon meaning. However, using only the lexicon's (dictionary's) meaning has several weaknesses: (1) lexicons report many different definitions and nuances depending upon the historical era and literary contexts of the appearances. For instance, the 1843 edition of Liddell, Scott, Jones and McKenzie's Lexicon includes more than 25 possible meanings of *kephale*. Bauer's lexicon also includes multiple meanings;[42] (2) the definition one selects may be done to support an *apriori* decision about the man-woman relationship;[43] (3) although it is appropriate to research how a specific word is used in other literature by other authors as by the same author.

The Mickelsens identify several different nuances in the New Testament such as source, top or crown, derivation, originator, and complete.[44] *Kephale* also refers to the literal physical head. Two different meanings dominate most discussions of *kephale* in this passage, "ruler" (authority over) and "source" (origin of).

Kephale as Ruler

Wayne Grudem researched 2,336 uses of kephale in various ancient Greek writings and opts for "authority over being the meaning in this text."[45] He noted that *kephale did* not carry the meaning of "source" in the literature researched. However, his work is too incomplete for a definitive conclusion, because *kephale* translated as or meaning "authority over" appeared in only 49 of the 2,336 places, and there are

---

[42] See expanded discussions of this by Berkeley and Alvera Mickelsen, "What Does Kephale Mean in the New Testament," in *Women, Authority & the Bible*, ed. by Alvera Mickelsen (Downer's Grove, IL: InterVarsity Press, 1986), 97-105. Philip Barton Payne's in the same book noted that the Michelsens' understated their case, since the 1968 supplement to Liddell and Scott lists 48, "Response," 118.

[43] Andrew Perriman notes that "too often a meaning is given to a word more for polemical reasons", 32.

[44] Michelsens, "What Does Kephale Mean," 105-110.

[45] Wayne Grudem, "Source," 38-59; see response to Grudem's article by Richard S. Cervin, "Does Kephale Mean Source or 'Authority Over' in Greek Literature? A Rebuttal," TJ 10 (Spring 1989); 85-112; see also Grudem's response to his critics in appendix 1 of *Recovering*, 425-468.

10,000 other listings in the same tool not researched by Grudem.[46] Fitzmyer[47] as well as all others holding the hierarchical (complementarian) view of the male-female relationship to each other opt for "authority over" or "supremacy of" as the meaning in this text.[48]

Kephale as Source/Origin

Some note that *kephale* seldom meant"authority over" in Greek literature,[49] and opt for "source" as the most natural meaning.[50] Stephen Clark combines "governing" with "source", and suggests when Paul uses "head" in this passage, "he is thinking of one body with one head .

---

[46] The resource is the database of the Thesaurus Linguae Graecae at the University of California, Irvine, which lists 12,000 places κεφαλη was used in Greek literature.

[47] Fitzmyer, "Another Look," 503-511.

[48] A sampling includes Wire, 117; Grosheide, 249; Thrall, who states that women are naturally inferior to men as seen by the fact she came from Adam's rib and was created to assist him, and thus cannot delegate as men can so it follows that women should obey them, 78-80. Boschman states that headship, means leadership that calls for submission, was God's intended plan, 46. Jack Cottrell, *Feminism and the Bible: An Introduction to Feminist for Christians.* (Joplin, MO: College Press, 1992); 308-313; Ortlund, 95-112; Thomas R. Schreiner, "Head Coverings, Prophecies and the Trinity: 1 Corinthians 11; 2-16," in *Recovering Biblical Manhood & Womanhood*, eds. John Piper and Wayne Grudem, 127, 138; George Knight III, "Husbands and Wives," 168-178.

[49] Michelsens "What Does Kephale Mean," 118-122; Bartchey, 78; Payne, 118; Barrett, 248; Fee, *1 Corinthians*, 503 n. 44. Some also opt for source citing that is rare that κεφαλη was used to translate the Hebrew word for a ruling authority (*ro'sh*) in the LXX. See Michelsons, 101-104; Perriman, 14-20; and Fee, *1 Corinthians*, 503 n. 44. However, any use of κεφαλη for *ro'sh* in the LXX is not determinative for the New Testament, since the old covenant emphasized legalism, which calls for human "authority over" people. But the new covenant emphasizes "lovalism" which calls for the inner guidance of the Spirit with only one head of the Church, Jesus. Jesus called for servant, not lords.

[50] In addition to the above see Fiddes, 371; Keener, 32-34; F.F. Bruce, 1-2 *Corinthians*, 103; Jervis, 241; Witherington III, *Origen*, 167-168; Murphy-O'Connor, CBQ 42, 492-493 and 1 *Corinthians, 103; Nolland, 108; Groothius rejects the idea that source is a new idea since kephale meant source in the writings of Athanasius, Chrysostom, Basil, Theodore of Mopsuestia, Eusebius, Cyril of Alexandria, and Photisus, 159; See also Fee, 504 n. 48 for a quote from Cyril of Alexandria; Scroggs, "Paul," 309; and several others.*

. . a person who is a head does more than govern. He is actually the source or origin of the kind of unity which makes many into one."[51]

"Source" is a possible for several reasons: (1) the Greek words for authority, ruler, or govern (*arche, archo, ezousia*) are not directly linked with *kephale* elsewhere in the New Testament; (2) 1 Corinthians 11:3 points toward the creation of the first man and woman in verses 7-9, which hi-lights source; (3) source/origin fits well the sequence of the historical appearance of the pairs listed. Historically, Adam appeared first, and so the man is listed first as a "non-head" who responds to his corresponding "head"; then historically Eve appeared, and so the woman is listed second as a "non-head responding to her corresponding head; then the earthly historical Christ appeared and so is listed third. The original source of the first man was Christ as co-creator.[52] The original source of the first woman was the man.[53] God was the source for the Son being incarnated into the Christ.

In several places, *kephale* clearly refers to a person's biological head (verses 4, 5-7). In verse 10, *kephale* seems also refers to the woman's own biological head, for it is her hairstyle that is upon her head.[54] "Authority" in this verse refers to her own power, liberty, or right. But what does the authority, liberty, or right permit her to do in the assembly when she is properly wearing her hair? The way she wore her hair, affirmed her dignity, modesty, and faithfulness to her husband which enhanced her right/authority to do what she was doing – praying and prophesying. Her enlistment through baptism into Christ (priesthood of all believers), her equipment through *charisma* (for ministry within and through the body of Christ), and her decorum (hairstyle on her head) which would not have caused others to stumble (angels – probably refers

---

[51] Clark, 180.

[52] For Christ as co-creator, see Jn 1:3,10; 1 Co 8:6; Col 1:16. Perhaps the reason "Christ" is used as the source of the first male is because God had decided *before* He created the world that humans would be redeemed through His son (Eph 1:3-5) as announced in the "pre-gospel" (Ge 3:15).

[53] Ge 2:2-22, 1 Co 11:8.

[54] The words "symbol" or "sign of" authority are not in any Greek manuscript. The words "to have authority" describe the woman having authority because of who she is. For those who view verse 10 describing a woman having authority to fulfill her leadership role in praying and prophesying, see Murphy-O-Conner, *1 Corinthians*, 109; Barrett, 255; Blomberg, 212; Caird, 272; Scorggs, "Paul," 301; Witherington III, *Genesis, 169; Orr and Walther, 261; Judy Brown, 258.*

to other human messengers) gave her that right.[55] Her appropriate hairstyle (on top) would not interfere with the attention of other worshippers. William Ramsay captures the "authority" that was hers when he states that the word "authority" here refers to the woman's power or right to be respected as a woman – not to be shamed, propositioned or talked against. With her identity clear, she can go anywhere with security and profound respect. But without that – the woman is a thing of naught – whom anyone may insult. So a woman's authority and dignity vanish."[56] Leon Morris agrees, "by covering her head the woman secures her own place of dignity and authority."[57]

Although ruler and source are 2 popular meanings of *kephale*, there is a third option that conditions the kind of relationship which happens or should happen between the "head" and the "non-head" within the triad.

Head as Initiator

Head as initiator adds a different dimension to the head to non-head relationship without automatically eliminating the meanings of "source" or "authority over.[58] What is common in all three pairs is an **inter**dependent relationship with an initiator (head) and a responder (non-head). The kind of relationship God initiated for the earthly Christ and Christ's "kind of response" to God is paralleled linguistically with the other pairs and should be applied relationally. It is the **character** of the "head" which is shared with the "non-head" that distinguishes,

---

[55] While some understand angels to be heavenly male types who can lust, we have no hint that angels have gender characteristics related to sexuality. The word "angel" in Greek literally means messenger and can refer to heavenly spirits or earthly humans. For discussions see Grosheide, 257; Barrett, 253-254; Hering, 106-107; Nolland, 23; Conzelmann, *I Corinthians*, 189; Murphy-O'Connor, *CBQ* 50, 272; Caird, 278; Thrall, 80; Calvin, 359: From the above are several different identities of the angels such as those who are always present in worship (Calvin), guardian angels (Thrall and Nolland), fallen angels (Caird), human messengers (Murphy-O'Connor), evil angels (Hering), demons (Conzelmann), universal angels (Barrett). Barrett is correct to write that what angels mean here is "notoriously obscure," 253.

[56] William Ramsay, *The Cities of St. Paul: Their Influence on His Life and Thought*. (New York: Hodder & Stoughton; George H. Doran Company, 1907), 202-203.

[57] Leon Morris, *The First Epistle of Paul to the Corinthians: An Introduction and Commentary*. (Grand Rapids: Eerdmans Publishing Company, 1966), 154.

[58] Perriman views *kephale* as commencement or beginning and thus is representative of relationships that is representative of relationships that determines the identity of a group, *Speaking*, 26-33. He reviews similar uses in Philo, Herodotus, Artemidorus, and the Orphic fragment.

characterizes, and conditions the reciprocal response from the "non-head" to its corresponding "head." The character initiated by the head provides the environment for a loving, servicing, graceful, forgiving, harmonious, peaceful, friendly, patient, kind, good, caring, faithful, gentle, self controlled, protecting, honoring, compassionate, understanding, adoring, pleasing, unselfish, not easily angered, encouraging, etc. kind of relationship with the non-head. In this kind of environment, the "non-head" can mature, fulfill his/her God-given potentials, and continue that same kind of relationship in the next set of head to non-head connection.

This initiating kind of **character-conduct** from the "head" brings development and strength to a relationship that empowers expanding interactions. It **energizes** mutual attraction and commitment between the members in each pair. It **liberates** rather than restrains and coerces the other in healthy and secure relationships. **The head to non-head relationship intended by God's creation models the kind of interactions that initiates and maintains community**. Judy Brown commended, "Perhaps the re-creation . . . gives the church what was originally made available at creation, namely, the capacity for men and women to reflect the harmonious relationship that exist within God."[59]

Restoring human community to pre-fall relationships was centered in the God to Christ relationship. Out of love, God transferred His Son into human flesh to function as the earthly Christ – the anointed one. God as "head" initiated protection, care, love, patience, honor, and so on, for His earthly Christ. More than once God verbally expressed His pleasure in the Christ.[60] God characterized His headship of love and support by such acts as sending angels to minister to Christ; answering His prayers to do the extraordinary; protecting Him until the fullness of time; expressing a friendship kind of love (*philos*) to Christ as well as *agape*.[61] The earthly Christ responded to this kind of character relationship initiated from the Father by pleasing God in everything He did and said.[62]

---

[59] Judy Brown, 21.

[60] This is my son, whom I love; with him I am well pleased." Mt 3:17 and 17:5.

[61] In addition to agape, Jesus used the Greek word for friendship love, *phileo*, to describe God's love to Him, Jn 5:20.

[62] Jesus said, "I always do what pleases him," Jn 8:29. See also Php 2:5-8, and in His statement, "The reason my Father loves me is that I lay down my life – only to take it up again. No one takes it from me, but I lay it down of my own accord. I have authority to lay it down and authority to take it up again..," Jn 10:17-18. *What a description of an interdependent relationship of mutuality with reciprocal respect and love.*

Jesus' submission was voluntary as seen in Philippians 2:5-8 and in His statement, "The reason my Father loves me is that I lay down my life – only to take it up again. No one takes it from me, but I lay it down of my own accord. I have authority to take it down and authority to take it up again . . .."

God as "head of Christ" is His **earthly** relationship to the **earthly** Christ and does not suggest an eternal (pre-incarnational) hierarchical-subordinate relationship between the Father and Son as some suggest, nor does the earthly nature of the relationship weaken the trinitarian relationship in heaven.[63]

In the three pairings, the "non-head" Christ becomes the "head" of every man. But that is problematic for some. Is not Christ also the head of women and the whole body, the Church? Why then restrict Christ's headship here to "every man?" Although "every man" can refer to every **male** "in Christ,"[64] it more likely means every Christian **husband**, because 1 Corinthians 11 points toward the relationship of husband and wife to each other as suggested by the woman disgracing her man/husband with an improper hair style.[65]

Christ as head of every man (husband) models him and initiates in him through the Spirit the same kind of relational characteristics God

---

[63] Some see eternal subordination of the Son in 1 Co 15:28. See the position developed by Stephen D. Kovach, "Equalitarians Revamp Doctrine of the Trinity," CBMW News 2 (Dec., 1996), 1, 3-5. However, to speculate from this one verse a pre-incarnational authority-subordination relationship is speculative. Cullmann correctly cautions, "The New Testament neither is able nor intends to give information about how we are to conceive the being of God beyond the history of revelation.... It intends rather to report the great even of God's revelation in Christ." Cullmann continues by stating that the Father and the Son "can be meaningfully distinguished only in the time of revelation history." 326-327.

Surely the total Godhead, which includes the total Trinity, is exempt from the "subjection under" to which all things are *placed under* Christ. It is the total Trinity that will be "all in all." 1 Co 15:28 probably refers to the conclusion of Christ's work on earth which for us happens with our resurrection – the content and context of 15:28. Jesus Himself did not seem to expect the identical relationship with the Father after the ascension. See Jn 17:5.

[64] For "every man" referring to the Christian, see Barrett, 249; Murphy-O'Connor, *CBQ* 42, 493; however Murphy-O'Connor is weak to suggest that "man" here refers to any human in Christ. Several others view the man as any male in the creation.

[65] The Greek word ανερ is used for "man" here. It is consistently used when the topic is a husband; although, it is also used for males in general. However ανφροποPaul more typically uses s when his topic is the general male. He used ανφροπος 27 times in 1 Co 11. In all of Paul's other writings, he used ανερ to refer to a husband; consequently, there is no objective reason to reject a husband-wife relationship in this chapter.

initiated for and in the earthly Christ – love, sacrifice, peace, joy, gentleness, acceptance, grace, protection, blessing, friendship, need-meeting, etc.

The man's (husband's) reciprocal response to Christ is to be the same kind as Christ's response to God's headship, i.e., to please His relational head with voluntary submission of love, sacrifice, respect, and honor. Responding to his head as Christ did to His head is surely what being Christ-like is about, "it is no longer I who live, but Christ lives in me."[66]

Now the "non-head" man becomes the "head" for the woman (wife). As Christ's headship mirrored God's relational characteristics, the Christian husband's headship is to mirror the same kind for his wife and, consequently, for the family which results from the union.

There is a direct correlation of "the head of the woman is man" in 1 Corinthians 11:3 with Ephesians 5:23, for the same Greek words are used.

1 Corinthians 11:3	Ephesians 5:23
Kephale gunaikos	*Kephale gunaikos*
. . .*aner*	. . .*aner*

Elsewhere the Bible does not connect *kephale* to a male-female relationship except for the husband-wife relationship, and nowhere does the Bible suggest that **any** man, because he is a male, is the head of **any** woman, because she is a female, (or **all** males are heads of **all** females). The only man who has headship responsibility for a woman is her husband.

By the pairings in the triad **and** by the descriptions in Ephesians 5:25-33, I am convinced that the "headship" responsibility in the husband-wife relationship is to correspond with the relational characteristics God initiated with the earthly Christ and which Christ in turn initiated with the "man in Christ." In his letter to the Ephesians, Paul develops this well by revealing that the husband's "head" responsibilities are to be as Christ's – love your wife as Christ loved the Church...sacrifice for her...initiate a family environment in which she can grow, be radiant, be fulfilled and be cleansed.

The wife's response to her husband's headship is to correspond with Christ's response to God's headship and the man's (her husband's) to Christ's. Only then will there be harmony in the church, and through the church to the world at large. That continuous flow of relational characteristics was evidently missing in many relationships within the Corinthian church, and accounts for divisions, quarrels, competition, immorality, immaturity, and so on – all of which saturated the Christian community in Corinth. Is it any wonder that Paul connected their internal problems to immaturity (1 Corinthians 3:1-3), and then with the need for love (chapter 13)?

---

[66] Ga 2:20.

Headship in the Church

Neither Jesus nor the apostles linked the word *kephale* to human leaders in the Church. The Church has only one head, Jesus who did not delegate surrogate heads to others. New Testament apostles and prophets are the foundation upon which the church was to be built,[67] not the head or heads under which members are to be governed. Christ equipped His apostles to lead by serving from the bottom-up, not from the top-down philosophy of leadership. He told them not to lord it over or exercise authority over others, but serve after the model of Jesus.[68] It is only by ministering from the bottom-up kind of servant philosophy, principles, and practices that better liberates members to recognize and utilize their gifts so every part can do its work so the church body can grow into the head's likeness.[69]

God initiated love with all its fruit that pleased Christ. Christ responded with His love and all its fruit, which pleased God. Christ then initiated that same love to the man that pleases him. The man is to respond to Christ with the same kind of love with all its fruit that pleases Christ. That man, as a husband, is to initiate the same kind of character relationship with his wife which pleases her. She is to respond with the same kind of love with all its benefits that pleases her husband. Pleasing and being pleased is the appropriate reciprocity in Christ-like living – God to Christ; Christ to God; Christ to man; man to Christ; the husband to his wife; the wife to her husband; the wife/mother to her children; and the children to their parents. Each is meeting the needs of others out of love – God's kind – a mutuality of interdependence with the intentionality of pleasing each other – mutual submission.[70] That kind of relational living builds up not only the biological family, but also the spiritual family, the Church, and from the Church the global village.

---

[67] Eph 2:20.

[68] Mt 20:25-28; Lk 22:22-27. See Paul's own servant leadership in 1 Co 3:5-10; 2 Co 11:28, and 2Ti 4:6.

[69] Eph 4:11-16.

[70] See Eph 5:2 and review the definition of submission in chapter 4. Mutual submission saturates the life of the" head" and the responding "non-head." "Pleasing" in the New Testament is a demonstration of and flows from God's kind of love that triggers reciprocal pleasing from the one who is pleased to the one who initiated it. Mt 3:17; 12:18; 17:5; Lk 2:14; 12:32; Ro 15:26-27; 1 Co 1:21; Ga 1:10, 15-16; Col 1:19; 1 Th 2:8; Ac 6:5. We are to please God and others, but not prioritize pleasing self (Ro 15:1,3), for prioritizing self, whether as an individual, or as a position holder, or as a member of a "privileged" gender fosters individualism and not community. Authentic pleasing helps initiate and maintain the relationships essential for community – the kind that will be in heaven, is God's will for life on earth.

Conclusion

The concept that "head" refers to the one who initiates a relationship of love, care, and grace to another for the purpose of enhancing closeness in partnership. Doing so actualizing the inherent potentialities of not only self, but also others and squares with God's intention for community in His initial creative act and subsequent activities throughout history. Out of His kind of headship, God established the environment that encouraged the first man and woman (husband and wife) to tap their inherent potentials as different genders with God's "breath of life" (His relational characteristics) in meaningful services to each other.

After the fall, God established His loving covenant with the Hebrew people when He showered them with **privileges** (blessings, love, grace, forgiveness, protection, etc.), so they could fulfill the **purpose** of being a blessing to all kinds of people (Genesis 12:2-3).

God's headship of love for them continued in spite of their reductionistic prostitution of His call. He continued to initiate concern and involvement for those who had been marginalized as people and excluded as partners in fulfilling God's call.

God's loving headship initiated and framed Jesus' kind of relational functions through which the untouchables were touched, the unwanted were wanted, the excluded were included, the shackled were liberated, the lost were found, and the potentials of the under achievers were released to extraordinary activities. While doing that, Jesus selected apostles who seemed to be unlikely prospects for mirroring His relational characteristics (two hot heads whom Jesus nicknamed "sons of thunder," a hard-head whom Jesus named "rock," a potential militant zealot, one prejudiced against the lowly, "can anything good come from Nazareth?" an exploiter of people's money—a tax collector, a thief, etc.). By initiating His relational headship characteristics of inclusiveness, love, patience, peace, kindness, and friendship, these apostles (except Judas) became the foundational teachers and models for God's colony of Heaven on earth, the Church—the on-going body of Christ to continue Jesus' kind of love to all and liberation of all. Thus these early leaders mirrored Jesus' love, patience, forgiveness, peace, kindness, friendship, mentoring and partnershipping as they included all kinds of people to not only salvation, but also to service. Thus all kinds were enlisted by baptism and equipped by charisma to be ministers with God's relational characteristics.

Today Christ continues to be the head of His body, the Church, by initiating/incarnating His character in Christians so they will mature, (grow up, not just grow old) into the relational likeness of the head, Jesus. For only as Christians develop Christ's kind of relational characteristics and will the Church be the kind of community on earth it will be in heaven.

The basic community within the larger church community is the biological family, and the basic relationship within the biological family is the husband/wife relationship. From that basic one-to-one relationship springs the relational characteristics of their children, the neighborhood, the church, the village, the city, the county, the state, the nation, and the world. No wonder when Paul wrote his Ephesian theological opus about church unity, he targeted husbands and wives as the first relationship to apply the principles priorities, and practices of love and unity amid diversity. All principles, attitudes, activities, and commands about unity and love in the first four chapters of Ephesians look to Ephesians 5:21-33 for their first practical expressions. If God's kind of relational headship is not caught in the husband/wife interactions, it will not likely be pervasive in their extended culture. Community will then become more individualistic, and solidarity will be weakened if not eliminated.

The man's/husband's headship is to do for his wife what God's headship did for Christ and Christ's headship did and continues to do for the man through the Spirit. His kind of servant headship initiates and maintains the environment of grace, love, fellowship, and encouragement that liberates **all** people to use all their gifts in ministry. It frees **all** people to grow from one degree of character to another — Christlikeness. It rescues the fallen and honors the faithful. It allows anyone to accept weaknesses without paralysis and to utilize strengths without excuses.

The relational male/husband headship (servant-leadership) does everything possible to help the woman/wife reach her God-given potentials in Christ without competition, jealousy, or envy from the husband or from others. It forgives faults and fosters successes. It allows women to be equal partners with men as God originally intended. It emancipates women from being viewed as second-rate citizens in the kingdom of God and in the culture of men to being equal citizens in both. It emancipates them to excellence and liberates them to leadership in whatever arena God allows.

As God expanded His relational characteristics through Christ, as Christ expanded His through the husband (man), so the wife (with her husband) is to initiate and expand those same relational characteristics through the rest of her family. Then others can be touched in the church family and in the secular community. Only as parents function in this way can the expanded Christian community on earth approximate what God intended in His original creation. Then His original responsibilities given to the first husband and wife can be fulfilled and His call to His people can be actualized – "all peoples will be blessed through you." (Genesis 12:3; Acts 3:24-25; Galatians 3:8)

When men and women (husbands and wives) function as co-partners, we may hear again, "God saw all that he had made, and it was very good." – people acting and reacting according to their created and re-created nature.

SO MAY IT BE

CHAPTER 8

FROM THE TRINITY OF DEITY TO THE "BI-UNITY" OF HUMANITY

Many times throughout history, theologians coined new words and/or utilized (and thus in some cases taken over) existing words to describe various theological concepts. Somewhere along the chronological line, people began using the words egalitarian and hierarchical (later complementarian) to describe the nature of two different male-female relationships to each other while fulfilling family, church, and cultural roles.

The position developed in the preceding chapters does not neatly fit into either the equalitarian or hierarchical models of male-female relationships. I am calling this collateral model the "bi-unitarian" position.

The triune God created male and female in His image and likeness. God squelched an individualistic model for humanity when He declared the situation of the male being alone was not good (Genesis 2:18). God instituted the "bi-unitarian" model when He formed the female as the male's counterpart.

The kind of oneness shared and expressed among the persons of the triune God is to be shared and expressed between males and females. The tri-unity of deity refers to the oneness amid the diversity of the three – Father, Son, and Holy Spirit.

Likewise, the bi-unity of humanity refers to the oneness amid the diversity of the two genders – male and female. God highlighted the bi-unity design when he declared, "they shall become one flesh". As the three persons of the trinity shared some of the same functions such as creating, inspiring, and judging; so the two genders share some of the same functions such as caring for the planet, judging, and prophesying. As there were some functional differences among the persons of the trinity, so there are functional differences between the two genders. As the functional differences of the persons of the trinity do not suggest a position of superiority or inferiority of each person within the trinity, so the functional differences of the genders do not suggest a position of superiority or inferiority of either one. There are a few functional differences of males and females, which are gender specific, but not many.

Rather than being rooted in one specified gender, most of the functional differences between men and women emerge from the diversity of interests, abilities, aptitudes, personalities, and propensities of each individual. Some of the basic differences are determined in conception (Psalms 139:13-16) and conditioned in various living environments. Each person is unique and God ordained that each one should live daily who he/she is, not who he/she is not. Through the delightfulness of our differences we serve God by serving others. The bi-unity relationship of males and females to each other is enhanced by the bi-unity source of conception.

At times what each person within the divine trinity did was conditioned by the situation, and so it is within the human bi-unity. The distinctions of one person from another in the trinity enhance their relationship with one another. Each one expresses his own uniqueness with commonality, mutual submission, respect and love for the others. Each points to the other one without competition or opposition. God sent the Son and the Spirit, and both responded accordingly. There is a magical oneness in the three. The Son prayed to the Father who responded accordingly. The Father gave commands to the Son who responded accordingly. Jesus spoke about the essentiality of the Holy Spirit and that Spirit testifies about Jesus.

The genders of the bi-unity are also to respond to each other without competition or opposition. Each is to express mutual submission to each other (Ephesians 5:21), while respecting each one's individual uniqueness. In certain activities, some men may do better than some women such as doing maintenance and financial management. However, some women may function better than some men in those identical activities. The recipients of those (and other competent) functions should respond with loving respect, regardless of the initiator's gender. There is a magical oneness in the two.

Diversities within the bi-unity should be mutually respected, honored, supported, and liberated for sacrificial service as representatives of God for benefiting all people (2 Corinthians 5:17-20). Living in God's righteousness is done when men and women experience and express the relational characteristics modeled by the divine trinity to and for each other.

The persons of the trinity share leadership abilities and functions with perfect *koinonia*. Likewise, both genders of the bi-unity are to share their leadership abilities and functions with mature *koinonia*. As leadership responsibilities were not restricted to only one member of the trinity, leadership responsibilities are not to be restricted to only one member of the bi-unity. The arena in which leadership abilities are to be expressed by either gender is rooted in an individual's aptitudes, *charismata*, personality, talents, training, understanding, competence, faith, and opportunities. Authentic leadership is the fruit of a charismatic root (Romans 12:8 and 1 Corinthians 12:28). However, leadership in one activity is not necessarily transferred into another one. One gender who displays a prominent leadership role in one area of responsibility does not erase that same kind of leadership role from the other gender, such as a woman denying leadership to a male in the church nursery because he is a man, or a man denying leadership to a woman on the church board because she is female. Throughout biblical history, the triune God gave identical kinds of leadership roles to the "bi-oneness" of humanity – lead-speakers, protectors of God's people, judges, teachers, and so on.

The trinitarian nature of deity functions as a shared partnership with one ultimate goal. So it is with the bi-unitarian nature of humanity. Throughout biblical history, men and women functioned as co-partners – Miriam with Moses, women prophets with male prophets, Deborah with male military leaders; Queen Esther with King Zerzes and with her cousin, Mordecai; Phoebe with Paul; Priscilla with Aquila, and so on.

The worldwide competitive spirit that pits men and women against each other because of gender does not represent the trinitarian nature of God in whose image men and women were created in the Garden and then re-created in the Christ. On the other hand, ignoring the differences between men and women also does not represent God's triune nature.

The bi-unitarian position affirms the unity amid the diversity of the two genders without animosity or assimilation. Our human bi-unity is to represent God's trinitarian relational characteristics. While the redeemed and re-created male and female citizenship is in heaven, both have received ambassadorial assignments on earth with the God-given purpose of blessing all peoples on earth (Genesis 12:2-3; Acts 3:24-25, Galatians 3:8).

Perhaps demonstrating our bi-unitarian relationship in principles and practices that imitate and mirror God's trinitarian relational characteristics is the only way to transform worldwide animosities into worldwide agape for the other gender, and to transform worldwide violence against the other gender into a worldwide valuing of the other gender.

Only as God's trinity fills us with His relational characteristics can men and women work together as God's ambassadors reconciling the world to God through Christ.

APPENDIX

WOMEN AS ELDERS: PONDERING THE ISSUE

It is possible for congregations to adopt the conclusions of this book, but be uncertain about women being elders. Some clearly excludes women. In those congregations, restricting elders to males only is mandated by two texts that list qualifying characteristics for elders (1Timothy 3:1-7 and Titus 1:5-9). Concluding that only males can be elders is gleaned from the "husband of one wife" qualification (1 Timothy 3:2 and Titus 1:6).

On the surface that nails down the issue; however, a broader analysis of the texts raises issues that deserve further consideration without dragging predetermined conclusions into the analysis. Below are some of those issues:

1. The "husband of one wife" qualification, as well as the other qualifications, is linked to the person being above reproach which is a "must." The word "must" is a translation of the Greek word, *dei*, which usually does not introduce a transcultural mandate unless there is a stated law elsewhere that dictates the mandate. Without the legal mandate, *dei* is a weakened and temporary necessity that relates to a particular situation. (In fact, *dei* is often not translated in the New Testament.) Thus *dei* in the eldership texts expresses obligations relative to specific circumstances in Ephesus and Crete. Thus, it is not likely that "must" introduces specific qualifications for all churches in all locations while excluding any other qualification for churches in other locations facing different circumstances. This understanding is supported by the fact that the set of qualifications for Ephesus (1 Timothy) is not identical with the set for Crete (Titus). We should not assume that a man who was not married, or whose wife died could no longer be "above reproach" in all cultures. If so, then how do we affirm the unmarried status and yet the "above reproach" character of Barnabus, Paul, and Jesus?

2. That the two lists were compiled for specific situations in their particular locations and during their particular time seem to be further supported by what items were not included such as the fruit of the Spirit in Galatians 5:22-23, Jesus' beatitudes in Matthew 5, other characteristics in the Sermon on the Mount, *charisma*, beliefs, and Peter's brief admonition to elders in 1 Peter 5:1-4.

3. If other qualifications in the two lists were culturally related, then would not the gender issue also be?

4. It behooves us to consider other teachings in 1 Timothy and Titus that were certainly culturally related and thus not mandated for all

churches in all cultures for all times. For instance, are we disobeying God if today we financially help widows who are not yet sixty years old (1 Timothy 5:9)? Do we seriously believe that if a husband dies leaving a thirty year old wife and three small children, the church leaders should tell her she must wait thirty more years before getting financial help from the church? Are we disobeying God if we help sixty-year-old widows who have never washed feet of other Christians (1 Timothy 5:10)? Should church leaders today counsel all younger widows to marry and have children (1 Timothy 5:14)? What will we do if they don't?

5. How do we square certain teachings in Timothy with other biblical passages unless *certain teachings in 1 Timothy were indeed situational for their time and place*? One example is the instruction for younger widows to marry in light of 1 Corinthians 7:39-40 and 7:27-35. Another would be the restrictions about helping widows in light of Galatians 6:10 and Jesus' teachings in Matthew 25:31-46.

6. Where in the Bible is a woman *directly* prohibited from being an elder? To assume that a "husband of one wife" serves as a direct prohibition against women is to argue from silence. If we do that with this passage, what about other passages in 1 Timothy that by the same logic would exclude women? One such passage would exclude women from being prayed for (2:1-2. While the NIV reads "anyone", the Greek is *uper panton anthropon*—on the behalf of all **men**). By the same argument, women would not be allowed to "be saved and to come to the knowledge of the truth," because the text records that God desires that for all **men** (*pantas anthropous*—2:4). Should women not be allowed to pray with uplifted hands because of 2:8? Since only widows are mentioned in chapter 5, should the church refuse to help a widower whose wife died and left small children—and refuse to do so by the silent argument—because widowers are not mentioned?

7. How can we square prohibiting women from serving as elders for **all times** and in **all locations** in light of the holistic teachings about women in the Bible including the following:

   A. God created both male and female in His image and likeness Genesis 1:26.
   B. God gave the first service/ministry responsibilities on earth to **both** the man and the woman in shared partnership (Genesis, chapters 1 & 2).
   C. God called women in the Old Testament to be prophets and inspired them to speak/teach with men present (Exodus 15:20, Judges 4:4, 2 Kings 22:14, Isaiah 8:3).
   D. Two Old Testament books are named after women (Ruth and Esther).

E. God drafted a woman (Deborah) to be His military, civil, and religious leader for His people.

F. The only known prophet between the Old Testament and the beginning of the Church was a woman, Anna (Luke 2:36-38).

G. Jesus' value and use of women.

H. Peter's announcement that the Christian era was pre-announced by God to include women prophets (Acts 2:17-18).

I. The early Church's value and use of women recorded in the book of Acts.

J. Not one *charisma* mentioned in the New Testament is gender specific.

K. Through the ages, the Church continues to build upon the foundation of the apostles and prophets (Ephesians 2:20), and women were included among those foundational prophets.

L. The New Testament function of elders certainly fits both genders, for elders were primarily relational caregivers to needy people. See how the verb *episkeptomai* describes compassionate caring activities of its corresponding noun, *episkopos*—elder. (Matthew 25:35,36,43; Luke 1:68, 78; 7:16; Acts 15:14, 36; Hebrews 2:6; James 1:27). The verb described servant-leaders who met specific needs of people. These leaders looked **over** people for the purpose of looking **after** them with care, compassion, and concern. Do we really believe men, because of their gender, can out do women, because of their gender, with these kind of caring functions?

M. If women are denied being elders because the word "must" overlays the qualifications, then men "must" be married with children in the plural. But how do we square that in all situations and locations with 1 Corinthians 7:32-25? And would that exclude Jesus and Paul from the eldership? Would we then be correct to exclude the "head", Jesus, and one of the Church's foundational apostles, Paul, from the eldership?

Past traditions, along with individual and congregational "comfort zones," help make this an issue with high potential for disharmony and disunity within congregations and across the Church at large. While we are given a mandate to "maintain the unity of the Spirit in the bond of peace" (Ephesians 4:3), we are not to maintain unity **for the sake of unity** if doing so restricts a church from being and doing what God desires as modeled by Jesus. Individually and corporately we are to mature into the likeness of Christ (Romans 8:29; 2 Corinthians 3:17-18;

Ephesians 4:11-16), to imitate God, the Father (Ephesians 4:24; 5:1), and please (not grieve nor quench) the Holy Spirit (Ephesians 4:30, 1 Thessalonians 5:19).

Sometimes I catch myself wishing the issue of women leaders in the Church were left alone so the traditional way I was taught would stand unquestioned and unchallenged. However, God wants all His children, male and female alike, to be liberated, encouraged, and enabled to use whatever *charisma* they have for whatever activity and role may need it in service to and through the whole body of Christ, so together we all can progress toward maturity- God's desire for us. One essential function of and challenge for congregational leaders is to enhance that liberation for all members even though it may be unpopular to do so.

May our courage rise to the challenge.

WORKS CITED

Anderson, Bonnie S.and Judith P. Zinsser. *A History of Their Own: Women in Europe from Prehistory to the Present,* Vol. 1. New York: Harper & Row, 1989.

Anderson, Janice Capel. "Matthew: Gender and Reading." *Semeia* 28 (1983): 3-27.

Alison, Stewart-Patterson. "The Mutuality of Women & Men in Ministry." D.Min. diss., Fuller Theological Seminary, 1991.

Arlandson, James Malcolm. *Women, Class, and Society in Early Christianity: Models from Luke-Acts.* Peabody, MA: Hendrickson, 1997.

Baldwin, Scott H. "A Difficult World: αυθεντεω in 1 Timothy 2:12," In *Women in the Church: A Fresh Analysis on 1 Timothy 2:9-15.* Edited by Andreas J. Kostenberger, Thomas R. Schreiner, and H. Scott Baldwin, 65-80. Grand Rapids: Baker Books, 1995.

Balsdon, J.P.V.D. *Roman Women: Their History and Habits.* London: The Bodley Heade, 1962.

Barnett, Paul W. "Wives and Women's Ministry (1 Timothy 2:11-15)." *Evangelical Quarterly* 61 (1989): 225-237.

Barrett, C.K. *The First Epistle to the Corinthians.* Harper's New Testament Commentaries. New York: Harper & Row Publishers, 1968.

Barron, Bruce. "Putting Women in Their Place: 1 Timothy 2:12 & Evangelical Views of Women in Church Leadership." *Journal of the Evangelical Theological Society* 33 (1990): 451-459.

Bartchy, S. Scott. *First-Century Slavery and 1 Corinthians 7:21.* Dissertation series, number eleven. Missoula, MT: Society of Biblical Literature, 1973.

_____. "Power, Submission and Sexual Identity Among the Early Christians." In *Essay's in New Testament Christianity.* Edited by Robert Wetzel. Cincinnati: Standard Publishing Company, 1978.

Barth, Karl. *Church Dogmatics.* Vol. III, Part 4. Edited by G.W. Bromiley and T.F. Torrance. Edinburgh: T & T Clark, 1952.

Barth, Markus. *Ephesians: Translation and Commentary on Chapters 4-6.* Garden City, N.Y.: Doubleday & Company, 1960.

Barton, Ruth R. *Becoming a Woman of Strength: 14 Life Challenges for Women – and the Men Who Love Them.* Wheaton: Harold Shaw Publishers, 1994.

Barton, S.C. "Paul's Sense Of Place: An Anthropological Approach to Community Formation in Corinth." *New Testament Studies* 32 (1986): 225-246.

Baugh, S.M. "A Foreign World: Ephesians in the First Century." In *Women in the Church: A Fresh Analysis of 1 Timothy 2:9-15.* Edited by Andreas J. Kostenberger, Thomas R. Shreiner and H. Scott Baldwin, 13-52. Grand Rapids: Baker Books, 1995.

Bedale, Stephen. "The Meaning of κεφαλη in the Pauline Epistles." *Journal of Theological Studies* 5 (1954): 211-215.

Bennett, Anne McCrew. *From Woman-Pain to Woman-Vision: Writings in Feminist Theology.* Minneapolis: Fortress Press, 1989.

Bilezikian, Gilbert. *Beyond Sex Roles: What the Bible Says About a Woman's Place in Church and Family.* 2d ed. Grand Rapids: Baker Book House, 1990.

_____. *Community 101.* Grand Rapids: Zondervan Publishing House, 1997.

Birney, John B. "Paul and Women." *Christian Standard* 28 (February 13, 1892): 136.

Blackwelder, Boyce W. *Light from the Greek New Testament.* Anderson, IN: Warner Press, 1958.

Blair, Christine Eaton. "Liberating Biblical Education with Women: The Implication of Gender for Methodology in Religious Education." Ph.D. diss. School of Theology, Claremont University, 1988.

Bledstein, Adrien Janis. "Was Eve Cursed? (Or Did a Woman Write Genesis?)" *Bible Review* 9 (1993): 42-45.

Blomberg, Craig. *1 Corinthians.* The NIV Application Commentary. Grand Rapids: Zondervan Publishing House, 1994.

Bock, Darrell L. *Luke*. Vol. 1, *1:1-9:50*. Grand Rapids: Baker Books, 1994.

_____. *Luke*. Vol. 2, *9:51-24:53*. Grand Rapids: Baker Books, 1996.

Borchert, Gerald L. "A Key to Pauline Thinking – Galatians 3:23-29: Faith and the New Humanity." *Review and Expositor* 91 (1994): 145-151.

Borland, James A. "Women in the Life and Teachings of Jesus." In *Recovering Biblical Manhood & Womanhood: A Response to Evangelical Feminism*. Edited by John Piper and Wayne Grudem, 113-123. Wheaton: Crossway Books, 1991.

Boschman, Ed. "Women's Role in Ministry in the Church." *Direction* 18 (1989): 44-53.

Bowen, Nancy R. "The Daughters of Your People: Female Prophets in Ezekiel 13:17-28." *Journal of Biblical Literature* 118 (1999): 417-433.

Bowman, Ann L. "Women in Ministry: An Exegetical Study of 1 Timothy 2:11-15." *Bibiotheca Sacra* 149 (1992): 193-213.

_____. "Women, Spiritual Gifts, and Ministry." *Faith & Mission* 14 (1996): 57-74.

Bristow, John Temple. *What Paul Really Said About Women*. San Francisco: Harper and Row, 1988.

Brooten, Bernardette. "Women Leaders in the Ancient Synagogue: In Scripture Evidence and Background Issues." *Brown Judaic Studies* 36 (1982): 5-33.

_____. "Early Christian Women and Their Cultural Context: Issues of Method of Historical Reconstruction." *Feminist Perspectives on Biblical Scholarship*. Edited by A.Y. Collins. (Chico, CA: Scholars Press), 1985.

Brown, Ann. *Apology to Women: Christian Images of the Female Sex*. Leicester: InterVarsity Press, 1991.

Brown, Judy L. *Women Ministers According to Scripture*. Kearney, NE: Morris Publishers, 1996.

Bruce, F.F. *1 and 2 Corinthians*. New Century Bible. London: Oliphants, 1971.

_____. *The Epistle to the Galatians: A Commentary on the Greek Text*. The New International Greek Testament Commentary. Grand Rapids: William B. Eerdmans Publishing, 1982.

_____. "Luke's Presentation of the Spirit in Acts." *Criswell Theological Review* 5 (1990): 20.

Bruner, Frederick Dale. *Matthew. Vol. 1: The Christbook*. Dallas: Word Publishers, 1987.

_____. *Matthew. Vol. 2: The Churchbook*. Dallas: Word Publishing, 1990.

Brunner, Emil. *The Christian Doctrine of Creation and Redemption*. Dogmatics. Vol. 2. Translated by Olive Wyon. Philadelphia: The Westminster Press, 1952.

Bullough, Byrne L. *The Subordinate Sex*. Baltimore: Penguin Books, 1973.

Burnet, J.F. *Early Women of the Christian Church*. Dayton, OH: Christian Publishing Assoc., 1921.

Butler, Thomas. "Woman's Work in the Church." *Millennial Harbinger* (1865): 377-382.

Cadbury, Henry. *The Making of Luke-Acts*. New York: Macmillan, 1928.

Caird, G.B. "Paul and Women's Liberation." *Bulletin of the John Rylands Library* 54 (1972): 268-281.

Calvin, John. *Genesis: An Introduction and Commentary*. The Tyndale Old Testament Commentaries. Downers Grove, IL: Inter-Varsity Press, 1967.

_____. *Commentaries on the Book of Genesis*. Vol. 1. Translated by John King. Reprint. Grand Rapids: Baker Book House, 1993.

_____. *Commentaries on the Epistles of Paul to the Galatians and Ephesians*. Translated by William Pringle. Reprint. Grand Rapids: Baker Book House, 1993.

_____. *Commentary on the Epistles of Paul to the Corinthians*. Vol. 1. Translated by John Pringle. Reprint. Grand Rapids: Baker Book House, 1993.

Campbell, Alexander. "Woman's Rights." *Millennial Harbinger* (1854): 203-206.

_____. "Woman and Her Mission." *Millennial Harbinger* (1856): 301-314.

Carson, D.A. "Silent in the Churches: On the Role of Women in 1 Corinthians 14:33b – 36." In *Recovering Biblical Manhood & Womanhood: A Response to Evangelical Feminism*. Edited by John Piper and Wayne Grudem, 140-153. Wheaton: Crossway Books, 1991.

Cassidy, Richard J. *Society and Politics in the Acts of Apostles*. Mary Knoll, N.Y.: Orbis Books, 1987.

Cerling Jr., C.E. "Women Ministers in the New Testament Church." *Journal of the Evangelical Theological Society* 19 (1976): 209-215.

Cervin, Richards. "Does *Kephale* Mean 'Source' or 'Authority Over' in Greek Literature? A Rebuttal." *Trinity Journal* 10 (1989): 85-112.

Chilton, Bruce D. "Opening the Book: Biblical Warrants for the Ordination of Women." *Modern Churchman* 20 (1977):

Christiansen, Ellen Juhl. "Women and Baptism." *Studia Theologila* 35 (1981): 1-8.

Clark, Gillian. *Women in Late Antiquity: Pagan and Christian Lifestyles*. Oxford: Clarendon Press, 1993.

Clark, Stephen B. *Man and Woman in Christ: An Examination of the Roles of Men and Women in Light of Scripture and the Social Sciences*. Ann Arbor, MI: Servant Books, 1980.

Clifford, Richard J. "Genesis 1-3: Permission to Exploit Nature?" *The Bible Today* 26 (1988): 133-137.

Cohen Shaye J.D. "Women in the Synagogues of Antiquity." *Conservative Judaism* 34 (1980): 23-29.

Cohen, A. ed. *The Soncino Chumash: The Five Books of Moses with Haptaroth.* London: Soncino Press, 1947.

Conzelmann, Hans. *The Theology of Luke.* Translated by G. Buswell. New York: Harper and Row, 1960.

_____. *An Outline of the Theology of the New Testament.* Translated by John Bowden. New York: Harper and Row, 1969.

_____. *1 Corinthians: A Commentary on the First Epistle to the Corinthians.* Translated by James W. Leitch. Philadelphia: Fortress Press, 1975.

Cook, Michael L. "The Image of Jesus as Liberating for Women." *Chicago Studies* 27 (1988): 136-150.

Corley, Kathleen. *Private Women, Public Meals: Social Conflict and Women in the Synoptic Traditions.* Peabody, MA: Hendrickson Publishers, 1993.

Cottrell, Jack.. "Male and Female Roles." *Christian Standard* CXXI (1986): 52-54.

_____. *Feminism and the Bible: An Introduction to Feminism for Christians.* Joplin, MO: College Press, 1992.

_____. "1 Tim 2:12 and the Role of Women." 4 parts. *Christian Standard* CXXVIII (1993): 20-22; 44-46; 68-70; 84-86.

_____. "Response to My Critics." 3 parts. *Christian Standard* CXXVIII (1993): 997-998; 1020-1023; 1036-1038.

_____. "Priscilla, Phoebe, and Company." *Christian Standard* CXXVIII (1993): 1060-1061.

_____. "The Husband is the Head of the Wife." *Christian Standard* CXXII (1997): 631-633.

Cranfield, C.E.B. *A Critical and Exegetical Commentary on the Epistle to the Romans.* Vol. 2. The International Critical Commentary. Edinburgh: T & T Clark, 1979.

Cullmann, Oscar. *The Christology of the New Testament.* Translated by Shirley C. Guthrie and Charles A.M. Hall. London: SCM Press, 1959.

Danby, Herbert, trans. *The Mishnah*. London: Oxford University Press, 1933.

Daniel-Rops, Henri. *Daily Life In The Time Of Jesus: An Authentic Reconstruction of Biblical Palestine and the Day-To-Day Lives and Customs of Its People*. New York: Hawthorn Books, 1962.

Davidson, Robert M. "The Theology of Sexuality in the Beginning: Genesis 3." *Andrews University Seminary Studies* 26 (1988): 121-131.

_____. *Genesis 1-2*. Cambridge Bible Commentary. Cambridge: Cambridge University Press, 1973.

_____. *Genesis 1-11*. Cambridge Bible Commentary. Cambridge: Cambridge University Press, 1973.

Delling, Gerhard. "υποτασσω." In *Theological Dictionary of the New Testament,* Vol. VIII.

Dillow, Joseph. *Speaking in Tongues: Seven Crucial Questions*. Grand Rapids: Zondervan Publishing House, 1975.

Domeris, W.R. "Biblical Perspectives on the Role of Women." *Journal of Theology for Southern Africa* 55 (1986): 58-61.

Dunn, James D.G. *Jesus and the Spirit*. London: SCM Press, 1975.

_____. *Romans 9-12*. Word Biblical Commentary, Vol. 38b. Dallas: Word Books Publisher, 1988.

_____. *Unity and Diversity in the New Testament: An Inquiry into the Character of Earliest Christianity*. Philadelphia: Trinity Press International, 1990.

_____. *The Epistle to the Galatians*. Black's New Testament Commentary. Reprint. Peabody, MA: Hendrickson Publishers, 1993.

Duraisingh, Christopher, ed. *Women's Perspectives: Articulating the Liberating Power of the Gospel*. Gospel and Culture Pamphlet 14. Geneva, Switzerland: WCC Publications, 1996.

Durant, Will. *The Story of Philosophy*. New York: Simon and Schuster, 1961.

Edersheim, Alfred. *Sketches of Jewish Social Life in the Day of Christ.* Grand Rapids: Eerdmans, 1976.

Edge, Findley B. *A Quest for Vitality in Religion.* Nashville: Broadman Press, 1963.

_____. *The Greening of the Church.* Waco, TX: Word Books Publisher, 1971.

Elliot, Elisabeth. "Why I Oppose the Ordination of Women." *Christianity Today* XIX (June 6, 1975): 12-20.

Emrey, Elizabeth Virigina. "Paul's Ethics and Feminism in Light of 1 Corinthians." D.Min. diss., School of Theology, Claremont University, 1980.

Erikson, Erik H. *Identity Youth and Crisis.* New York: W.W. Norton & Company, 1968.

Esler, P.F. *Community and Gospel in Luke-Acts: The Social and Political Motivation of Lucan Theology.* New York: Cambridge University Press, 1987.

Estep, JR., James Riley. "The Problem with Women." *Christian Standard* CXXVII (1993): 741-743.

Evans, Mary J. *Women in the Bible.* Downers Grove, IL: InterVarsity Press, 1986.

"Fallen Asleep." *Christian Standard* 61 (July 25, 1925): 1045.

_____. *Christian Standard* 84 (November 6, 1948): 737.

Fee, Gordon D. *The First Epistle to the Corinthians.* New International Commentary on the New Testament. Grand Rapids: Eerdmans Publishing, 1987.

_____. *1 and 2 Timothy, Titus.* New International Biblical Commentary. Peabody, MA: Hendrickson Publishers, 1988.

_____. "Issues in Evangelical Hermeneutics, Part III: The Great Watershed— Intentionality & Particularity/Eternality: 1 Timothy 2:8-15 As a Test Case." *Crux* 26 (1990): 31-37.

Fender, Helmut. *St. Luke, Theologian of Redemptive History.* Translated by R.H. and Ilse Fuller. Philadelphia: Fortress Press, 1967.

Fiddes, P.S. "Woman's Head is Man: A Doctrinal Reflection Upon a Pauline Text." *Baptist Quarterly* 31 (1986): 370-383.

Fiorenza, Elisabeth Schussler. "Women in the Pre-Pauline and Pauline Churches." *Union Seminary Quarterly Review* XXIII (1978): 153-166.

Fitzmyer, Joseph A. *The Gospel According to Luke* (I-IX). Garden City, N.Y.: Doubleday & Co., 1981.

_____. *The Gospel According to Luke* (X-XXIV). Garden City, N.Y.: Doubleday & Co., 1985.

_____. "Another Look at ΚΕΦΑΛΗ in 1 Corinthians 11.3." *New Testament Studies* 35 (1989): 503-511.

_____.. "Fidelity to Jesus and the Ordination of Women." *America* 175 (Dec. 28, 1996): 9-12.

Foh, Susan T. "What is the Woman's Desire." *Westminster Theological Journal* 37 (1974-75): 376-383.

Ford, J. Massyn Gberde. "Biblical Material Relevant to the Ordination of Women." *Journal of Ecumenical Studies* 10 (1973): 664-669.

Foster, Lewis A. "Marks of a Christian Woman in a Changing Society – Roads and Pitfalls." *Christian Standard* CXVI (1981): 692-693.

_____. "Marks of a Christian Woman in the Continuing Church – Views and Virtue." *Christian Standard* CVI (1981): 720-721.

_____. "Marks of a Christian Woman in a Continuing Society – Problems and Pressures." *Christian Standard* CVI (1981): 746-747.

_____. "Marks of a Christian Woman in the Continuing Church – Conflicting Voices and Opposition to Paul." *Christian Standard* CXVI (1981): 766-767.

_____. "Marks of a Christian Woman in the Continuing Church – Conculsions." *Christian Standard* CVI (1981): 788-789.

Foster, Richard J. *Celebration of Discipline: The Path to Spiritual Growth.* 20th Anniversary Edition. San Francisco: HarperSanFrancisco, 1998.

Fowler, James W. *Stages of Faith: The Psychology of Human Development and the Quest of Meaning.* San Francisco: HarperSanFrancisco, 1981.

Fretheim, Terence E. *The Book of Genesis: Introduction, Commentary, and Reflections.* The New Interpreter's Bible. Nashville: Abingdon Press, 1994.

Gaventa, Beverly Roberts. "Toward a Theology of Acts." *Interpretation* 42 (1988): 146-147.

Gifford, Swarte, ed. *The Defense of Women's Rights to Ordination in the Methodist Episcopal Church.* n.p. New Garland Publishing, 1988.

Gill, Deborah Menken. "The Female Prophets: Gender and Leadership in the Biblical Tradition." Ph.D. diss., Fuller Theological Seminary, 1991.

Greenhalgh, Stephen. "Creative Partnership in Genesis." *Scripture Bulletin* 22 (1992): 9-14.

Grenz, Stanley J. and Denise Muir Kjesbo. *Women in the Church: A Biblical Theology of Women in Ministry.* Downers Grove, IL: InterVarsity Press, 1995.

Groothius, Rebecca Merrill. *Women in the Conflict: The Cultural War Between Traditionalism and Feminism.* Grand Rapids: Baker Books, 1994.

_____. *Good News for Women: A Biblical Picture of Gender Equality.* Grand Rapids: Baker Books, 1997.

Grosheide, F.W. *Commentary on the First Epistle to the Corinthians.* The New International Commentary on the New Testament. Grand Rapids: Wm. B. Eerdmans Publishing Company, 1968.

Grudem, Wayne. "Does κεφαλη (Head) Mean "Source" or "Authority Over" in Greek Literature? A Survey of 2, 336 Examples." *Trinity Journal* 6 (1985): 38-59.

Guingnebert, Charles. *The Jewish World in the Time of Jesus.* New Hyde Park, N.Y.: University Books, 1959.

Gunkel, Hermann. *Genesis*. Translated by Mark E. Biddle. Macon, GA: Mercer University Press, 1997.

Guthrie, Donald. *The Pastoral Epistles: An Introduction and Commentary*. 2d ed. The Tyndale New Testament Commentaries. Grand Rapids: William B. Eerdmans Publishing Company, 1990.

Haenchen, Ernst. *The Acts of the Apostles: A Commentary*. Oxford: Basil Blackwell, 1971.

Hagner, Donald A. *Matthew 1-13,* Word Biblical Commentary, Vol. 33a. Dallas: Word   Books Publisher, 1993.

_____. *Matthew 14-28,* Word Biblical Commentary, Vol. 33b. Dallas: Word Books Publisher, 1995.

Harnack, Adolph Von. *The Mission and Expansion of Christianity in the First Three Centuries*. Vol. II. Translated and Edited by James Moffatt. New York: Williams and Norgate, 1908.

Harris, Timothy J. "Why Did Paul Mention Eve's Deception? A Critique of P.W. Barnett's Interpretation of 1 Timothy 2." *Evangelical Quarterly* 62 (1990): 335-352.

Harrison, Everett F. *Acts: The Expanding Church*. Chicago: Moody, 1975.

Hasel, Gerhard. "The Meaning of 'Let Us' in Genesis 1:26." *Andrews University Seminary Studies* 13 (1975): 58-66.

Hayden, Morgan P. "Women Pastors and Evangelists." *Christian Standard* 29 (June 10, 1893): 450-451.

Hauerwas, Stanley and William H. Willimon. *Resident Aliens: A Provocative Christian Assessment of Culture and Ministry for People Who Know That Something is Wrong*. Nashville: Abingdon Press, 1989.

Hering, Jean. *The First Epistle of St. Paul to the Corinthians*. Translated by A.W. Heathcote and P.J. Allcock. Reprint. London: Ephworth Press, 1969.

Hill, C.E. "Paul's Understanding of Christ's Kingdom in 1 Corinthians 15:20-28." *Novum Testamentum* 30 (1988): 297-320.

Hirsch, Samson Raphael. *The Pentateuch/ Genesis*. Vol. 1, 2d ed. Translated by Isaac Levy. Gateshead: Judaica Press Ltd., 1989.

Holladay, C. *The First Letter of Paul to the Corinthians*. Austin, TX: Sweet, 1979.

Holton, Thomas T. "The Subjection of Women." *Christian Standard* 29 (March 11, 1893): 198-199.

Hommes, N.J. "Let Women Be Silent in Church: A Message Concerning the Worship Service and the Decorum to be Observed by Women." *Calvin Theological Journal* 4 (1969): 5-22.

Hooker, Morna D. "Authority on her Head. An Examination of 1 Corinthians 11. 10." *New Testament Studies* 10 (1963-64): 410-416.

House, H.W. "A Biblical View of Women in Ministry. Part 3 (of 5 parts): The Speaking of Women and the Prohibition of the Law." *Bibliotheca Sacra* 145 (1988): 301-318.

Howe, Margaret. *Women & Church Leadership*. Grand Rapids: Zondervan Publishing, 1982.

Hugenberger, Gordon P. "Women in Church Office: Hermeneutics or Exegesis? A Survey of Approaches to 1 Tim. 2:8-15." *Journal of the Evangelical Theological Society* 35 (1995): 341-360.

Hull, William E. "Women in Her Place: Biblical Perspectives." *Review and Expositor* 72 (1975): 5-17.

Hurley, James B. *Man and Woman in Biblical Perspective*. Grand Rapids: Zondervan Publishing, 1981.

Ilan, Tal. *Jewish Women in Greco-Roman Palestine*. Peabody, MA: Hendrickson Publishers, 1981.

Irvin, Dorothy. "The Ministry of Women in the Early Church: The Archeological Evidence." *Duke Divinity School Review* 45 (1990): 76-86.

Jansen, J.F. "1 Cor. 15. 24-28 and the Future of Jesus Christ." *Scottish Journal of Theology* 40 (1987): 543-570.

Jeremias, Joachim. *Jerusalem in the Time of Jesus: An Investigation into Economic and Social Conditions During the New Testament Period*. London: SCM, 1969.

Jervis, L. Ann. "'But I Want You to Know': Paul's Midrashic Intertextual Response to the Corinthian Worshipers (1 Cor 11:2-16)." *Journal of Biblical Literature* 112 (1993): 231-246.

Jewett, Paul K. "Why I Favor the Ordination of Women." *Christianity Today* XIX (June 6, 1975): 7-12.

_____. *Man as Male and Female: A Study in Sexual Relationships from a Theological Point of View*. Grand Rapids: Eerdmans Publishing, 1975.

Johnson, S. Lewis. "Role Distinctions in the Church." In *Recovering Biblical Manhood & Womanhood: A Response to Evangelical Feminism*. Edited by John Piper and Wayne Grudem, 154-164. Wheaton: Crossway Books, 1991.

Kahl, Brigitte. "Human Culture and the Integrity of Creation: Biblical Reflection on Genesis 1-11." *The Ecumenical Review* 39 (1987): 128-137.

Keener, Craig S. *Paul, Women & Wives: Marriage and Women's Ministry in the Letters of Paul*. Peabody, MA: Hendrickson Publishers, 1992.

Keil, C.F. and F. Delitzsch. *Commentary on the Old Testament I: The Pentateuch*. Reprint. Grand Rapids: William B. Eerdmans Publishing Company, 1981.

Kelly, J.N.D. *A Commentary on the Pastoral Epistles*. London: Adam & Charles Black, 1963.

Kent, Homer A. *The Pastoral Epistles*, Revised. Chicago: Moody, 1982.

Kidner, Derek. *Genesis: An Introduction and Commentary*. The Tyndale Old Testament Commentaries. Downers Grove, IL: Inter-Varsity Press, 1967.

Kirschbaum, Charlotte von. *The Question of Women: The Collected Writings of Charlotte von Kirschbaum*. Translated by John Shephard. Edited by Eleanor Jackson. Grand Rapids: Eerdmans Publishing, 1996.

Knight III, George W. "The New Testament Teaching of the Role Relationship of Male and Female." *Journal of the Evangelical Theological Society* 18 (1975): 81-91.

_____. "The Number and Function of Permanent Offices in the New Testament Church." *Presbyterian* I (1975): 111-116.

_____. "Male and Female Related He Them." *Christianity Today* XX (April 9, 1976): 709-713.

_____. *The New Testament Teaching on the Role and Relationship of Men and Women.* Grand Rapids: Baker Book House, 1977.

_____. "The Ordination of Women: No." *Christianity Today* XXV (February 20, 1981): 16-19.

_____. "AYϑENTEΩ in Reference to Women in 1 Timothy 2.12." *New Testament Studies* 30 (1984): 143-157.

_____. "Husbands and Wives as Analogues of Christ and the Church: Ephesians 5:21-33 and Colossians 3:18-19." In *Recovering Biblical Manhood & Womanhood: A Response to Evangelical Feminism.* Edited by John Piper and Wayne Grudem, 165-178. Wheaton: Crossway Books, 1991.

_____. *The Pastoral Epistles: A Commentary on the Greek Text.* The New International Greek Testament Commentary. Grand Rapids: William B. Eerdmans Publishing Company, 1992.

Kostenberger, Andreas J. "A Complex Sentence Structure in 1 Timothy 2:12." in *Women in the Church: A Fresh Analysis of 1 Timothy 2:9-15.* Edited by Andreas J. Kostenberger, Thomas R. Schreiner, H. Scott Baldwin, 81-103. Grand Rapids: Baker Books, 1995.

_____. "The Crux of the Matter: Paul's Pastoral Pronouncements Regarding Women's Roles in 1 Timothy 2:9-15." *Faith & Mission* 14 (1996): 24-48.

Kovah, Stephen D. "Egalitarians Revamp Doctrine of the Trinity." *CBMW News* 2 (1966): 1, 3-5.

Kraemer, Hendrik. *A Theology of the Laity.* Philadelphia: The Westminster Press, 1958.

Kraemer, Ross, "Hellenistic Jewish Women: The Epigraphical Evidence." *SBL Sources for Biblical Studies* (1986): 183-200.

Kroeger, Catherine C. "Ancient Heresies and a Strong Greek Verb." *The Reformed Journal* 29 (1979): 12-15.

Kroeger, Catherine and Richard. "Strange Tongues or Plain Talk." *Daughters of Sarah* 12 (1986): 10-13.

_____. *I Suffer Not a Woman: Rethinking 1 Timothy 2:11-15 in Light of Ancient Evidence.* Grand Rapids: Baker Books, 1992.

Kuhn, H.B. "God, names of," In *The Zondervan Pictorial Encyclopedia of the Bible.* Vol. 2. 1975.

Kummel, W.G. *Introduction to the New Testament.* Translated by A.J. Mattel Jr. Nashville: Abingdon Press, 1966.

_____. *The Theology of the New Testament: According to its Major Witnesses Jesus-Paul-John.* Translated by John E. Steely. Nashville: Abingdon Press, 1973.

Kung, Hans. *Truthfulness: The Future of the Church.* New York: Sheed and Ward, 1968.

_____. *The Church.* Garden City, N.Y.: Doubleday, 1976.

Lambrecht, J. "Paul's Christological Use of Scripture in 1 Cor. 15. 20-28." *New Testament Studies* 28 (1982): 502-527.

Lane, William L. *The Gospel According to Mark.* Grand Rapids: Eerdmans Publishing, 1974.

Lantzer, Mary Ellen. "An Examination of the 1892-1893 *Christian Standard* Controversy Concerning Women's Preaching." MA. diss., Emmanual School of Religion, 1990.

Lee, Sung Hee. "Woman's Ordination: An Administrative Necessity and Effectiveness in the Presbyterian Church of Korea." D.Min. diss., Fuller Theological Seminary, 1991.

Leonard, Augenie Andruss. "St. Paul on the Status of Women." *Catholic Biblical Quarterly* 12 (1950): 311-320.

Leslie, William Houghton, "The Concept of Woman in the Pauline Corpus in Light of the Social and Religious Environment of the First Century." Ann Arbor, MI: Xerox University Microfilms, 1976.

Litke, Wayne. "Beyond Creation: Galatians 3:28, Genesis and the Hermaphrodite Myth." *Studies in Religion/Sciences Religieuses* 24 (1995): 173-178.

Longenecker, Richard N. *Galatians.* Word Biblical Commentary. Vol. 41. Dallas: Word Books Publishers, 1990.

Longstaff, Thomas R.W. "The Ordination of Women: A Biblical Perspective." *Anglican Theological Review* 57 (1975): 316-327.

Low, M. "Can Women Teach? A Consideration of Arguments from 1 Tim 2:11-15." *Trinity Theological Studies* [Singapore] 3 (1994): 99-123.

Lowery, Robert. "Reflections on God's Desire for Women." *Christian Standard* CXXIX (1994): 567-568; 590-591; 612-613; 628-629.

Luter, Boyd and Kathy McReynolds. *Women as Christ's Disciples.* Grand Rapids: Baker Books, 1997.

Luther, Martin. *Lectures on Genesis: Chapters 1 – 5.* St. Louis: Concordia Publishing, 1958.

_____. *Commentary on Galatians.* Translated by Erasmus Middleton. Reprint. Grand Rapids: Kregel Publications, 1979.

Maier, Walter A. "An Exegetical Study of 1 Corinthians 14:33b-38." *Concordia Theological Quarterly* 55 (1991): 81-104.

Malcolm, Kari Torjesen. *Women at the Crossroads: A Path Beyond Feminism and Traditionalism.* Downers Grove. IL: InterVarsityPress, 1982.

Mann, S. Schatz. *A Pauline Theology of Charismata.* Peabody, MA: Hendrickson Publishers, 1987.

Marshall, Howard I. *Luke: Historian and Theologian.* Exeter: Paternoster Press, 1970.

_____. *Commentary on Luke*. Grand Rapids: Eerdmans, 1978.

_____ *Acts of the Apostles: An Introduction and Commentary*. Grand Rapids: Eerdmans, 1980.

Marshall-Green, Molly. "When Keeping Silent No Longer Will Do: A Theological Agenda for the Contemporary Church." *Review and Expositor* 83 (1986): 27-33.

Martyn, J. Louis. *Galatians: A New Translation with Introduction and Commentary*. The Anchor Bible. New York: Doubleday, 1997.

Massey, Lesly F. *Women and the New Testament: An Analysis of Scripture in Light of New Testament Era Culture*. Jefferson, N.C.: McFarland & Co, 1989.

McEleney, Neil J. "Gifts Serving Christ's Body." *Bible Today* 33 (1995): 134-137.

Mickelsen, Alvera and Berkely. "The 'Head' of the Epistles." *Christianity Today* XXV (February 20, 1981): 20-23.

_____. "What Does *Kephale* Mean in the New Testament?" In *Women, Authority & The Bible*. Edited by Alvera Mickelsen, 97-117. Downers Grove, IL: InterVaristy Press, 1986.

Mitton, C. Leslie. *Ephesians*. New Century Bible Commentary. Reprint. Grand Rapids: Wm. B. Eerdmans Publishing Company, 1983.

Mollenkott, Virginia Ramey. *Women Men & the Bible*. Nashville: Abingdon, 1977.

Moltmann, Jurgen. *The Church in the Power of the Spirit: A Contribution to Messianic Ecclessiology*. Translated by Margaret Kohl. Minneapolis: Fortress Press, 1993.

Moo, Douglas. "1 Timothy 2:11-15: Meaning and Significance." *Trinity Journal* 1 (1980): 62-83.

_____. "What Does It Mean Not to Teach or Have Authority Over Men?" In *Recovering Biblical Manhood & Womanhood: A Response to Evangelical Feminism*. Edited by John Piper and Wayne Grudem, 179-193. Wheaton: Crossway Books, 1991.

Moore, George Foot. *Judaism in the First Centuries of the Christian Era: The Age of Tannam*. Reprint, Peabody, MA: Hendrickson Publishers, 1997.

Moore, William. "Woman's Share and Responsibilities." *Millennial Harbinger* (1860): 590-591.

Morris, Leon. *The First Epistle of Paul to the Corinthians: An Introduction and Commentary*. Grand Rapids: Eerdmans Publishing Company, 1966.

_____. "Luke and Early Catholicism." *Journal of Theology of South Africa* (1982): 4-16.

_____. *Luke: An Introduction and Commentary*. Revised. Grand Rapids: Eerdmans Publishing, 1990.

Murch, James DeForest. *Christians Only: A History of the Restoration Movement*. Cincinnati: Standard Publishing, 1962.

_____. "Today in Christendon." *Christian Standard* CVI (1971): 15.

Murphey-O'Connor, Jerome. "The Non-Pauline Character of 1 Corinthians 11: 2-16." *Journal of Biblical Literature* 95 (1976): 615-621.

_____. "Sex and Logic in 1 Corinthians 11:2-16." *Catholic Biblical Quarterly* 42 (1980): 482-500.

_____. "Interpolations in 1 Corinthians." *Catholic Biblical Quarterly* 48 (1986): 81-94.

_____. "1 Corinthians 11: 2-16 Once Again." *Catholic Biblical Quarterly* 50 (1988): 265-274.

Murray, John. *The Epistle to the Romans*. The New International Commentary on the New Testament. Grand Rapids: Wm. B. Eerdmans Publishing Company, 1968.

Nardoni, E. "Charism in the Early Church Since Rudolph Sohm: An Ecumenical Challenge." *Theological Studies* 4 (1992): 646-662.

Neil, William. *The Letter of Paul to the Galatians*. The Cambridge Bible Commentary. Cambridge: University Press, 1967.

Neyrey, Jerome H., ed. *The Social World of Luke-Acts: Models of Interpretation.* Peabody, MA: Hendrickson Publishers, 1991.

Niccum, Curt. "The Voice of the Manuscripts on the Silence of Women: The External Evidence for 1 Cor. 14:34-35." *New Testament Studies* 43 (1997): 242-255.

Nock, Arthur Darby. *Early Gentile Christianity and Its Hellenistic Background.* New York: Harper & Row Publishers, 1964.

Nolland, John. "Women in the Public Life of the Church." *Crux* 19 (1983): 17-23.

Norris, Judy. "Jesus My Lord, Emancipator of Women." *Christian Standard* CXV (1980): 793-794.

Odell-Scott, David W. "Let the Women Speak in the Church: An Equalitarian Interpretation of 1 Cor. 14:33b-36." *Biblical Theology Bulletin* 13 (1983): 90-93.

_____. "In Defense of an Equalitarian Interpretation of 1 Cor. 14:34-36: A Reply to Murphy-O'Connor's Critique." *Biblical Theology Bulletin* 17 (1987): 100-103.

Oepke, Albert T. "γυνη." In *Theological Dictionary of the New Testament*, Vol. I.

Ogden, Greg. *The New Reformation: Returning the Ministry to the People of God.* Grand Rapids: Zondervan Publishing House, 1990.

Omanson, Roger L. "The Role of Women in the New Testament Church." *Review and Expositor* 83 (1986): 15-25.

Orr, William F. and James Arthur Walther. *1 Corinthians: A New Translation, Introduction with a Study of the Life of Paul, Notes, and Commentary.* The Anchor Bible. Garden City, N.J.: Doubleday & Company, 1976.

Ortund Jr, Raymond C. "Male-Female Equality and Male Headship: Genesis 1-3."in *Recovering Biblical Manhood & Womanhood: A Response to Evangelical Feminism.* Edited by John Piper and Wayne Grudem. 95-112. Wheaton: Crossway Books, 1991.

Osborne, Grant R. "Women in Jesus Ministry." *Westminster Theological Journal* 51. (Fall, 1989): 263-268.

Osburn, Carroll D. "Women in the Church: Refocusing the Discussion." Abilene, TX: *Restoration Perspectives*, 1994.

O'Toole, Robert F. *The Unity of Luke's Theology.* Wilmington, DE: Michael Glazier,1984.

Otwell, John. *And Sarah Laughed: The Status of Women in the Old Testament.* Philadelphia: Westminster Press, 1977.

Packer, J.I. "Let's Stop Making Women Presbyters." *Christianity Today* XXXV (February 11, 1991): 18-21.

Padgett, Alan. "Wealthy Women at Ephesus 1 Timothy 2: 8-15 in Social Context." *Interpretation* 41 (1987): 19-31.

Page, Franklin S. "Toward a Biblical Ethic of Women in Ministry." Ph.D. diss., *Southwestern Baptist Theological Seminary*, 1980.

Payne, Philip. "Libertarian Women in Ephesus: A Response to Douglas G. Moo's Article, 1 Timothy 2:11-15 Meaning and Significance." *Trinity Journal* 2 (1981): 169-197.

Pendelton, W.K. "Shall Women Pray or Exhort in Public?" *Millennial Harbinger* (1864): 325-330.

Perriman, A.C. "What Eve Did. What Women Shouldn't Do: The Meaning of αυθεντεω in 1 Timothy 2:12." *Tyndale Bulletin* 44 (1993): 129-142.

_____. *Speaking of Women: Interpreting Paul.* Leicester, England: Apollos, 1998.

Philsy, S.R. "Diakonia of Women in the New Testament Church." *Indian Journal of Theology* 32 (1983): 1-17.

Pilch, John J. and Bruce Malina, eds. *Biblical Social Values and Their Meaning: A Handbook.* Peabody, MA: Hendrickson Publishers, 1993.

Pinnock, Clark H. *Flame of Love: A Theology of the Holy Spirit."* Downers Grove, IL: InterVarsity Press, 1996.

Piper, John and Wayne Grudem, eds. *Recovering Biblical Manhood & Womanhood. A Response to Evangelical Feminism.* Wheaton: Crossway Books, 1991.

Plumacher, Eckard. "Alta-Forschunn 1974-1982." *Theologische Rundschau* 49 (1984).

Plummer, Alfred. *A Critical and Exegetical Commentary on the Gospel According to S. Luke.* 5th ed. Edinburgh: T & T Clark, 1922.

Power, B.W. "Women in the Church: The Application of 1 Tim 2:8-15." *Interchange* 17 (1975): 55-59.

Ramsay, Wm. *St. Paul The Traveler and the Roman Citizen.* 3d ed. London: Hodder & Stoughton, 1897.

_____. A Historical Commentary St. Paul's Epistle to the Galatians. 2d ed. London: Hodder and Stoughton, 1900.

_____. *The Cities of St. Paul: Their Influence on His Life and Thought.* New York: Hodder & Stoughton; George H. Doran Company, 1907.

Redekop, Gloria Neufeld. "Let the Women Learn: 1 Timothy 2:8-15 Reconsidered." *Studies in Religion/Sciences Religieuses* 19 (1990): 235-245.

Reid, Barbara E. *Choosing the Better Part? Women in the Gospel of Luke.* Collegeville, MN: The Liturgical Press, 1996.

Reike, Bo. "προιστημι" In *Theological Dictionary of the New Testament*, Vol. VI.

Richards, Lawrence O. and Clyde Hoeldtke. *A Theology of Church Leadership.* Grand Rapids: Zondervan Publishing House, 1980.

Richards, Lawrence O. and Gib Martin. *A Theology of Personal Ministry: Spiritual Giftedness in the Local Church.* Grand Rapids: Zondervan Publishing House, 1981.

Richardson, Alan. *An Introduction to the Theology of the New Testament.* London: SCM Press, 1958.

Rohrbaugh, Richard, ed. *The Social Sciences and New Testament Interpretation.* Peabody, MA: Hendrickson Publishers, 1996.

Rowthorn, Anne. *The Liberation of the Laity.* Wilton, CT: Morehouse-Barlow, 1986.

Ruether, Rosemary Radford. *Women and Redemption: A Theological History*. Minneapolis: Fortress Press, 1998.

Sanday, William and Arthur C. Headlam. *A Critical and Exegetical Commentary on the Epistle to the Romans*. 5th ed. The International Critical Commentary. Edinburgh: T & T Clark, 1980.

Sanders, James A. *God has a Story Too*. Philadelphia: Fortress Press, 1979.

_____ "Isaiah in Luke." *Interpretation* 36 (1982): 144-155.

Scalise, Pamela J. "Women in Ministry: Reclaiming Our Old Testament Heritage." *Review and Expositor* 83 (1986): 7-13.

Scanlon, Regis. "Women Deacons: At What Price?" *Homiletic and Pastoral Review* XCVI 10 (1996): 6-14.

Scanzoni, Letha Dawson and Nancy A. Hardesty. *All We're Meant to Be: Biblical Feminism for Today*. 3d ed. Grand Rapids: Eerdmans Publishing, 1992.

Schaffer, Francis. *Genesis in Space and Time: The Flow of Biblical History*. Downers Grove, IL: Inter Varsity Press, 1972.

Schatzmann, S. *A Pauline Theology of Charismata*. Peabody, MA.: Hendrickson Publishers, 1987.

Scherman, Nasson and Meir Zlotowitz, eds. *The Chumash: Bereishis/Genesis*. The Stone Edition. Brooklyn: Mesorah Publications, 1995.

Schmitt, John J. "Like Eve, Like Adam: MSL in Gen 3,16." *Biblica* 72 (1991): 1-22.

Scholer, David M. "Women in the Church's Ministry: Does 1 Timothy 2:9-15 Help or Hinder Them?" *Daughters of Sarah* 16 (1990): 7-12.

Schotroff, Luise. *Let the Oppressed Go Free: Feminist Perspectives on the New Testament*. Translated by Annemarie S. Kidder. Louisville, KY: Westminster/John Knox Press, 1993.

Schreiner, Thomas R. "An Interpretation of 1 Timothy 2:9-15: A Dialogue with Scholarship." in *Women in the Church: A Fresh*

Analysis of 1 Timothy 2:9-15. Edited by Andreas J. Kostenberger, Thomas R. Schreiner, H. Scott Baldwin. 105-154. Grand Rapids: Baker Books, 1995.

Schurer, Emil. *A History of the Jewish People.* Revised. 2d division, Vol. II. Translated by Sophia Taylor and Peter Christie. Peabody, MA: Hendrickson Publishers, 1995.

Schweizer, Eduard. *Church Order in the New Testament.* Translated by Frank Clarke. London: SCM Press, 1959.

_____. "The Source of Worship: An Exposition of 1 Corinthians 14." *Interpretation* XIII (1959): 402.

Scroggs, Robin. "Paul and the Eschatological Woman." *Journal of the American Academy of Religion* XL (1972): 283-303.

_____. "Paul: Chauvinist or Liberationist?" *The Christian Century* 89 (1972): 307-309.

Shoemaker, Thomas P. "Unveiling of Equality: 1 Cor. 11:2-16." *Biblical Theology Bulletin* XVII (1987): 60-63.

Simpson, E.K. *The Pastoral Epistles: The Greek Text with Introduction and Commentary.* Grand Rapids: Wm. B. Eerdmans Publishing Company, 1954.

Skinner, John. *A Critical and Exegetical Commentary on Genesis.* The New International Critical Commentary. Edinburgh: T & T Clark, 1910.

Smith, George T. "Does Woman Keep Silence in the Churches?" *Christian Standard* 29 (August 12, 1893): 638.

Smith, Robert. "The Theology of Acts." *Currents in Theology and Missions* 42 (1971): 53.

Snyder, Howard A. *The Community of the King.* Downers Grove, IL: InterVarsity Press, 1977.

_____. *Liberating the Church: The Ecology of Church & Kingdom.* Reprint. Eugene, OR: Wipe & Stock Publisher, 1996.

_____. *A Kingdom Manifesto.* Reprint. Eugene, OR: Wipe & Stock Publisher, 1997.

_____. *Signs of the Spirit: How God Reshapes the Church*. Reprint. Eugene, OR: Wipe & Stock Publishers, 1997.

Songer, Harold S. "Isaiah in Acts." *Review and Expositor* 65 (1968): 459-70.

Spencer, Aida Besancon. "Eve at Ephesus." *Journal of the Evangelical Theological Society* 17 (1974): 215-222.

_____. *Beyond the Curse*. Peabody, MA: Hendrickson Publishers, 1985.

Stagg, Frank. "The Purpose and Message of Acts." *Review and Expositor* XLIV (1947): 3-21.

_____. *The Book of Acts: The Early Struggle for an Unhindered Gospel*. Nashville: Broadman Press, 1955.

_____. *Studies in Luke's Gospel*. Nashville: Convention Press, 1967.

_____. "The Unhindered Gospel." *Review and Expositor* 71 (1974): 451-462.

_____. "The Domestic Code and Final Appeal Ephesus 5:21-6:24." *Review and Expositor* 76 (1979): 541-552.

Stagg, Frank & Evelyn. *Woman in the World of Jesus*. Philadelphia: Westminster Press, 1978.

Staton, Julia. *What the Bible Says About Women*. Joplin, MO: College Press, 1980.

_____. "Is God a Male Chauvinist?" *Christian Standard* CXVI (1981): 239-240.

_____. "The Apostle Paul and Women." *Christian Standard* CXVI (1981): 544-545.

Staton, Knofel. *Jesus and Paul Agree: You Don't Have To Stay The Way You Are*. Cincinnati: Standard Publishing Company, 1976.

_____. *How to Understand the Bible*. Cincinnati: Standard Publishing, 1978.

_____. *1 Corinthians*. Cincinnati: Standard Publishing, 1987.

_____. *Timothy-Philemon.* Cincinnati: Standard Publishing, 1988.

_____. *Hearing God: 8 Steps to Understand the Bible.* Cincinnati: Standard Publishing, 1993.

Stendahl, Krister. *The Bible and the Role of Women: A Case Study in Hermeneutics.* Translated by Emilie T. Sander. Philadelphia: Fortress Press, 1966.

Stott, John. *The Spirit, the Church and the World.* Downers Grove, IL: InterVarsity Press, 1990.

Stouffer, Austin H. "Hierarchy or Equality: Biblical Implications for Modern Marriage." D.Min. diss., Fuller Theological Seminary, 1976.

_____. "The Ordination of Women: Yes." *Christianity Today* XV (February 20, 1981): 12-15.

Strauss, Richard L. "Like Christ: An Exposition of Ephesians 4:13." *Bibliotheca Sacra* 143 (1986): 260-265.

Stuhlmacher, Peter. *Paul's Letter to the Romans: A Commentary.* Translated by Scott J. Hafemann. Louisville: Westminster/John Knox Press, 1994.

Sukenek, Elizezer. *Ancient Synagogues in Palestine and Greece.* London: SCM Press, 1984.

Sumner, Sarah. *Men and Women in the Church.* Downers Grove, IL.: InterVarsity Press, 2003.

Swindler, Leonard. *Women in Judaism: The Status of Women in Formative Judaism.*Metuchen, N.J.: The Scarecrow Press, 1976.

_____. *Biblical Affirmation.* Philadelphia: Westminster Press, 1979.

"Theological Reflections on the Ordination of Women." [no author named] *Journal of Ecumenical Studies* 10 (1973): 693-699.

Thrall, M.E. *The Ordination of Women to the Priesthood: A Study of the Biblical Evidence.* London: SCM Press, 1958.

_____. *1 & 2 Corinthians.* The Cambridge Bible Commentary. Reprint. Cambridge: Cambridge University Press, 1986.

Towner, Philip H. *1 – 2 Timothy & Titus*. The IVP New Testament Commentary Series. Downers Grove, IL: InterVarsity Press, 1994.

Trible, Phyllis. *God and the Rhetoric of Sexuality*. Philadelphia: Fortress, 1978.

Tucker, Ruth A. *Women in the Maze: Questions & Answers on Biblical Equality*. Downers Grove, IL: InterVarsityPress, 1992.

Tucker, Ruth A. and Walter L. Liefeld. *Daughters of the Church: Women in Ministry from New Testament Times to the Present*. Grand Rapids: Zondervan Publishing, 1987.

Van Leeuvwen, Mary, Annelies Knoppers, Margaret L. Koch, Douglas J. Schurman, and Helen M. Sterk. *After Eden: Facing the Challenge of Gender Reconciliation*. Grand Rapids: Eerdmans Publishing Company, 1993.

Walker, Wm. O. "1 Corinthians 11:2-16 and Paul's Views Regarding Women." *Journal of Biblical Literature* 94 (1975): 94-110.

Waltke, Bruce K. "1 Timothy 2:8-15: Unique or Normative?" *Crux* 28 (1992): 22-27.

Webb, Joseph M. "Where is the Command to Silence?" *Christian Standard* CXXIII (1989): 460-462; 487-488.

Webber, George W. *God's Colony in Man's World*. Nashville: Abingdon Press, 1960.

Weber, Hans-Ruedi. *Salty Christians*. New York: The Seabury Press, 1969.

Wedderburn, A.J.M. "A New Testament Church Today." *Scottish Journal of Theology* 31 (1967): 517-532.

Wenham, Gordon J. *Genesis 1-15*. Word Biblical Commentary. Vol. 1. Waco, TX: Word Books Publisher, 1987.

Whitehead, James D. and Evelyn Eaton Whitehead. *The Emerging Laity: Returning Leadership to the Community of Faith*. Image Book Edition. New York: Doubleday, 1988.

Wiebe, Ben. "Two Texts on Women (1 Tim. 2:11-15; Gal. 3:26-29): A Test of Interpretation." *Horizons on Biblical Theology* 16 (1994): 54-85.

Wilshire, Leland E. "The TLG Computer and Further References to AYϑENTEΩ in 1 Tim. 2.12." *New Testament Studies* 34 (1988): 120-134.

_____. "1 Timothy 2:12 Revisited: A Reply to Paul W. Barnett and Timothy J. Harris." *Evangelical Quarterly* 65 (1993): 43-54.

Wire, Antoinette. *The Corinthian Women Prophets.* Minneapolis: Fortress Press, 1990.

Witherington III, Ben. "Rite & Rights for Women – Galatians 3.28." *New Testament Studies* 27 (1981): 593-604.

_____. *Women in the Ministry of Jesus.* New York: Cambridge University Press, 1984.

_____. *Women and the Genesis of Christianity.* Edited by Ann Witherington. New York: Cambridge University Press, 1990.

Zlotowitz, Meir. *Bereishis Genesis: A New Translation with a Commentary Anthologized from Talmudic, Midrashic, and Rabbinic Sources.* Vol. 1. Brooklyn: Mesorah Publications, 1986.

POSTSCRIPT

Our unity with other Christians is not based upon being in conformity with them, but rather with Christ. Anyone who is in Christ is a child of God, belongs to all of the other children of God, and is commanded to love those others (Jn 13:34-35, 1 Jn 4:20-5:3).

As long as we are in this world with different minds and come from different experiences and traditions, we will have differences in interpretations and understandings of the Bible. It is important that we recognize our brothers and sisters in Christ in spite of the differences. Let us receive one another as Christ has received us. God accepts our differences, but not our arrogances about those differences.

As long as maturity is hindered, we will be less than God intended. That should cause us to quit condemning and rejecting our brothers and sisters for differing in opinions and interpretations. It should also cause us to remain humble with our own understandings and conclusions. All of us can practice an essential slogan from antiquity, "In essentials unity, in non-essentials liberty, in all things charity."

If many of the opinions that are now dividing Christians had not been heightened into controversies, they might have died and vanished long ago – particularly as tests of fellowship. There will be no tests of fellowship dividing Christians from one another on the other side of the grave. May those tests cease on this side.

After stating that Christ died for all so that those who live should no longer live for themselves but for Christ who died for them, Paul immediately mentioned viewing people differently from the culture does. In context that practice surely refers to the first demonstration of living for Christ and not for self. We can begin to view people and to use them differently because Christians have been re-created into the image and likeness of Christ (in Christ) and thus have the relational characteristics of Christ and the new responsibility as members in Christ on-going earthly body to accept and actualize a ministry of reconciliation to and for all (2 Co 5:15-19).

May we not allow our differences in interpretations to block God's unifying work in Christ. And that unifying work began with men and women, having been created and then recreated in the image and likeness of God.

About the Author
e-mail: knofelee@earthlink.net

Korean War Vetern: 8 years active service; 5 medals; Letters of Commendation from General Burns (3 Stars), General Wooten (I Star) and Colonels.

Served in Korea as well as being the youngest supervisor ofthe world's busiest Air Force control tower.

Former: Senior F.A.A. Air Traffic Controller at O'Hare Airport, Chicago, IL, where he also wrote the first training manual for controllers at that airport.

Education: Lincoln Christian College, Illinois State University, Indiana University, Southern Baptist Theological Seminary, Kentucky State University, Wheaton Graduate School of Theology, University of Iowa-Graduate School of Religion, Harvard Medical School-Dept. of Continuing Education, Azusa Pacific UniversityHaggard Graduate School of Theology. (Fellow and Doctoral Honor's Program at Southern Seminary.)

Degrees: Bachelor of Arts (Summa Cum Laude), Master of Divinity, Doctor of Divinity, Doctor of Ministry (Outstanding Doctoral Award). Dissertation, "The Biblical Liberation of Women for Leadership."

Author: 35 books, over 200 periodical articles, chapters in 5 other books.

Served as: Executive Committee Member, Vice President and President of the North American Christian Convention

An initial Director of the International Disaster Emergency Service

An initial Director of the Institute for Church Leadership and Church Funding Corporation

Chair of New Testament Department, Lincoln Christian Seminary

Professor at Ozark Christian College, Missouri

2-term President of a local PT A

Consultant to RAPHA, nation's leading Christian psychiatric hospital care

National Task Force on the Study of Women's Role in the Church

President of Pacific Christian College, Fullerton, California

Presently: Professor of Biblical Literature at Hope International University

Commissioner on the Chaplaincy Endorsement Commission which works with Pentagon in endorsing! selecting Chaplains for military services and with entities for CAP, hospital, and prison chaplains.

Listed in: International Who's Who in Education (England).

Who's Who Among American Teachers

International Dictionary of Biography (England)

Personalities in the West and Midwest

Men of Achievement (England)

Who's Who of International Society

Who's Who in Religion

Who's Who of International Leaders

Who's Who in California

International Authors and Writers

Who's Who in the West and Midwest

Who's Who in America

The Directory of Distinguished Americans

International Book of Honor

International Directory of Distinguished Leadership

5,000 Personalities of the World